THE NEW ENCYCLOPEDIA OF
JEWELLERY MAKING
TECHNIQUES

JINKS McGRATH

Search Press

For Suzy and Tom, my favourite jewels

A QUARTO BOOK

Published in 2010 by Search Press Ltd
Wellwood
North Farm Road
Tunbridge Wells
Kent TN2 3DR

ISBN   978 1 84448 621 2

QUAR.EJM2

Conceived, designed and produced by
Quarto Publishing plc
The Old Brewery
6 Blundell Street
London N7 9BH

Senior Editor: Ruth Patrick
Art Editor: Jacqueline Palmer
Art Director: Caroline Guest
Designer: Simon Brewster
Photographers: Paul Forrester, Colin
Bowling, Jon Wyland, Phil Wilkins
Picture Researcher: Sarah Bell
Creative Director: Moira Clinch
Publisher: Paul Carslake

Colour separation by Modern Age Repro
House Ltd, Hong Kong
Printed in China by 1010 Printing
International

10 9 8 7 6 5 4 3 2 1

CHAPTER 1: **INTRODUCTION**

About the new edition   6
Basic tools and materials   8
All about metal   12
Recovering and reusing metal   16
Design   18

CHAPTER 2: **CUTTING METAL**

Piercing   20
Filing   24
Drilling   27

Inlaying   29
Making blanks   32
Lathe work   34
Engraving   38

CHAPTER 3: **HEATING METAL**

Annealing   42
Pickling and quenching   44
Soldering   48
Fusing   52

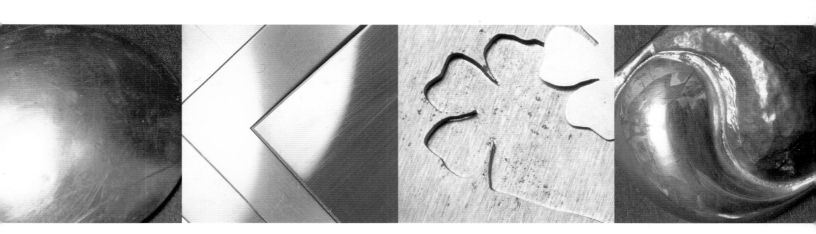

THE NEW ENCYCLOPEDIA OF
JEWELLERY MAKING
TECHNIQUES

CONTENTS

CHAPTER 4: **MOVING METAL**

Bending — 56
Hammering — 60
Doming and swaging — 62
Forging — 66
Chasing and repoussé — 70

CHAPTER 5: **SURFACE DECORATION**

Texturing — 74
Polishing — 78
Reticulation — 80
Stamping and embossing — 82

CHAPTER 6: **WORKING WITH WIRE**

Using wire — 86
Chain making — 92
Catches and joints — 98
Fittings and findings — 106
Riveting — 111

CHAPTER 7: **SPECIALIST TECHNIQUES**

Enamelling — 114
Etching and photoetching — 120
Casting — 124
Stone setting — 130

CHAPTER 8: **USING OTHER MATERIALS**

Wood — 138
Acrylics — 140
Metal clay — 144
Resizing and removing stones — 150

Suppliers and services — 153
Conversions and tool shapes — 154
Glossary — 156
Index — 158
Acknowledgments — 160

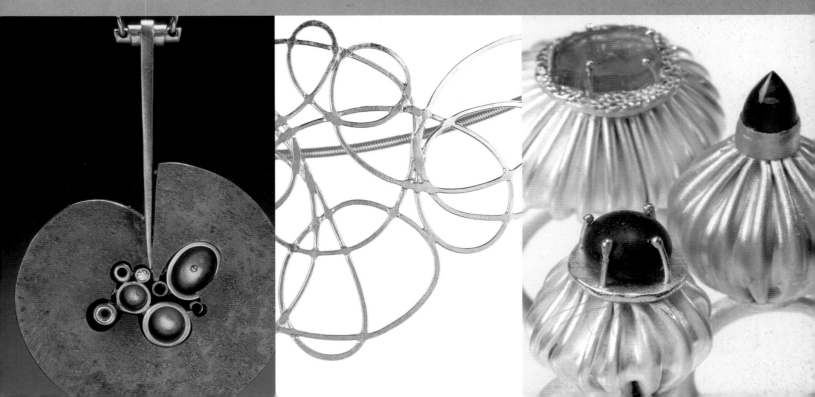

INTRODUCTION

This section includes everything you need to know in order to get started. It introduces the basic tools you will need as well as the many different materials you could work with. Then you are ready to go!

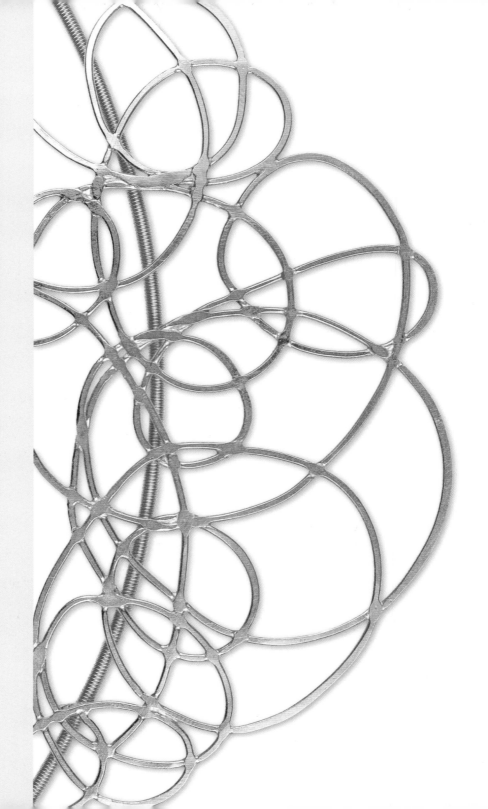

ABOUT THE NEW EDITION

Since the first edition of this book was published, there have been several new developments in the world of jewellery making. Some are best left to commercial enterprise, but others, such as metal clay, have also become very popular and can be a useful alternative way of making a piece of jewellery.

There have also been advances in soldering techniques. Micro welders, which produce a very small flame, are useful for soldering in awkward places, and laser welders are brilliant for being able to make a join without worrying about introducing a flame onto your work. The drawback is that they cost a lot of money, so are only really applicable if they are going to be used on a large scale.

In this new edition of the book, the order of techniques has now been set out in eight distinct chapters. For example, I have put together different techniques that involve cutting metal, whether with a piercing saw or with a file. This will enable you to see at a glance the alternative ways of doing a similar action and what each action achieves. These alterations will make the book easier to follow and a little more logical. I have also introduced some new techniques and expanded on some others.

There are, of course, different aspects and procedures within every technique, and in a book of this kind it is impossible to cover every variation and permutation. If a technique really interests you, try to find further, more specialized reading on the subject. Alternatively, experiment for yourself – experimentation is one of the most rewarding ways to discover how metal works and how you can use it.

You will find that several techniques – annealing, piercing and soldering, for example – are essential to all stages of jewellery making, and you should master these basics before you try anything too elaborate. Where techniques are used in different procedures, cross-references will guide you to the relevant information.

Jewellery making is a rewarding and fascinating pastime. Although you may find that you enjoy some aspects of jewellery making more than others, the techniques described in this book will give you a thorough understanding of all the basic information you need to create unique and professional-looking pieces.

Jinks McGrath

BASIC TOOLS AND MATERIALS

WHEN YOU ARE FIRST BEGINNING TO WORK WITH JEWELLERY YOU WILL NEED ONLY A FEW TOOLS AND MATERIALS; KEY ITEMS ARE SHOWN ACROSS THESE FOUR PAGES. BUY TOOLS ONLY AS YOU NEED THEM. THERE IS NO NEED TO ACQUIRE THE FULL RANGE WHEN YOU ARE BEGINNING.

ALTHOUGH IT IS POSSIBLE TO WORK IN THE KITCHEN, YOU SHOULD, IF POSSIBLE, TRY TO HAVE A SPECIAL WORKING AREA THAT CAN BE EITHER CLOSED OFF OR SECURED IN SOME WAY, BECAUSE SOME OF THE TOOLS AND PICKLES YOU WILL USE COULD BE DANGEROUS IN THE WRONG HANDS.

DIVIDERS (BELOW)

A pair of stainless steel dividers are used for many types of measurements. They can be used for making the same measurement many times, for example when marking wire for cutting pieces of equal lengths accurately, and many other drawing applications.

There is no need to buy a sophisticated work bench. An old table will suffice, as long as it is reasonably sturdy and does not wobble. Make sure that the table is a comfortable height. When you are working your elbows should be able to rest easily on the surface of the table, but try to keep your back straight while you work.

The wooden bench pin, which is the central working point, can be attached to the table with a G-clamp. Try to arrange the bench and working area so that the tools you use most often – pliers, snips and piercing saw, for example – are easily accessible. A hook or rack near to the bench pin is a neat and convenient method of keeping them near at hand. A small vice, which has numerous uses, can be screwed to the edge of the table.

Make sure that you work under a good light. An adjustable table lamp is ideal, because the light can be directed to shine onto your work so that no shadows are cast. Bear in mind that when you are soldering and annealing you need to be able to turn off the light, so make sure that the switch is within easy reach. Protect the area of your bench or table that you use for soldering with a metal plate of some kind – an old roasting pan would be ideal – and stand the soldering block or charcoal block on the metal so that the surface of the bench is not damaged by the flame of the torch. Small soldering jobs can be done with a portable gas cylinder torch, but for everyday use, you will probably find a blow torch that uses propane gas and your own breath more than adequate.

Most polishing can be done by hand, especially at first. If and when you do acquire a polishing motor, make sure that it has its own housing or that it has an integral dust extraction system. The dust created by polishing is dirty and gets everywhere.

The following tools and equipment are those you will need to get started. Buy other items as you need them so that you gradually acquire a fully equipped workshop.

WOODEN RING CLAMP (1)

Ring clamp with leather jaws for holding pieces securely without damage.

SMALL VICE (2)

Once it is firmly attached to the work bench, a vice will have dozens of uses, including holding formers, bending right angles, holding metal steady while it is being filed and holding draw plates. When working with metal, use 'safe' jaws with the vice so that the metal is not damaged.

PARALLEL PLIERS (3)

These open with a parallel action, unlike other pliers that work with a scissor-action, so can be used to hold work without damaging it.

RING SIZER (4)

Handy steel device for measuring ring sizes (A to Z).

STEEL RULER (5)

A steel ruler usually comes with both metric and imperial measurements, and is an invaluable tool.

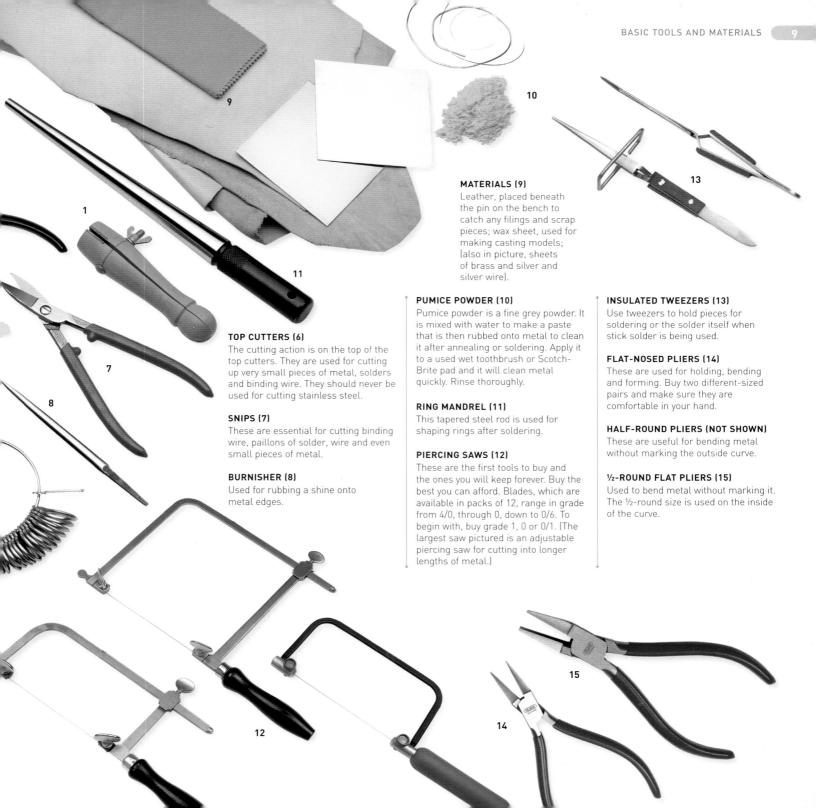

MATERIALS (9)

Leather, placed beneath the pin on the bench to catch any filings and scrap pieces; wax sheet, used for making casting models; (also in picture, sheets of brass and silver and silver wire).

TOP CUTTERS (6)

The cutting action is on the top of the top cutters. They are used for cutting up very small pieces of metal, solders and binding wire. They should never be used for cutting stainless steel.

SNIPS (7)

These are essential for cutting binding wire, paillons of solder, wire and even small pieces of metal.

BURNISHER (8)

Used for rubbing a shine onto metal edges.

PUMICE POWDER (10)

Pumice powder is a fine grey powder. It is mixed with water to make a paste that is then rubbed onto metal to clean it after annealing or soldering. Apply it to a used wet toothbrush or Scotch-Brite pad and it will clean metal quickly. Rinse thoroughly.

RING MANDREL (11)

This tapered steel rod is used for shaping rings after soldering.

PIERCING SAWS (12)

These are the first tools to buy and the ones you will keep forever. Buy the best you can afford. Blades, which are available in packs of 12, range in grade from 4/0, through 0, down to 0/6. To begin with, buy grade 1, 0 or 0/1. (The largest saw pictured is an adjustable piercing saw for cutting into longer lengths of metal.)

INSULATED TWEEZERS (13)

Use tweezers to hold pieces for soldering or the solder itself when stick solder is being used.

FLAT-NOSED PLIERS (14)

These are used for holding, bending and forming. Buy two different-sized pairs and make sure they are comfortable in your hand.

HALF-ROUND PLIERS (NOT SHOWN)

These are useful for bending metal without marking the outside curve.

½-ROUND FLAT PLIERS (15)

Used to bend metal without marking it. The ½-round size is used on the inside of the curve.

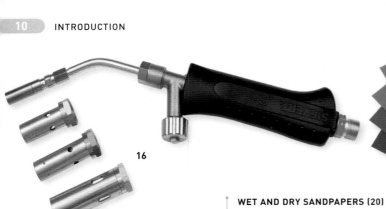

WET AND DRY SANDPAPERS (20)
Keep a good selection in stock, beginning with grade 240 and working through grades 400 and 600 down to grade 1200.

LEATHER OR FELT STICK (NOT SHOWN)
The final stage in polishing is buffing on a stick.

SAFETY PICKLE, ALUM OR SULFURIC PICKLE (NOT SHOWN)
A pickle of some kind is needed to clean metal after soldering.

WATER (NOT SHOWN)
Wherever you work, make sure that you have easy access to running water.

HAND DRILL (23)
This hand-held drill is for use with very small drill bits. The drill is operated by pushing the ridged piece at the top up and down and turning the handle.

SOLDERING TORCH (16)
Make sure that there is somewhere near the soldering area to keep the torch.

BORAX DISH AND CONE (17)
Flux is produced by rubbing the borax cone in a little water in the dish.

BINDING WIRE (18)
Before soldering, hold two pieces of metal firmly together with wire. Always remove the wire before pickling.

SOLDERING WIG (19)
A soldering wig looks a little like a wire bird's nest. Place articles to be soldered on the wig, which will help to distribute heat around them evenly. The wires can be moved to form different supports.

CHARCOAL BLOCK (21)
Charcoal blocks are used during certain heating processes, especially when small work requires a high temperature. Charcoal holds heat and prevents it from dissipating, meaning that work will take less time and energy to reach the required temperature.

FLAT METAL PLATE (22)
Flat metal plates can be used in a vice for forging, on the bench, or on a sandbag to reduce the noise created from hammering. The plate provides a hard, resistant surface to support metal while it is being worked, and will prevent sheet metal from distorting as it would if hit on a wooden surface.

27

28

29

HEAVY HAMMER (24)

A heavy hammer can be used for all heavy work. It can forge out lumps of molten silver, give a heavy texture on metal and be used for reshaping.

BALLPIEN HAMMER (25)

A lightweight jeweller's, or riveting, hammer can be used for all delicate work. It has one flat end, which can be used for riveting and other small jobs, and one wedge-shaped end that can be used for texturing metal.

WOODEN MALLET (26)

Used to shape metal on a mandrel, for instance, without leaving any marks.

FILES AND NEEDLEFILES (27)

Files vary in quality – get the best you can afford. Flat file – for flat surfaces, filing between joins to be soldered, edges and outside curves; Half-round file – for inside curves and edges; Triangular file – for filing around the top edges of bezels, grooves for right angles and other difficult edges; Square file – for making right angles true and filing inside areas; Knife – with one thick edge and one thinner edge, it is used for getting in between small areas.

LARGE FLAT FILE (28)

This tool is essential for removing lumps of excess solder, for straightening edges and for generally cleaning up your work. Make sure that it is not too coarse.

LARGE HALF-ROUND FILE (29)

Use this for cleaning up the inside surfaces of rings and inside curves.

JEWELLER'S HAMMER (30)

A general-purpose hammer that has dozens of uses.

PLANISHING HAMMER (31)

Planishing hammers are used to remove marks made by other hammers, imparting a subtle, even texture to the surface of the metal. One face of the hammer is completely flat and the other has a gentle curve – both faces should be kept highly polished so that the planished surface of the metal is reflective.

DOMING BLOCK AND GRADED ROUND PUNCHES (32)

A doming block is a brass or metal cube with different size half-spheres depressed into each side. It is used to form round metal disks into domes. Doming punches are shaped to fit into each different size of half-sphere in the doming block. They can be made of wood or steel, and are placed on top of the metal disk and hit with a hammer or mallet to form the dome.

32

31

30

ALL ABOUT METAL

ALL METALS HAVE CHARACTERISTICS RELATING TO STRENGTH, MALLEABILITY, DENSITY, SPECIFIC GRAVITY, HARDNESS AND MELTING POINT. THE METALS MOST CONDUCIVE TO JEWELLERY MAKING ARE REASONABLY STRONG, AND HAVE GOOD MALLEABILITY, A HARDNESS ACHIEVED THROUGH WORKING, A MEASURABLE DENSITY AND A MELTING TEMPERATURE ACHIEVABLE WITH A HIGH-TEMPERATURE TORCH, USUALLY A COMBINATION OF OXYGEN AND PROPANE. AS WELL AS THEIR COMMON NAMES, ALL METALS HAVE AN ATOMIC SYMBOL AND MANY METALS ARE MADE UP OF A COMBINATION OF TWO OR MORE DIFFERENT METALS, KNOWN AS ALLOYS.

STATEMENT RINGS – FELICITY PETERS
Silver- and gold-formed rings with dramatic stone settings.

Metals for jewellery fall into two categories: the first, precious metals, are platinum, gold, palladium and silver; the second, non-precious or base metals, are copper, brass (an alloy of copper and zinc), bronze (an alloy of copper and tin), zinc, tin, nickel, lead, titanium, and niobium. The above precious metals and base metals are all non-ferrous (do not contain iron). The ferrous metals of iron and stainless steel can also be used in jewellery making.

WORKING WITH PRECIOUS METALS

Precious metals are the ones usually associated with jewellery making. Keep any base metal workings away from precious metal ones as they can contaminate when heat is applied.

PLATINUM

Platinum has only been used extensively in the jewellery world for the last 100 years or so. Its strength and resistance to oxidization, plus the attractiveness of its whitish-grey colour have made it a very practical and desirable metal, not only for diamond settings, but for all kinds of other fine jewellery pieces. Currently the price of platinum is almost double that of gold.

Pure platinum, with the pureness of 999, is rarely used for jewellery because, as for other pure precious metals, it would be too soft. Platinum for most jewellery manufacture is an alloy of 950 parts platinum and 50 parts copper. For a casting alloy, the 50 parts would be made up of a mixture of copper and cobalt.

Other alloys of recognized quality are:
800 parts plat. 200 parts iridium.
950 parts plat. 50 parts gold.

When purchasing platinum it is a good idea to find out what the alloy is. Different alloys have different working properties about which your supplier should be able to inform you.

Platinum has a high soldering temperature, which requires special soldering torches. These can either be a mixture of oxygen and propane, or oxygen/hydrogen. Special dark goggles should be worn when soldering platinum, as the intense yellow light of the metal at high temperatures is harmful to the eyes.

Platinum should be kept very clean as it is being worked. After contact with metal tools in the workshop – when rolling, hammering, drawing down wire, etc. – it should be pickled in a warm nitric acid (10 parts water to 1 part nitric acid) to make sure there is no contamination. Better still, clean your tools before using them with platinum. Any particles of other metals that are accidentally deposited onto platinum will, when heated, burn and leave small holes in the surface of the platinum, which are difficult to remove.

Work to be soldered should be placed on a special platinum soldering block and not on a charcoal block because this can release carbon into the metal. Do not hold the work with insulated tweezers. If tweezers are necessary they should be tungsten.

As platinum does not oxidize, work may be finished to a very high level before soldering. The joins should be closely butted and do not require flux. In fact, flux can contaminate platinum with silicone deposits. Hard, medium and easy solders are available, but large joins may be welded together by placing a small piece of the platinum being used for the main article through the join and filing to shape after welding.

A separate set of files should be kept for platinum work, but if this is not possible, other files should be brushed with a file cleaner before use. Fine abrasives of 800, 1,500 and 4,000 up to 8,000 are used to polish the surface. These are available either as finishing papers or polishing wheels, and should be used exclusively for platinum. Polishes should be for white metals – use Hyfin for a general polish and a green or white rouge containing chromium or aluminium oxides for a high finish.

PALLADIUM

Palladium is a relatively new metal. It has only recently been given its own mark of quality, which is 950. It is a bright white metal with a lower density and specific gravity than either platinum or white gold. For a precious

CASTING GRAIN
24-carat gold casting grain (right) and
fine silver casting grain (far right).

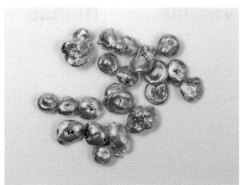

metal palladium is fairly light, so designs
that would look and feel a little heavy in
gold, for example, can be very well suited to
palladium. The advantage of palladium over
white gold is that it does not need plating after
finishing as it holds a beautiful white shine that
does not deteriorate as plating always does.

Palladium alloyed for jewellery is mostly 95
per cent pure. Its usual alloys are ruthenium
and iridium, which are palladium group metals.

The melting temperature of palladium
is quite high at 1552°C (2826°F). As with
platinum, special soldering goggles should
be worn when soldering, since the heat
is very intense, which is harmful to the
naked eye. Palladium does not need flux to
solder and can be soldered with the lower
platinum solders and some white gold solders,
as well as special palladium ones. Due to some
gold content in these solders, the solder line
will just remain visible, but after cleaning and
polishing, a smoothing over with the burnisher
will help to reduce it.

Name	Symbol	Specific gravity	Melting °C	Melting °F
Platinum	Pt78	21.45	1769°	3217°
Gold	Au79	19.32	1063°	1945°
Palladium	Pd 46	12.02	1552°	2826°
Silver	Ag47	10.49	960.5°	1760°
Copper	Cu29	8.94	1083°	1981.4°
Zinc	Zn30	7.131	419.4°	786.9°
Tin	Sn50	7.29	231.9°	449.4°
Nickel	Ni28	8.9	1453°	2647°
Lead	Pb82	11.36	325.6°	618°
Brass	Cu + Zn	Zinc is added to copper to make brass		
Gilding metal	95Cu–Zn5	Alloy of 95 parts copper and 5 parts zinc		
Red brass	85Cu–Zn15	Alloy of 85 parts copper and 15 parts zinc		
Yellow brass	65Cu–Zn35	Alloy of 65 parts copper and 35 parts zinc		
Titanium	Ti22	4.5	1800°	3272°
Niobium	Ni41	8.57	2467°	4474°
Iron	Fe26	7.87	1536°	2797°
Stainless steel	Chromium, or a mixture of chromium and nickel, is added to iron			

FOR JEWELLERY PURPOSES, GOLD IS AVAILABLE IN THE FOLLOWING CARATS AND COLOURS:

CARATS

24 carat

Pure gold. Rarely used on its own for an entire piece, due to the very soft nature of the metal. Would typically be used for adding decoration to a stronger metal and can also be purchased in very thin sheets known as gold foil. (The gold leaf used for gilding wood and plaster is not suitable for jewellery as it is too thin.)

22 carat

This alloy is 22 parts pure gold and 2 parts other metals, usually copper or silver. The colour is usually a buttery yellow or, if the alloyed metal is mainly copper, it will have a slightly redder look. 22 carat is used extensively in the jewellery of Eastern and Middle Eastern countries. It is a beautiful metal to work with but, owing to its high gold content, is too soft for some delicate pieces.

Annealing
Between 650 and 750°C (1200 and 1292°F). The metal should become a deep orange red and does not need annealing too often.

Soldering
Around 800°C (1472°F). Metal appears bright orange-red.

18 carat

This alloy is 18 parts pure gold and 6 parts other metals such as silver, copper and palladium. By varying the amount of these alloying metals, different colours of 18-carat gold can be achieved.

14 carat, 10 carat and 9 carat golds are all used in jewellery. The lower the carat the less fine gold makes up the content. These golds are also available in different colours and the same applies when annealing, quenching and soldering.

COLOURS

White gold

This colour is achieved by adding silver and palladium to pure gold. It is a very suitable metal for delicate work as it is malleable, while remaining strong. After finishing and polishing, white gold is usually rhodium-plated to maintain a bright finish. Soldered lines can remain visible in white gold so the rhodium plate helps to disguise this.

Red gold

The colour for red gold is achieved by alloying more copper than silver to pure gold. Can become quite hard when working, so should be regularly annealed.

Green gold

A small amount of cadmium mixed with copper and silver is the alloy for making green gold. It is not used very often, but is malleable and has a very pretty appearance.

Yellow gold

This is usually an alloy of just copper and silver. Yellow gold is the most commonly used in 18 carat and is very malleable and a pleasure to work with.

Annealing golds
Between 650 and 750°C (1200 and 1382°F). A dull red colour can be seen in all the coloured golds when annealing.

Quenching gold
Different alloys of gold need quenching at different times after annealing.
1   Quench straight after turning off the flame.
2   Quench once the metal has cooled to black heat (i.e. about 450 to 500°C/ 842 to 932°F).
3   Should not be quenched but allowed to air cool.

If your alloy feels hard to work after annealing and quenching in the usual way, try either method 2 or 3 until the metal feels soft. This applies to all colours and all carat golds.

Soldering gold

White, red and yellow gold all have solders to match their colours. The solders are available in hard, medium and easy, and are applied in the usual way.

To achieve a neat solder join in gold, the pieces to be soldered should have a really close fit (gold solder will not run and fill gaps the way silver solder may do) and the paillons of solder should be quite tiny. Using more tiny pieces rather than fewer bigger pieces will give a much better result.

Low-karat easy solders will melt between 650 and 720°C (1200 and 1328°F).
High-karat easy solders will melt between 700 and 715°C (1292 and 1319°F).
Low-karat hard solders will melt between 755 and 795°C (1390 and 1463°F).
High-karat hard solders will melt between 790 and 830°C (1454 and 1526°F).

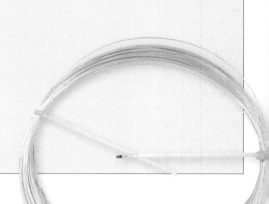

DISK NECKLACES – FAITH TAVENDER
Made from sterling silver and sterling silver with 22-carat gold plating. This is a cast piece but the original was handmade. A circle cut from a flat sheet with a hole drilled in the centre, then fine wire wrapped from the centre all the way round. The piece was flooded with solder to make it solid and filed at the edges.

GOLD

In its pure form, gold is arguably the most beautiful, soft, lustrous and tactile metal of all. The fact that it is also so durable means that there remain thousands of stunning examples in museums around the world of gold pieces fabricated over the last 6,000 years or more. Gold has been and remains to this day the metal most desired by human beings.

Pure gold of 999.9 quality is rarely used for jewellery. The higher-carat golds are alloyed with other metals such as silver, copper, cadmium, platinum and palladium, and golds lower than 15 carat would typically have zinc and nickel as part of their makeup.

SILVER

In its pure form, silver is a soft white metal classed as 999.9 silver. For jewellery purposes, this metal is too soft to be practical so 75 parts of copper are added to the pure silver to make 925, known as standard silver. Britannia silver, used mainly by silversmiths for large vessels and bowls and which has slightly less copper content than standard silver, is classed as 958. This too, is too soft to be used for jewellery. From time to time, different alloys of silver come on the market to fill a particular

need, but for the purposes of this book, standard silver will be used throughout.

After it is annealed, silver is soft and will work easily. As it is being worked, because of the copper content, it will become gradually harder. It should then be annealed again. After annealing, enough time should be left to turn off the flame and replace the torch before quenching and pickling.

There are five different solders for silver. Enamelling solder, which has the highest melting temperature, followed by hard, medium, easy and extra easy, each one in turn needing a little less heat in order to flow.

Annealing

Around 600°C (1112°F). This will show as a dull red appearance on the metal.

Soldering

Hard solder between 745 and 790°C (1373 and 1454°F), easy solder between 705 and 725°C (1300 and 1337°F). The areas being soldered

PENDANT/BROOCH – FELICITY PETERS
18-carat gold, granulated pendant/brooch with a striking watermelon tourmaline at its centre.

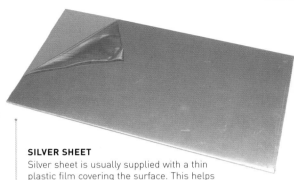

SILVER SHEET
Silver sheet is usually supplied with a thin plastic film covering the surface. This helps prevent scratches and should be removed before heating.

need to have a good fit and should be clean and dry. Silver will become a bright orange-red as it is being soldered.

BUYING METALS

There are several bullion dealers to buy your precious metal from listed at the back of this book. Until you are able to know exactly what you want to order, the choice can be a little daunting. Do your research: get a brochure, or look on-line to see what is available from your chosen dealer.

To begin with, buy a sheet of standard silver 1 x 100 x 100 mm (1/32 x 4 x 4 in.), which should allow enough metal to make some rings and a pendant. 0.8 mm, 1 mm, 1.5 mm and 2 mm round silver wire is also useful to have to hand. Lengths of 30–60 cm (12–24 in.) should be good to start with.

You can buy silver, gold, platinum and palladium in sheets, wire with several different profiles, tubing (chenier), casting grain and in all sorts of different fittings. Copper and brass are not usually available from precious metal dealers, but look on-line to find your local metal suppliers.

Most precious metal sheets are supplied with a plastic film covering both sides. This should be removed when heating, otherwise it is a good idea to leave it on for as long as possible so that the surface does not become scratched as it is being worked.

RECOVERING AND REUSING METAL

AT SOME TIME OR OTHER AS A JEWELLER YOU WILL WANT OR NEED TO REUSE SOME OF THE METALS THAT YOU HAVE CAREFULLY KEPT IN YOUR SCRAP BOX. CUSTOMERS ALSO SOMETIMES LIKE TO REUSE THE METAL OF AN OLD RING OR PIECE OF JEWELLERY THAT HOLDS SOME SENTIMENTAL VALUE, BUT IS NEVER WORN.

There are some metals that are just not worth melting up and reusing, since the time can outweigh any financial advantage that there may be in doing this. More often than not, the best way of dealing with your scrap is to wait until you have a good amount, i.e. at least 1 kg (2 lb 4 oz) of standard silver and at least 30 or 40 g (1 or 1½ oz) of 9-, 10-, 14-, 15- or 18-carat gold before you sell it through a reputable dealer.

It is not advisable to recover low-carat golds or silver, since they tend to crack when subsequently being worked, although clean scrap can be used for casting. Fine silver, fine gold and 22-carat gold present fewer problems when being reused in the workshop though you do need a high-firing torch to melt the golds and hold them at the correct temperature before pouring into the ingot maker.

CLEAN UP YOUR SCRAP

If you are taking scrap metals to a dealer to sell, try to make sure that they are relatively clean. For instance, remove any broken saw blades with a magnet and burn off any paper that may still be attached to the metal. The less rubbish there is in your scrap, the better price you will be paid for it.

CASTING GRAIN

Most metals can be bought as 'casting grain'. This is more often used for lost-wax, sand or cuttlefish castings as the tiny pieces are easier to melt. Grain is also clean, which means there are no impurities within so making the melt smoother. If you need a wire or sheet of a particular measurement that is not readily available, grain can be melted and poured into different-shaped ingot moulds and then rolled or beaten.

RECOVERING YOUR OWN METAL

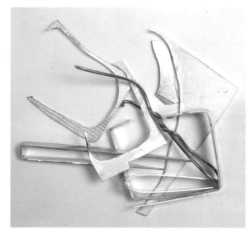

Scrap silver that has had all solder remains removed, and which can be melted up for pouring into a wax, sand or cuttlefish casting.

Two 22-carat gold rings that can be melted up and poured into an ingot mould prior to being put through the rollers, or beaten with a hammer to make sheet or wire.

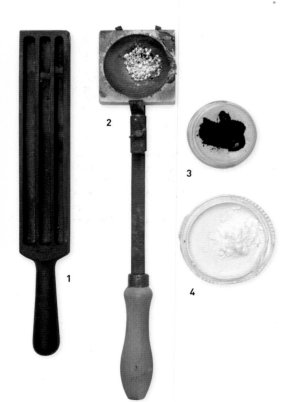

REUSING METAL TOOLS

1 Ingot mould for making wire; **2** small crucible and holder with fine silver casting grain (notice the small pouring lip on the right-hand side of the crucible – make sure this is always in the right position!); **3** ground charcoal, which helps with the flow of the melt-up; **4** powdered flux, which is sprinkled over the metal to help prevent oxidization.

SEE ALSO

- Annealing, pages 42–43
- Hammering, pages 60–61
- Texturing, pages 74–77

22-carat gold rings that have been annealed and are therefore oxidized so that any previous solder join becomes clearly visible. Any solder must be removed before the melt-up begins. Cut it away with the piercing saw and use a file on any obvious patches.

MAKING A FINE SILVER INGOT

1 Place the silver grains in the crucible with a little powdered flux and charcoal. Place the crucible on top of the ingot mould so that some of the heat from the flame will transfer to it and keep it warm for the pour. Have the flame as high as possible and in such a position that the silver shows shiny once it has started to melt.

2 Push any stray pieces of silver grain into the rest with a titanium rod as it starts to melt. Do not remove the flame while you are doing this.

3 Watch carefully as the silver forms up into a glistening ball. With the hand that is holding the crucible, give it a gentle rocking movement back and forth to check whether there are still unmelted pieces in the mass. Before pouring, you need to be sure that all the silver is completely liquid. A good tip is to hold the flame over the melt and count up to twenty to be certain!

4 When you are ready to pour, keep the flame exactly where it is and move the crucible into position just over the slot in the ingot mould and pour quickly in. Try to pour as quickly as possible without spilling any metal. If the pour is a little slow you will get little lumps on the ingot and small balls of metal will remain behind in the crucible. After turning off the torch, turn the ingot mould upside down to remove the ingot. Quench and pickle as necessary.

ALWAYS USE SEPARATE CRUCIBLES FOR SILVER AND GOLD. DOING MELT-UPS OF DIFFERENT METALS COULD RESULT IN SERIOUS CONTAMINATION.

5 Now place the ingot in the wire plates of the rolling mill and pass through until you have the desired dimensions. Remember to anneal the ingot as soon as it starts to feel a little hard. This should help to prevent any cracking.

6 Alternatively, beat the ingot to size using a stretching hammer and an anvil. Hold one end of the ingot between your finger and thumb off the anvil and work half of it with the hammer, beating from the middle outward. Then change around and do the same with the other end.

DESIGN

DESIGN IS OFTEN A SUBJECT THAT
STUDENTS FIND A BIT INTIMIDATING OR
DAUNTING AND WONDER: A) HOW TO
FIND IDEAS; AND B) HOW TO TRANSLATE
THOSE IDEAS INTO SOMETHING
TANGIBLE. A GOOD WAY TO START IS BY
IDENTIFYING THE STYLES THAT YOU LIKE,
WHETHER IT BE JEWELLERY, GRAPHICS,
TEXTILES, ARCHITECTURE, COLOURS,
FURNITURE OR NATURAL OBJECTS.
IT IS WORTH MAKING A NOTE OF
WHATEVER DRAWS YOU IN.

Embroidered and sewn cuffs

FINDING INSPIRATION

Photographs, postcards, things you see on the
Internet and cut-outs from magazines can all
be collected and stored in a scrap book. By
making a collection like this, it will soon
become clear what sort of direction you will
take in your design. Keep adding to your
collection and see how and when your ideas
might change. If possible, join a jewellery class.
It is always a good idea to talk to others who
are interested in making jewellery and who like
to share ideas and see what everyone else is
making. It can be helpful too, to see how others
execute a technique as there are always more
ways than one of getting something to work.

Books too are a wonderful source of
information and inspiration, and of course they
need not necessarily be books about jewellery.
For example, books about African, Asian and
South American textiles and their patterns,
weaves and colours provide an amazing
amount of ideas that can be played with before
being translated into designs for jewellery. So
too are books on the natural world. Details of
flowers, leaves, stones, trees and shapes of the
landscape will all set your mind racing with
inspiration. Sometimes, instead of simply
copying what you see, try to pare it down to a
bare outline, or just take one small section of it

and work with that until you have something
that you think will work.

AVOID DESIGN PLAGIARISM

These days it is very easy to print out pictures
of jewellery from the Internet. Although they
may be providing inspiration, they should not
be copied per se. Apart from infringement of
copyright, the designer who has made the
piece certainly wouldn't thank you for taking his
or her ideas and using them for yourself! It is
always so much more rewarding to come up
with your own idea.

DESIGN GUIDELINES

At first, keep everything simple. Often the best
and most appealing designs are really simple.
Some of the best pieces in either jewellery,
paintings or ceramics are incredibly simple
ideas, but are truly beautifully executed.

Once you have started to make something,
ideas for the next piece are probably already
forming in your mind. It is a good idea to keep a
sketchbook handy so that as ideas arrive they
can just be roughly drawn as a reminder. Many
students worry that they can't draw – as long
as you understand what you have sketched and
can work out the method of construction from
it, it will be good enough!

The real aim of design is to create something
that is made as well as you can make it. With
time, design will simply happen – initially,
finessing the techniques will make you really
pleased with your finished piece.

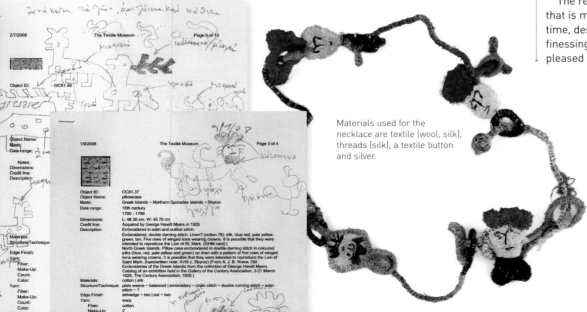

Materials used for the
necklace are textile (wool, silk),
threads (silk), a textile button
and silver.

LOUKIA RICHARDS

These pieces were inspired by the motifs
found in the Greek embroidery collection
of the Textile Museum in Washington DC.
Notes on the collection show the artist's
sketches for her textile jewellery pieces.
Techniques include sewing and
embroidery. Loukia's work is often
inspired by 17th and 18th century Greek
embroidery motifs that she finds amusing
and contemporary in design.

ERICA SHARPE

This piece, 'Indian Summer', was inspired by Erica's interest in the natural world. She started by making a series of rough sketches of flowers, then worked these up into the highly detailed sketches above, from which the final pendant design was taken. This piece is made from 22-carat gold decorated with granulation, the petals are made from carved amethyst. The piece is meant to be worn as a forehead ornament.

CHRISTINE KALTOFT

Christine uses a sketchbook to work up her design ideas. The pieces shown here (left and below) play on the looseness and freedom of such drawings. Many of these sketches have resulted in more formal pieces, such as her 'Que?' brooch (see page 138).

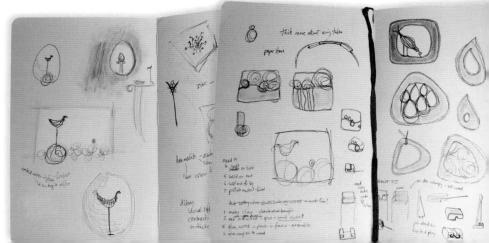

CUTTING METAL

The techniques included in this first section all involve cutting metal in different ways, whether the cut is being made with a piercing saw, a file, an engraving tool, a drill or even by a machine such as a lathe.

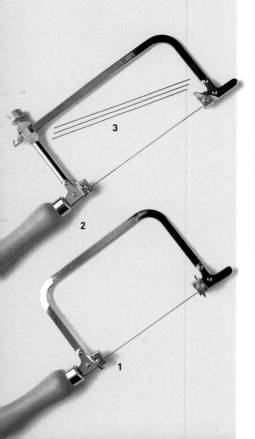

PIERCING TOOLS
1 Standard piercing saw; **2** piercing saw with adjustable frame for different lengths of saw blade; **3** saw blades.

PIERCING

THE PIERCING SAW IS ONE OF THE MOST ESSENTIAL TOOLS IN A JEWELLER'S WORKSHOP. AT FIRST, WORKING WITH A PIERCING SAW CAN BE RATHER FRUSTRATING BECAUSE THE BLADES USED ARE SMALL AND THEY CAN BREAK EASILY. SOMETIMES A SINGLE BLADE WILL LAST FOR WEEKS; SOMETIMES YOU WILL GET THROUGH AN ENTIRE PACK IN AN AFTERNOON. DON'T WORRY – IT HAPPENS TO EVERYONE!

FRILLS PENDANT – RUI KIKUCHI
This silver 'snowflake' pendant consists of several layers of pierced silver sheet placed on top of one another to create a lovely light effect.

Blade sizes range from 4, through 0 to 06, which is the finest and is used with metal that is as thin as 0.3 mm (1/90 in.). Use a No. 4 blade for cutting metal 2 mm (1/16 in.) thick, or for cutting acrylic that is up to about 6 mm (1/4 in.) thick.

Begin by practicing on a piece of metal about 1 mm (1/32 in.) thick and with a size No. 1 or 01 blade.

A coping saw is about one-and-a-half times larger than a piercing saw, but it is used in the same way. It has much larger saw blades and is useful in the workshop for cutting wood and plastic.

ATTACHING A BLADE
Sit so that you can hold the handle of the saw in one hand and the blade in the other, and so that you can push the head of the saw against something solid, such as the side of your workbench.

Hold the blade with the teeth facing toward you but pointing down toward the handle of the saw. Run your fingers down the blade. If it feels smooth, the blade is correctly positioned; if it does not, turn it the other way up. Place the top end of the blade into the top anchor point of the saw and tighten it. Push the handle of the saw against the bench and fasten the lower end of the saw into the bottom anchor point. The blade should be taut before you start work.

HOLDING THE SAW
Hold the handle of the saw as lightly as possible and let the saw do the work. The cut is made on the downstroke, so try to develop a rhythm whereby the saw almost falls through the work and needs only a gentle hand to guide it up again. Keep it upright, so that the blade is at an angle of 90 degrees to your work, unless you are deliberately cutting an angle.

USING THE SAW

Hold the saw upright, with the blade just touching the line on the metal you wish to cut. Place the index finger of your other hand against the side of the saw and use it as a guide as you move the saw up and down and gently forward into the metal.

When you begin to use the piercing saw, you may find it helpful to cut between two close parallel lines. For example, when you are cutting a strip of metal to make a ring, set a pair of dividers to the required width, place one side of the dividers on the straight edge of the metal, and use the other side of the dividers to draw a line parallel to it. Open out the dividers by a fraction, and draw a second line, parallel to the first. Pierce between the two lines.

You may also find it helpful to cut circles in this way at first. Use dividers to scribe the circle on the metal, open them a fraction, and scribe a second circle. Cut between the lines and use a file to clean up the edge down to the first scribed line.

TURNING CORNERS

Cut to the edge of a corner and, while you keep the saw moving in rhythm, use the smooth back edge to work around the corner. Pretend to be cutting backwards and, once the corner is turned, continue with the forwards movement.

PIERCING OUT CENTRAL AREAS

If the pattern has enclosed areas, use a small drill to make a hole in the corner of each area. Unfasten the bottom end of the blade, thread it through a hole and refasten the blade tightly. Pierce out the area, undo the blade and thread it through the next area to be removed.

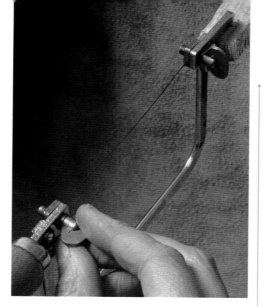

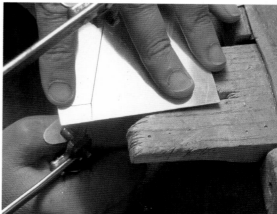

USING A PIERCING SAW
1 Push the saw against the pin or against the side of the work bench and tighten the blade until it is firm and springy. A loose blade will be difficult to use and will break easily.

3 Turn a corner by pushing the back edge of the blade against the outside edge of the metal. Move forward again only when the turn is complete.

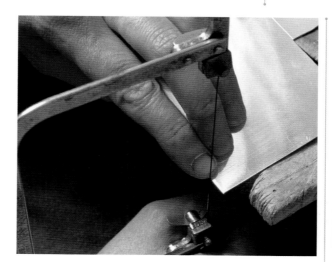

2 To make the first cut, use your finger as a guide at the side of the blade and move the saw gently up and down until it has a purchase on the metal.

4 If the blade gets stuck, lift the saw and metal away from the pin and allow the metal to find its own balance by simply holding the saw and letting go of the metal. Carefully replace the metal in that position on the pin, and the blade should be free to start cutting again.

SEE ALSO
• Drilling, pages 27–28
• Soldering, pages 48–51
• Bending, pages 56–59

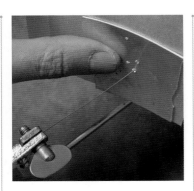

WORKING LARGE PIECES

1 An extra-large piercing saw is useful if you need to cut out one shape from a large piece of metal. Use it in exactly the same way as an ordinary piercing saw.

2 Use a coping saw for large items. Here a block of model-making wax is being cut to size. A coping saw can be used to cut wood – oak, for example.

PIERCING CENTRAL AREAS

When you need to cut areas from the centre of a piece of metal, drill a small hole and thread the bottom of the saw blade through the hole. Refasten it tightly and cut out the required area. Clean the inside edges with a fine saw blade (size 04/02), working with a gentle stroking action down the edge of the metal.

PIERCING OUT THE CENTRAL SECTION FOR A COMPLEX DESIGN

1 Draw the pattern on a piece of tracing paper. Rub the surface of the metal with clay or putty and stick the tracing onto the metal.

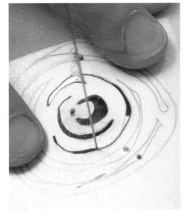

CUTTING OUT A DESIGN

1 Draw the design on tracing paper, then coat the back of the tracing with spray adhesive and place it on the metal.

2 Beginning in the centre, drill a hole in the areas to be cut out. Pierce along the lines of the tracing.

3 Complete all the piercing of the inside of the design before cutting out the outside shape. Peel off the tracing paper. If some paper is left, it will burn off during annealing.

2 Transfer the pattern to the surface of the metal and cut out the edges with a piercing saw. Remove the tracing paper and use a scriber to outline the traced lines of the pattern.

3 Solder together the ends of the ring and shape it on a triblet.

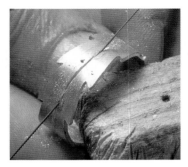

4 Draw a line around the centre of the ring and use the piercing saw to cut the ring into two halves.

5 Clean up the sawn edges with a flat file.

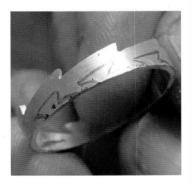

6 Go over the scribed lines of the pattern with a sharp pencil to make the lines easier to follow with the piercing saw.

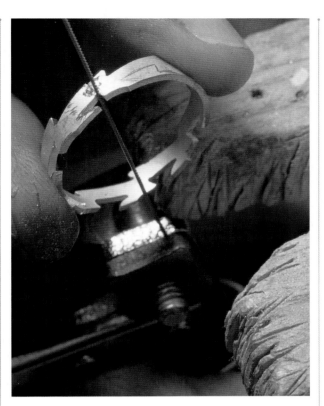

7 Carefully pierce out the pattern from both sides.

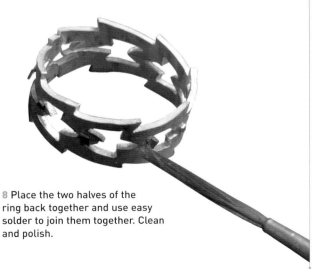

8 Place the two halves of the ring back together and use easy solder to join them together. Clean and polish.

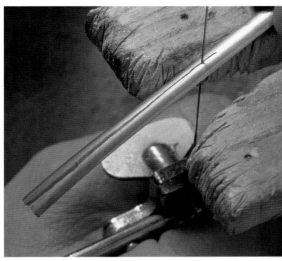

CUTTING WIRE AND CHENIER USING A PIERCING SAW

1 Mark the centre line with a pair of dividers, set to half the width of the metal. Place one side of the dividers against the edge of the wire and draw a line down the centre, then cut the line with the saw.

2 Use a jointing tool to hold chenier or wire if you want to cut a straight edge. Place the chenier through the tool until it is the right length and fasten the little screw to hold the chenier in place. Lean the blade of the saw against the edge of the tool to cut straight down through the chenier.

FILING

THE PURPOSE OF FILING IS TO REMOVE EXCESS METAL. JEWELLERY MAKERS USE DIFFERENT GRADES OF FILE TO ACHIEVE DIFFERENT FINISHES, BUT LARGE ESCAPEMENT AND ENGINEERING FILES ARE NOT SUITABLE FOR DELICATE JEWELLERY. FILING IS ALSO THE FIRST STEP TOWARD FINISHING A PIECE, AND IT IS IMPORTANT THAT YOU USE THE FILES IN THE CORRECT SEQUENCE, SO THAT ANY MARKS MADE BY ONE ARE REMOVED BY THE NEXT. THE FINISHED ARTICLE SHOULD NOT BEAR ANY FILE MARKS. YOU SHOULD ALWAYS TAKE GREAT CARE WHEN FILING – IT IS IMPOSSIBLE TO REPLACE THE METAL REMOVED BY EACH STROKE OF A FILE.

CASTLE RING – KAT ZAHRAN
The grooves in this cast ring are filed to different widths and some are oxidized. The stone reflects the contrasting colours of the oxidization.

Files are graded by the coarseness of the cut. A 'zero' or 0 file is the coarsest, 2 gives a medium cut, and 4 is the finest. Some needle files are graded down to 6. If quite a large amount of metal has to be removed, a large 0 file will do the work most efficiently, but any further filing should be done with a finer grade, and this should be followed by an even finer needle file.

Choose a correctly shaped file for each job. On an inside curve, you should use an oval or a half-round file. If you need a crisp right angle, use a square file. Grooves are best worked with a triangular file. A groove for chenier can be filed with either a round file or a joint round-edge file. Some files have 'safe' edges, so if you need to file close to an area that you do not want to mark, you can work with the safe area next to the area to be protected.

USING FILES
When you use a file, it is important to keep the direction level. For example, if you are straightening a line, use a flat file and keep it absolutely parallel to the line. If you do not, the corners at the ends of the line will tend to curve and drop below the line.

Files usually cut in only one direction, so place the article on the bench pin and hold it steady with one hand while you hold the file in the other hand, and then work with a forward cutting movement. Rubbing a file back and forth over a piece is ineffective.

USING WET AND DRY SANDPAPERS
After filing you should clean the area with wet and dry sandpapers. These are available in grades ranging from 240, through 400 and 600, to 1,200, and you should keep a variety of grades in your workshop so that you can work through each grade if you want a highly polished finish. As their name suggests, these papers can be used with or without water. Water helps to keep the surface smooth by washing away the metal particles as they are removed by the paper. When you are sitting at your work area, however, it is often impracticable to have a bowl of water in front of

you and water dripping on the bench. The papers are, therefore, often used dry.

When you are rubbing a flat metal surface with wet and dry sandpapers, place the paper on a flat surface – an old tile or a piece of mirror, for example, or a metal flat plate – and rub the work along it.

MAKING AN EMERY BOARD
Small sections of paper can be cut from a large sheet and wrapped around a file to remove file marks. Papers can also be glued to wooden sticks. Take a small piece of wood, approximately 6 × 50 × 200 mm (¼ × 2 × 8 in.) and glue a section of wet and dry sandpaper, about 50 × 130 mm (2 × 5 in.), around one end of the stick. The wood creates a firm, flat base that can be pulled across the metal. This is used dry.

BURNISHING
A burnisher is a highly polished, hard steel tool that is rubbed firmly back and forth on metal to create a polished, shiny surface.

A curved burnisher can be used to polish the top edge of the bezel for a cabochon stone setting. This is a delicate operation, but you do need to exert quite a lot of pressure on a burnisher to polish a surface, and it is easy to slip and damage the stone, especially a soft stone such as an opal, which could crack under sudden pressure. Use your other hand as a brake on the burnisher to avoid damaging the stone.

Use your burnisher to remove scratches caused by slips of engraving tools or other little mishaps. Put a drop of oil on the affected area and rub the burnisher sideways, along the direction of the scratch. If you rub the burnisher across the direction of the scratch, you may make it worse. Finish off with fine-grade wet and dry sandpaper, again working in the same direction as you smooth over the burnished area.

SEE ALSO
• Bending, pages 56–59

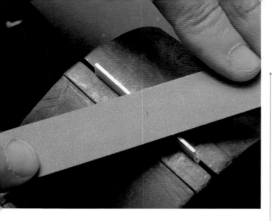

USING FILES

1 When you file a straight edge, keep the file level by balancing it with your non-working hand. Cut across the edge at a slight angle, rather than directly across it, and make sure that you do not drop the file at the ends of the piece of metal.

4 Flatten uneven edges of a ring by rubbing it on a broad flat file, held steady on a flat surface.

MAKING A CHAMFERED EDGE

1 Use a pair of dividers to draw a line 2 mm (1/16 in.) from the top edge of the ring.

2 When you file a curved surface with a flat file, use stroking, upward movements. On the ring, for example, the file is moved against the curve of the metal, and the ring is moved around so that the file covers the whole surface.

5 Use a round needle file to clean up the inside surface of a ring.

2 Hold a broad flat file at an angle of 45 degrees, working around the edge down to the line marked in step 1. Remove the marks made by the large flat file with a flat needle file and clean the edge thoroughly with wet and dry sandpaper before polishing.

3 Use an oval file on the bottom curve of the inside of a ring, working with sweeping movements. Turn the ring around so that the file can make the same movement, but from the other side. Always take care that you do not file away too much metal, especially around a soldered joint.

TYPES OF FILE

1 Large flat file; **2** large oval file; **3** riffler files, designed to reach inside awkward places and useful for filing inside little holes between twisted wires, in convex and concave areas, and for removing traces of solder; **4** needle files.

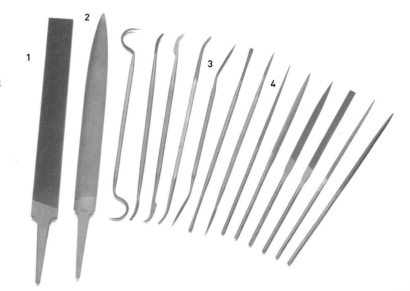

FILING OTHER SURFACES

1 Use a three-cornered or square file to make a groove in the metal that is to be bent to a right angle. Begin the groove with a scriber or by making a cut with a saw blade. Use the file only when the line has been established.

FINISHING OFF FILED SURFACES

1 When a flat edge is required on a flat surface, use wet and dry paper to clean the area.

3 Wrap wet and dry paper around an oval needle file, and working with the same sweeping movement, clean away the marks left by the needle file.

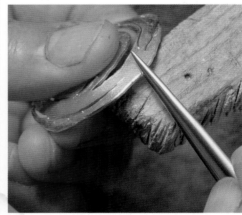

2 A riffler file can be used to remove paillons of solder from areas that other files cannot reach.

2 Emery boards can be used to clean up flat surfaces.

4 Use a burnisher to give polished highlights to edges and raised areas. Keep the burnisher highly polished for the best results.

RIFFLER FILES
Riffler files are available in various shapes. This one is being used to clean up a cast ring.

DRILLING

THE MOST IMPORTANT RULE TO OBSERVE IN DRILLING IS TO MAKE SURE THAT THE HOLE IS DRILLED WHERE YOU WANT IT. THIS IS NOT AS SIMPLE AND OBVIOUS AS IT MAY SOUND, AND IT IS WORTH SPENDING A LITTLE TIME THINKING ABOUT THE POSITION BEFORE YOU BEGIN WORK.

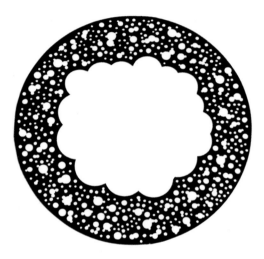

BLACK COLLAR PIECE – ISABELLA METAXA
This piece is made from industrial rubber and shows the effectiveness of drilling lots of different-size holes. Some holes are drilled up close to another, which joins the holes together and makes the appearance less uniform.

MARKING YOUR POSITION

Always mark the position for the hole before you begin to drill. This can be done with a sprung centre punch, by punching a small mark, or with the point of a scriber. Choose one of the above that is a suitable size for the hole to be drilled and for the thickness of metal.

When using a scriber, hold it firmly on the metal and push down with a quick side-to-side motion. If you use a sprung centre punch, lay the piece to be drilled on a flat metal surface, place the centre punch squarely on the metal, and push it firmly downward. The centre punch has a fairly strong action and will usually displace a little of the metal around it, but this is not important if the hole to be drilled is fairly large.

USING A DRILL

Another element to plan ahead is the stage at which you drill. It is much simpler to drill into a large area of uncut metal than to have to make an accurate hole in a small, neatly cut piece. If you need a centrally positioned hole, it is often easier to drill the hole and then cut the shape around it.

You will need to hold the piece securely while you drill. If the metal can move, it will just spin around with the drill. Usually, it can be held comfortably in your hand on the pin of the bench, but metal drilled with a bit held in a pendant motor or with an electric pedestal drill can become very hot. In this case, clamp the piece with some wood, which can be held in the hand, or dip the drill into oil and water as you work to keep it cool. It is easier to drill a large hole if you drill a small hole first and then enlarge the hole gradually.

DRILLING TOOLS
1 Bow drill with cord at correct tension; **2** handheld pin drill with four different chucks.

DRILLING IN A CURVED SURFACE

Do not try to drill straight into a curved surface because the drill bit will not be able to gain purchase and will slide around and may even break. File a small, flat area on top of the curve, mark the spot to be drilled with a pencil and then mark it firmly with a scriber.

MAKING A SMALL DRILL

Small drills can be made from sewing needles. Hold the eye end of the needle in a pair of flat-nosed pliers and snap off the last, pointed one-third with another pair of pliers. Rub the snapped-off end on an oiled carborundum stone, working on opposite sides to create a wedge shape with an angle of about 45 degrees. Lightly smooth away the two opposite corners, which form the sides of the wedge. Drill bits made in this way are very useful and strong, but they are not suitable for drilling metal that is thicker than 1 mm ($\frac{1}{32}$ in.).

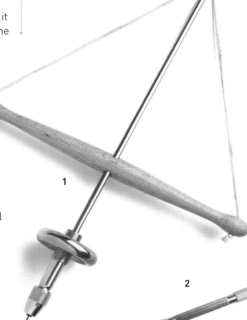

1

2

DRILLING A HOLE IN FLAT METAL

1 Use a centre punch or a scriber to mark the centre of the hole you wish to drill.

2 Hold the metal in one hand while you make the hole with a small hand drill.

DRILLING A HOLE IN A CURVED SURFACE

Carefully flatten the area you want to drill with a flat needle file. Mark the centre and use a drill held in the pendant motor to make the hole. If you want a slightly larger hole, move the drill in and out of the hole, pushing it gently against the edges to widen the circle.

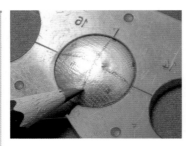

DRILLING A HOLE IN A DOME

1 Place the dome in a circular template and use a pencil to mark the centre point.

2 Slightly flatten the top with a flat needle file and mark the centre again before drilling through. Use a small hand drill or hold the drill in the chuck of a pendant motor.

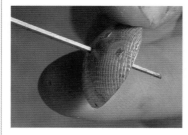

3 Twist a reamer through the hole to enlarge it.

WORKING ON SMALL PIECES

When you are drilling through a tiny piece, hold it firmly in a pair of parallel pliers.

USING A BOW DRILL

1 Place your second and third fingers on top of the handle of the bow drill, with your thumb and fourth and fifth fingers positioned under the handle to guide the handle up and down the shaft.

2 The bow will find its own momentum as the tensioned string winds and unwinds around the shaft. It is possible to use very fine drill bits with a bow drill.

INLAYING

FINE METAL LINES CAN BE LAID INTO CONTRASTING METALS OR INTO OTHER MEDIA, SUCH AS WOOD, TO PRODUCE INTRICATE PATTERNS AND DESIGNS IN A FINELY FINISHED SURFACE. THE TRADITIONAL METHOD IS FOR THE INLAID METAL TO BE HELD IN CHANNELS OR GROOVES THAT ARE CHISELLED FROM THE BACKGROUND METAL. THE GROOVES ARE CUT IN SUCH A WAY THAT A BURR IS RAISED ON EACH SIDE OF THE CUT; THESE BURRS ARE PUSHED DOWN AND BURNISHED OVER THE FINE METAL WIRE THAT IS LAID IN THE CHANNELS.

There are some remarkable examples of extraordinarily detailed Japanese metal inlay work, and it is worth looking in a museum to see some of the finest work of this kind.

The technique illustrated here will enable you to achieve the same effect without having to master completely the skills of accurate chisel and tool work that are essential for traditional inlay work. It is, however, important to understand the principles underlying the traditional method by which fine wire is laid into the surface of another metal.

THE METAL

Use a metal that contrasts well with the wire that is to be inlaid. The metal should be 1 mm (1/32 in.) thick, so that a deep enough channel to accommodate the wire can be cut without a mark appearing on the back when the wire is hammered in. The thinner the metal you use, the finer should be the wire that is inlaid.

The metal should be annealed and then held flat in firm pitch or in jeweller's wax. The lines for inlay should be transferred directly onto the metal by tracing through the design, or by marking the metal with a pencil or scriber.

THE WIRE

You can use either round or rectangular wire. It should be well annealed and fit closely into the channel. Fine silver and gold wires, which are soft and flexible, are ideal for inlay work, but whatever you use must be a strong contrast with the background metal.

THE TOOLS

A **chasing hammer** is used to hit the top of the **chisel** as it cuts into the metal. The chisel is held at the same angle as a tracing punch – that is, it is held between the thumb and index finger of one hand, with the handle pointing away from your body while your other fingers rest on the metal. The chisel is worked toward you along the prepared line.

The cut, which is the essence of inlay, must be undercut. This means that the edges are raised slightly during cutting so that when the wire is laid in position, the edges are hammered down and so hold the wire in position.

The chisel has a cutting edge, of which the bottom edge is somewhat ground away to enable a very fine line to be cut. Chisels used for cutting metal do not have wooden handles, like those used for working with wood. The handles are made of steel stock, and the cutting end should be tempered.

A **matting or embossing punch** is used to beat the wire into the channel. It is held vertically above the wire and hammered with a chasing hammer or a heavier hammer if necessary. The face of the punch must be wide enough to spread across both the inlaid wire and the raised edges of the channel.

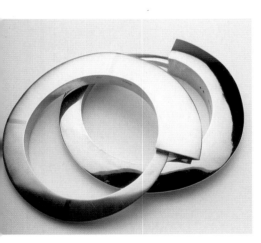

CHINESE CIRCLE BANGLES – JINKS McGRATH
Strips of 9-carat gold sheet were inlaid into the construction of these bangles to form a geometric pattern.

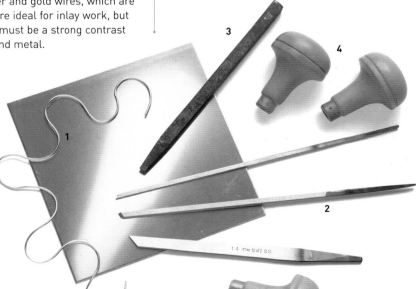

TOOLS FOR INLAY
1 Brass sheet with contrasting silver wire; **2** chisel-type gravers with different-sized cutting edges; **3** large punch for tapping wire into grooves; **4** wooden handles for graver chisels.

The groove or channel can also be cut with **engraving tools**. The first line is cut with a graver with a lozenge-shaped head, and the base of this line is broadened by a flat-edged graver. Wire can be punched into the groove, but it will need to be held in place with solder because there is no raised edge to push down to hold the wire in place. Use the smallest possible amount of solder and file the surface level after soldering.

INLAYING THE WIRE

Place one end of the wire at the start of the chiselled groove and tap it into place with a punch to make sure that it is held firmly. The wire is then inserted gradually into the line, pressed into place by the punch as you work along the channel. The main object of the process is to push over the edges of the groove that were raised during chiselling. When the wire has been pushed into place, a burnisher can be used to smooth the top of the wire and any rough edges.

If you are using a rectangular wire for the inlay, burnish along the bottom edge to create a slight overhang that will fit snugly into the chiselled groove.

INLAYING LARGER PIECES OF METAL

When you are inlaying larger areas of metal into each other, the piece being inlaid should fit exactly into the receiving metal. If you cut the shape to receive the inlay first, use the cut-out piece as a template around which you can scribe the shape onto the inlay metal. The shape should be fractionally larger than the template to allow for the width of the saw blade in the receiving metal. File the inlay piece so that it fits exactly.

SEE ALSO

• Annealing, pages 42–43
• Using wire, pages 86–91

INLAYING WIRE

1 Draw the pattern to be inlaid on the surface of the silver.

2 Use a punch that is no wider than the wire that is to be inlaid and, holding the punch above the work, strike it with a medium-weight hammer. Work smoothly along the lines of the design, overlapping each stroke as you make the next one.

3 Cut the wire into appropriate lengths and bend each piece to fit the line made by the punch. Lay all the pieces in position, making sure that none of the wires is longer than the punched groove and that no wire protrudes over the edges of the groove in which it is positioned.

4 Place the piece on a flat plate and place another flat plate over it. Strike the plate with a heavy hammer, held upright over the plate.

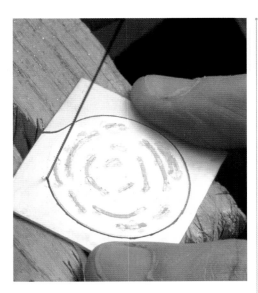

5 Flux all around the flattened wires and place a paillon of solder at each end of each wire. Solder them in place. Pierce around the shape. This piece was then domed (see Doming and swaging, pages 62–65), and further soldering was completed with medium and easy solder.

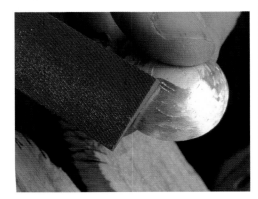

6 Use a coarse file to remove the sections of wire protruding above the surface of the metal. Then use a finer file before working through the grades of wet and dry sandpapers until the surface of the metal is absolutely smooth and the two metals look like one.

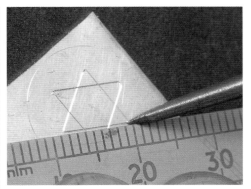

INLAYING LARGER PIECES OF METAL
1 Draw accurately the area to be removed from the main piece of metal.

2 Drill a fine hole just in from the scribed line, thread the saw blade through the hole and pierce out the shape. The piercing must be done as precisely as possible because the success of the technique lies in accurate cutting.

3 Place the cut-out pattern onto the metal that is to be used for the inlay. Hold it steady and scribe around the outside. Pierce around the line and use a file to smooth the shape until it fits exactly into the cut-out shape.

4 Press the cut-out shape into the metal and paint flux in the area to be joined. Turn the piece over so that solder can be applied to the back of the piece. Solder it in place.

5 A circle was scribed around the star and the shape cut out and domed before being polished.

MAKING BLANKS

THE RT BLANKING SYSTEM IS A METHOD FOR REPRODUCING A LARGE NUMBER OF IDENTICAL TWO-DIMENSIONAL PIECES (OR BLANKS). ALTHOUGH IT TAKES A LITTLE GETTING USED TO, THE SYSTEM DOES WORK WELL.

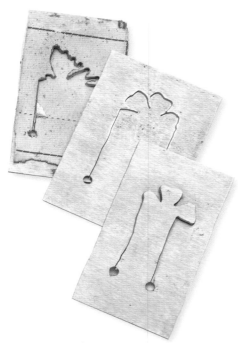

BLANKING TOOLS
Stainless steel blanks; cut and used with the RT blanking system.

SEE ALSO

• Piercing, pages 20–23
• Stamping and embossing, pages 82–85

The system is, basically, a hand-operated fret saw, except that the table through which the saw passes can be tilted at a variety of angles according to the thickness of the metal being cut to create the blank. A chart accompanying the system is used to get the angle correct. The blanks are cut from stainless steel, which, because of its strength, can be used for at least 500 blankings. The blade of the saw is tightened by a long screw arm, which is tricky to do at first, but it does work, so it is worth persevering. Follow the instructions to make the first cut-out shapes, and you will quickly see how you can adapt the system to create your own designs. You may find it easier to cut half a design first, then to turn it over and cut the other half rather than cutting the whole design at once.

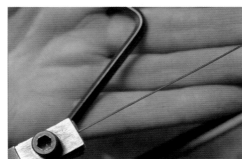

MAKING STAINLESS STEEL BLANKS
1 Position the saw blade so that the teeth point down but sideways in the saw. Anchor the blade with the Allen key provided.

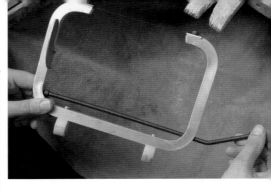

2 Tighten the blade with the long screw that fits through the saw.

3 Use the chart provided with the saw to adjust the angle of the table. This angle will depend on the thickness of the steel sheet you are using, so you should measure that first.

4 Hold the saw loosely at the base and let it fall through the steel as you saw around the pattern.

5 Press apart the pattern through the steel sheet with your finger and thumb.

MAKING SILVER MOTIFS USING THE PREPARED BLANK

1 Slide the silver sheet up between the two pieces of steel, making sure that you push enough silver into place to allow the second cut of the pattern.

4 Reverse the position of the silver in the jig to prepare for the second cut.

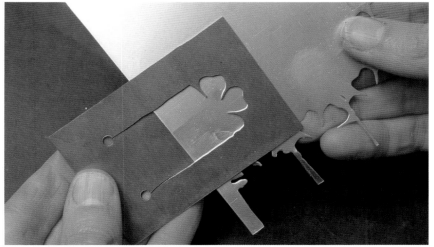

5 Place the silver/ steel sandwich between the two flat plates as before to produce the blank.

6 You can now make as many pieces, all exactly the same, as you wish.

2 Place the silver-and-steel 'sandwich' between two flat plates and hit it sharply with a heavy hammer.

3 One side of the pattern is now cut.

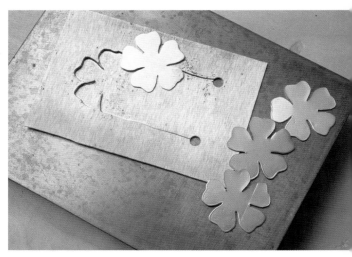

LATHE WORK

A LATHE IS A USEFUL ADDITION TO THE JEWELLERY WORKSHOP. ITS BASIC FUNCTION IS TO CUT, SHAPE AND DRILL A BLOCK OR ROD OF METAL, WOOD OR WAX. THE MATERIAL IS HELD IN A CHUCK THAT REVOLVES, SO THE BLOCK IS FIRST TURNED INTO A TRUE CYLINDER, AFTER WHICH THE CUTTING AND SHAPING CAN BEGIN.

Lathes come in different shapes and sizes. The most suitable for a small jewellery workshop is one which will sit on a bench top. Multipurpose lathes, which turn themselves inside-out to become drilling or milling machines are available, but they are usually overcomplicated and require a large amount of time to convert them from one application to another. A simple lathe, with additions as you need them and a simple drilling machine, will serve you much better.

If you have a lot of floor space in your workshop, a heavier duty, floor-standing lathe can be a good investment. When making a purchase, make sure that the lathe is steady and does not have any 'play' when turning.

HOW A LATHE WORKS

A lathe comes supplied with a chuck (called the headstock), which is usually three-jawed, allowing for different sizes of cylinder to be fixed into it. At the other end, the tailstock – a different chuck for holding drills – slots into the other end, to provide an accurate location for drilling down the centre of the piece being held in the headstock. When working on a long length of rod, a tailstock centre is used to hold the loose end in a straight line.

Other accessories include a 'compound slide', which allows you to cut into the cylinder at an angle; a four-jaw chuck, used for holding irregular shapes to be turned down into a cylinder; and a large variety of cutting tools.

As with any tool with a motor, great care must be taken when operating the machine. It is always better to remove jewellery and make sure that any loose clothing is either covered or kept well out of the way. Long hair should always be tied back.

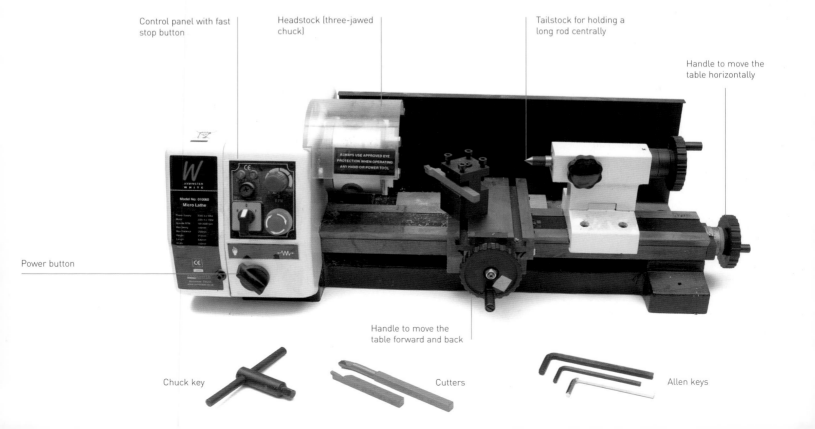

Control panel with fast stop button

Headstock (three-jawed chuck)

Tailstock for holding a long rod centrally

Handle to move the table horizontally

Power button

Handle to move the table forward and back

Chuck key

Cutters

Allen keys

USING A LATHE

After the piece is inserted and tightened in the chuck, the first thing to do is to make sure it is centred. Turn the lathe on and see how the piece turns. If it is very wobbly, it is either too long or it is in the wrong position in the chuck. If it is long, use the tailstock centre to hold it steady by placing the tip into the centre of the piece, otherwise reposition it in the headstock.

If you are not using the tailstock centre, the first cut to make is usually to 'face' the piece. Place the cutter so that the cutting edge is in the centre of the piece. When the lathe is switched on, the cutter should just touch the face. Turn the handle so that the tool comes toward you. All cutting should be done gradually. It is much better to remove small amounts at a time than trying to cut larger areas, since this can cause the machine to stall.

To make the second cut across the face, turn the handle on the tail end a little so that the cutter removes a little more from the face. Only take the cutter to the centre of the piece, not all the way across. Once the face is flat, change the position of the cutting tool so the work on the length of the piece can begin.

The cutting point of the tool should be positioned so that it can run freely along the edge of the piece and that it is not impeded by the guard over the headstock too soon. For the first cut the tool should just skim off the outer edge and then gradually move in. After travelling the length required along the piece for the cut, bring the tool back to the beginning, without turning it in for a further cut. Only move the cutting tool in to make a further cut at the beginning of its run, NOT on the return journey.

Materials such as wax or wood are easier to cut on the lathe than metal, so cuts can be a little deeper with these softer materials. Never try to remove too much metal and always make sure that your piece is securely fastened before starting work.

TURNING WAX FOR A RING

1 Position the cutting tool in the centre of the piece. Adjustments to the height are made on this lathe by altering the position of a wedge underneath the cutting tool and securing that position with the screws on top.

2 Turn the handle counterclockwise to bring the cutting tool toward you. This will remove the first layer of wax. To remove the second layer, turn the handle at the tail clockwise to move the cutting tool a fraction more into the wax face and then repeat the first movement.

3 Reposition the cutting tool so that it can start the cutting along the side of the piece. Make sure that the tool has room for the length of travel required. Only remove thin layers at a time.

4 To hollow out the inside of the ring, a different cutting tool is required. This one has a longer head that will reach down inside the piece. Centre the tool as before and then cut as far down as necessary.

6 With the machine switched off, make a groove with a needle file, by turning the chuck by hand. After the groove is made, saw the ring off with a piercing saw while holding the chuck.

5 This cutting tool has a broad, straight cut, which is being used to angle the sides of the ring.

7 The finished wax ring (enlarged to show detail). This would now have a sprue attached and be prepared in the flask ready for casting.

TURNING A SILVER ROD
This long length of rod is held steady at the centre of the right-hand end with the tapered tailstock. The cutting tool is ready to skim down the length of the rod.

This shorter length of silver rod only needs to be held in the headstock chuck. The cutting tool is positioned so that the rod can be skimmed down as far as required.

This fine-tipped cutter is used to cut into the silver rod to make a decorative groove. This could be filled with either vitreous enamel, an acrylic or left as it is. The advantage of a lathe is that the groove is absolutely accurate, which is difficult to achieve with a file or a piercing saw.

The table on the lathe is called a compound slide and can be set to an angle. This allows the cutting tool to make a cut at a chosen angle in the silver.

ENGRAVING

ENGRAVING IS THE ART OF REMOVING
SURFACE METAL TO CREATE A
DECORATION. MUCH OF THE FINELY
WORKED SILVER AND GOLD THAT IS SEEN
IS THE WORK OF HIGHLY SKILLED
PROFESSIONAL ENGRAVERS, WHO USE
TECHNIQUES AND PRACTICES ACQUIRED
OVER MANY YEARS. HOWEVER, MOST
JEWELLERY MAKERS CAN LEARN THE
RUDIMENTS OF ENGRAVING, AND IT CAN
BE USED TO GOOD EFFECT IN
A VARIETY OF WAYS.

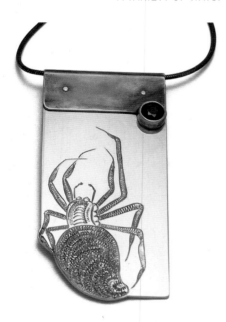

SPIDER PENDANT – ANASTASIA YOUNG
This engraved piece is made from silver, 18-carat
gold and garnet. It is a great example of the
incredible detail and delicacy that can be achieved
by using this technique.

THE TOOLS

The cutting edges most often used in
engraving are:
• Lozenge – for lines
• Square or diamond – for lines
• Dotter or round
• Square scorper – for removing metal
• Spitstick – for cleaning up edges
• Chisel
• Liner – for making background channels

The steel engraving tool is made or bought
separately from the handle, and can be made
to the appropriate shape and length to suit
individual needs. For example, straight gravers
are suitable for working on flat or convex
surfaces, while angled or curved ones are
better for working on concave or repoussé
surface. See Stamping and embossing (pages
82–85) for making steel tools.

The handles are made from wood and can be
either round or have one flat side, which makes
it possible to hold the tool almost level with
the work.

Always keep the cutting edge crisp and
sharp. The belly of the tool – that is, the area
where it meets the cutting edge – can be
rubbed back to a slight angle with a stone to
prevent drag lines being made on the metal. If
necessary, the tool can be shortened by holding
it in a vice and snapping off the shaft.

HOLDING THE WORK

Work that is to be engraved must be held
steady and flat, but you also need to be able to
turn it freely as you work. There are several
options. Work can be held in a wooden vice that
is itself held on a revolving sandbag, or it can
be held in the pitch bowl, which you can turn by
hand. If you are working on a small, flat piece,
an engraver's hand-held vice is useful. The
piece is held by pins that can be located in any
of the holes covering the surface of the vice.

Other pieces can be placed on the pin on
the bench and held by hand. Hold the work
between your thumb and index finger so that
you can make a smooth movement when the
work has to be turned. Take care to keep your

fingers out of the line of the engraving tool. If
it slips, you may cut your fingers badly. Holding
work by hand can be quite tiring, so if you are
working on a complex piece that will take some
time to complete, try to find another way.

HOLDING THE TOOL

The wooden handle of the tool should sit
comfortably in the palm of your hand. Your
index finger should extend so that it lies along
the top of the tool, and the thumb of the hand
holding the tool should rest on the surface of
the metal being engraved or on the medium
in which it is being held. This thumb acts as a
guide and a brake and sometimes as a pivot.

CUTTING

Select a tool that is the correct shape for the
cut to be made. It must be sharpened on a
stone to an angle of 45 degrees. If it is less than
45 degrees, the tip will be too long and may
snap. If it is more than 45 degrees, it is more
difficult to work and tends to dig into the metal.

To start a cut on a straight line, hold the tool
almost vertically so that it gets some purchase
in the metal, then quickly lower it so that your
thumb can be placed horizontally on the work.
Push the tool along the line to raise a tiny curl
of metal, then flick up the tool to remove the
sliver. Continue in this way along the line.

Curved lines are made with a tool that has
been stoned away on one side edge. Turn the
work smoothly as the line is being cut – the
hand that is holding the tool should remain in
more or less the same position while the work
beneath it is turned.

When engraving is used to remove areas
of metal, the area should be outlined with
a lozenge chisel and then a second line,
approximately 1–2 mm (1/32 in.) inside the first,
should be cut. The area within the second line

SEE ALSO
• Stamping and embossing,
pages 82–85

is then removed with a square scorper or chisel. The base can then be engraved with a lined tool and the edges cut away with a smaller square scorper before being cleaned up with a spitstick.

SHARPENING THE GRAVER

Use a fine carborundum stone or an Arkansas stone to sharpen your engraving tools. Put a small amount of oil on the stone and hold the tool flat on its face at an angle of 45 degrees from the stone. Rub the tool along the stone, to and fro, making sure that the whole face remains in contact with the top of the stone. Turn the tool over and rub the stone square along the belly or hold it at an angle if you want to smooth away part of the belly. If the side needs to be shaped or sharpened, hold it at the correct angle and rub in a circular motion.

PREPARING THE TOOLS
1 Line up the bottom edge of the engraving tool with the flat side of the handle.

2 Hold the tool in the safe jaws of the vice and use a mallet to hammer down the handle onto it.

1 Engraver's vice – adjustable hand-held vice which holds varying sizes of metal to be engraved; **2** four assorted gravers; **3** flat-sided handles; **4** Arkansas sharpening stone, which should be used with oil.

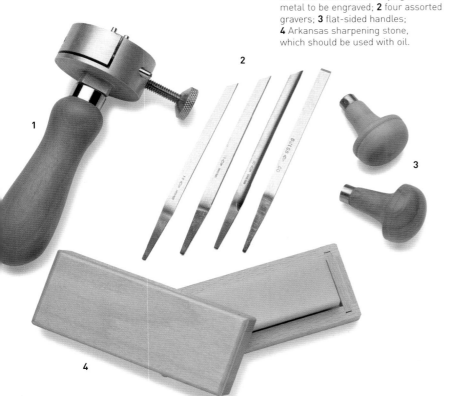

3 Put a little oil on the stone and sharpen the graver by rubbing it straight along its cutting angle.

ENGRAVING A DESIGN

1 Rub the surface of the metal with putty and then trace it through to transfer the design to be engraved to the surface of the metal; make sure that the lines are clear and easy to follow.

2 Follow the line with a lozenge engraving tool. Remove small slivers and flick up the tool to clear away the sliver.

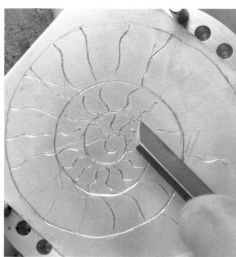

3 When you need to turn to the left or right, grind the edge of the tool so that it naturally turns that way.

4 Use a chisel-end tool to dig out a little edge up to the main line of the pattern.

5 Use the lozenge tool for the pattern. Here it is being used to cross-hatch shaded areas.

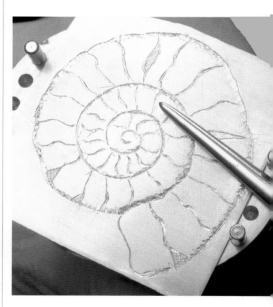

6 Unintentional slips with the graver can be disguised by dropping a spot of oil on the area and rubbing along the scratch with a polished burnisher. Keep the burnisher low so that it straddles the line and do not rub across the line, since it will accentuate the error.

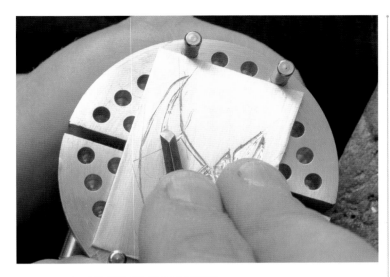

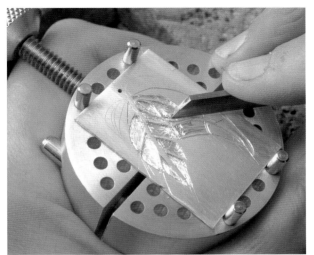

REMOVING METAL FOR INLAY OR ENAMEL

1 To remove metal for inlay or enamel, outline the pattern with a lozenge tool, then engrave another line close to the first.

4 Remove the edges up to the first line.

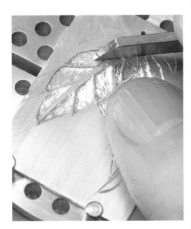

2 Remove the area within this second line with a chisel-type tool.

3 Use a flat-faced tool to level the base of this area. Press some plasticine clay down into the areas from which you have removed the metal to check that it is perfectly level.

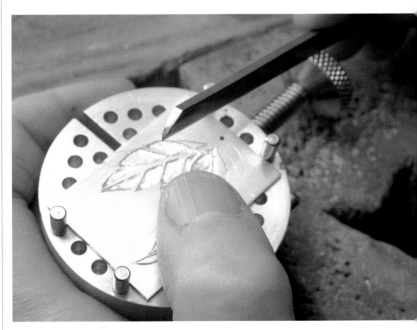

5 Clean up all the edges with a spitstick.

HEATING METAL

At some stage while working with metal, you will need to apply heat. This is usually by means of a flame from a torch that is hot enough to achieve the temperatures necessary to: keep the metal soft by annealing, which makes it easier to work; to permanently join one surface to another by soldering; or to join one piece to another by fusing the surfaces together.

ANNEALING

ANNEALING IS THE PROCESS USED TO SOFTEN METAL BY HEATING IT BEFORE YOU BEGIN TO WORK WITH IT. METAL IS ALSO ANNEALED WHEN IT BECOMES 'WORK-HARDENED' – THAT IS, WHEN IT BECOMES INFLEXIBLE AFTER BEING BENT, DRAWN, HAMMERED OR BEATEN.

Each metal has its own melting point, and each metal, therefore, must be annealed at a different temperature. Some metals – fine (pure) gold and fine silver, for instance – need little or no annealing because they will remain pliable throughout most processes and can be reduced by up to 70 per cent before they require annealing. Other metals, especially copper, quickly become work-hardened and need regular annealing. Metal is usually annealed with a torch, and there are several types to choose from: air- or oxygen-assisted propane torches; mouth 'blow' torches; propane gas torches; and natural gas torches. When you use a torch, a large 'reducing' flame is played over the surface of the metal until it turns the right colour. The most effective part of the flame for annealing purposes is about 2.5 cm (1 in.) or so from the end, at the point at which the orange centre meets the blue section.

Metals should be held at the correct temperature for about 10 seconds. It is, of course, impossible to measure the temperature of a piece of metal while it is being heated, but it is possible to estimate the temperature from the ways in which metals change colour as they become hot – the ability to identify the different colours will come with time. It is easier to identify the colour of a piece of metal as it is being heated if the annealing is done on the dark area of a charcoal block. Close the curtains to cut out any direct sunlight, and switch off your bench light when you are using a torch to anneal or solder.

Metal can also be annealed in a kiln, although by the time the kiln has warmed to the correct temperature, it is usually quicker and more practical to use a hand-held torch. A kiln can be useful, however, if you are working with a large piece of metal or a coil of fine wire. It can, for example, be difficult to anneal wire with a gauge of 0.5 mm or less because the wire could easily melt in the direct flame of a blow torch. Coil the fine wire into an old tin can and place it in a preheated kiln for a minute or two.

The chart opposite indicates the different annealing and melting temperatures of the metals you will be working with. It also indicates how the metal should be cooled or quenched after annealing. These figures should be regarded as guidelines, and you should always check the technical data supplied by your metal dealer because they will always include precise instructions.

SEE ALSO
• Pickling and quenching, pages 44–47

ANNEALING TOOLS
1 Soldering block can be placed straight onto the bench with the charcoal block **(2)** on top.

1

2

COPPER

1 Place the copper on a charcoal block.

3 When the metal is a deep pink, extinguish the flame and quench the copper.

2 Heat 18-carat yellow gold until it is deep pink before quenching.

4 Anneal 18-carat white gold by heating it until it is deep pink. Hold it at that colour for a few seconds before quenching.

2 Heat the metal with a large reducing flame.

GOLD

1 Anneal 9-carat gold by heating the metal until it is a dull red. Hold it at that colour for a few seconds, then allow it to cool to black heat before quenching.

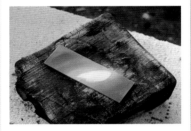

3 Heat 18-carat red gold until it is deep red. Hold it at that temperature for a few seconds before quenching.

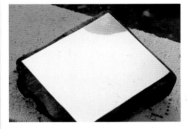

SILVER

Place the silver on the charcoal block and heat with a large reducing flame until the metal is a dull pink. Hold the silver at that colour for a few seconds before quenching.

ANNEALING AND QUENCHING TEMPERATURE

METAL	ANNEALING TEMPERATURE	MELTING TEMPERATURE	QUENCH
Copper	600–700°C (1110–1290°F)	1083°C (1981.4°F)	Immediately
Silver	600–650°C (1110–1200°F)	960.5°C (1760°F)	Below 500°C (930°F)
Gold	650–750°C (1200–1380°F)	1063°C (1945°F)	As indicated on technical data
White gold	650–750°C (1200–1380°F)	929°C (1704°F)	As indicated on technical data
Platinum	600–1000°C (1110–1830°F)	1769°C (3217°F)	Allow to cool in air, then quench in water

PLATINUM
Heat the metal until it is a deep cherry red; allow to cool before quenching in water.

PICKLING AND QUENCHING

PICKLING IS THE WORD USED TO DESCRIBE CHEMICALLY CLEANING A PIECE OF METAL AFTER IT HAS BEEN HEATED. QUENCHING DESCRIBES THE COOLING OF METAL AFTER HEATING. BOTH PROCESSES CAN BE CARRIED OUT IN A VARIETY OF WAYS.

'SPLASHES' – PHILIP SAJET
This 18-carat gold necklace is based on a mistake – when the artist accidentally poured fluid gold on a wet surface. After about 20 attempts to imitate these forms, this beautifully delicate piece emerged.

PICKLING

While they are heated, brass, copper, nickel silver, silver and golds up to and including 22 carat will oxidize to different degrees. The oxidization appears on the surface of the metal as a greyish-black film, which is removed chemically in an acid solution. Oxides can also be removed with wet and dry papers, fine files and so on, but this also removes minute amounts of metal, so chemical methods are, therefore, preferred.

Dirty or greasy metal must be annealed and then pickled in an acid solution to clean it before soldering can take place. After soldering, use pickle to remove any residual flux because if it is not removed immediately, the flux becomes crusty and is awkward to remove by hand.

QUENCHING

Metal can be quenched either in water or in a pickling solution. You should quench in water if you are using a warm sulfuric acid solution.

After annealing or soldering, allow the metal to cool slightly before quenching. If you do not, you may cause stresses within the structure of the metal that will distort it, and the pickling solution will spit violently and give off fumes.

Leave copper and silver for a few seconds, then use a pair of brass tweezers to place the hot metal in the pickling solution. Remove any binding wire that was used to hold pieces together for soldering. If you place binding wire or steel or iron tweezers in a pickling solution containing sulfuric acid, you will contaminate the solution and everything that is subsequently placed in it.

Before quenching gold, check the technical specifications that will have been supplied with the metal when you obtained it from the dealer. Some golds do not require quenching at all, and others must be quenched below specific temperatures.

SAFETY PROCEDURES

Some pickling solutions contain acid, and they are, therefore, potentially dangerous. When you are mixing a pickle, take a few obvious precautions:

- Make sure that you have easy access to running water in case of spills.

- Always store bottles containing acid where they cannot accidentally be knocked over and, ideally, in a lockable cupboard. Make sure that all bottles are clearly labelled.

- Wear rubber gloves, safety glasses and, preferably, a heavy-duty apron or overall.

- Work in a well-ventilated room or even outdoors because acids give off pungent fumes.

- Always add acid to water; never add water to pure acid.

PREPARING AND USING PICKLING SOLUTIONS

If you spill sulfuric acid, even when it is diluted, onto clothing, a hole will appear after the next washing. There is nothing you can do about this, which is why you should wear a thick apron or, at the very least, old clothes. If you get any sulfuric acid on your skin, rinse it under clear running water; it will leave your skin feeling sore and inflamed. Nitric acid solution splashes on your skin will cause black stains and make your skin feel itchy. Again, rinse the affected area under clear running water. A suitable solution for pickling silver, gold or copper can be made from 1 part sulfuric acid to 10 parts water.

For pickling gold, use a solution of 1 part nitric acid to 8 parts water. Keep this separate and use it only for gold, because if you clean

PREPARING PICKLES

1 Wear thick rubber gloves when you prepare a pickle that contains acid and always add the acid to water – not the other way around.

USING PICKLES

1 When it is used warm, alum will remove oxides and flux residues as effectively as sulfuric acid. Use an ovenproof bowl or jug with a lid.

2 If you leave binding wire on a piece of silver that is being pickled, the metal will turn red when the iron in the wire reacts with the acid. Anything subsequently pickled in the solution will be contaminated.

2 Placing a piece of silver in a hot sulfuric acid solution (10 parts water to 1 part acid) will remove any black oxides.

3 Mix 50 g (1½ oz) alum with 0.5 l (1 pt) water. You can buy alum in most pharmacies.

3 After being quenched in cold water, pieces can be placed in a hot pickle tank to remove the oxides.

4 Make a solution of soda crystals dissolved in hot water. If you are not sure that all the acid has been rinsed away, submerge the piece in the solution of soda crystals and boil it for a minute or two.

gold in a solution that has been used mainly for silver, a silver deposit may be left on the surface of the gold.

Sulfuric-acid solution can be used hot or cold. Mix it in an ovenproof glass bowl or jug with a lid to prevent evaporation. If you are using a warm pickle, place the bowl containing the solution in a second bowl of warm water, which is then heated. Do not place sulfuric acid in a pan or bowl that is subjected to direct heat.

It is possible to obtain special hot pickle tanks made of reinforced plastic. The outer casing containing the water has a thermostatically controlled heater, while the acid solution is held in an inner section.

ALUM PICKLE

Alum is most often used as an astringent or paper mordant, but it is also very effective as a pickling solution for precious metals. It acts more slowly than an acid solution, but is safer for use in the home workshop. Make a solution of 50 g (1½ oz) in 0.5 l (1 pt) of warm water. Mix it either in a fireproof bowl or a jug with a cover so that it can be kept warm over a gentle heat or in a ceramic slow cooker.

Quench heated work in cold water, then place it in the warm alum and leave until clean.

COMMERCIAL PICKLING SOLUTIONS

Your tool and equipment supplier will stock a ready-made commercial pickling solution, such as safety pickle. Read the manufacturer's instructions carefully before use.

'SPENT' PICKLE

After it has been used several times, pickle becomes 'spent' – that is, inactive. This will be obvious as the colour turns deeper and deeper blue, and the pickle takes longer to work.

When you dispose of spent pickle, run the cold tap for a while before slowly pouring away the pickle. Leave the water running while you do this and for a short time afterwards. **Never pour away fresh acid in this way.**

GREENER CHEMICALS FOR YOUR STUDIO BY UTE DECKER

Chemicals used in jewellery making can be extremely toxic and a hassle to dispose of safely. One of the simplest things you can do to lessen the negative health and environmental impact is to reduce chemical use in the studio and select less toxic alternatives for those that can't be avoided.

The most commonly used studio chemical is pickle and with increasing interest in green and ethical jewellery, many jewellers have already made the change back to traditional pickles such as citric acid or a vinegar and salt solution as nontoxic alternatives.

This panel details the main kinds of nontoxic pickle.

CITRIC ACID PICKLE

Component Citric acid, $C_6H_8O_7$, occurs in the metabolism of virtually all living things – particularly rich in citric acid are citrus fruits such as lemons, limes and oranges. It is a fairly common preservative and flavouring agent used in food and beverages as well as an environmentally benign cleaning agent.

Supplier Citric acid is widely available in supermarkets, Indian grocery stores and pharmacies. However, many suppliers are still promoting toxic pickle, including 'Safety pickle', which is a misnomer as it is both toxic and corrosive.

Preparation Mix 1 part citric acid powder with 5–7 parts of water,

depending on the strength required. Always add the citric acid to the water, not the water to the acid. Ideally, use distilled water, alternatively bottled spring water, to prevent the growth of microorganisms. As water evaporates from the solution, simply add more water. If the pickle is weak, add more acid.

Application Citric acid should be used warm for best results in removing flux, oxides and firescale on silver, gold, brass and copper after soldering. It takes slightly longer than other types of pickle, but citric pickle is still quite effective, and many jewellers prefer it. It has several advantages over the traditional pickles: it is gentler to your own health; does not burn holes into your clothes; and does not react with steel, thus steel tweezers and binding wire immersed into the pickle will not plate out copper onto your piece.

Do not overheat or put a hot piece of metal into pickle to quench it. The steam that rises from doing so will be acidic and may irritate the lining of your lungs. This health hazard is considerably greater when using a toxic pickle variety. Borax flux and glass reacts with citric acid and may cause foaming for a few seconds. This is not a problem as long as the pickle container is not overfilled as the frothing will subside quickly.

Copper (as well as gold, silver and platinum) is a heavy metal. Pernicious effects may result from long-term exposure through inhalation of dust, fumes or vapours in the workplace.

Therefore, pickle should only ever be used warm and never overheated to produce excessive evaporation you may then inhale.

Disposal A citric acid pickle solution will work effectively for many months. Citric acid itself is non-toxic and biodegradable and could be poured down the drain, however any pickling solution becomes saturated with copper, which can cause major problems for sewer treatment facilities.

In general, collect all spent pickle in clearly labelled plastic containers with tight lids for storage in the studio and during transportation, preferably with their original labels. Contact your local council for details about disposing of hazardous waste.

VINEGAR AND SALT PICKLE

Many jewellers report excellent results with a mixture of vinegar and salt, which is a simple, cheap and eco-friendly pickle.

Component White wine vinegar plus iodized or kosher salt is recommended by many, even though ordinary table salt works effectively, too.

Preparation About 240 ml (one cup) of vinegar to one teaspoon of salt or slightly more, if required.

Application Vinegar and salt pickle should be used warm for best results. It works quicker than citric acid and good results have been reported for both silver and gold. It does tend to evaporate with

beautiful salt crystals forming around the edge of the pot. You can just top up the solution with vinegar and salt. Leave the lid askew when you cool the solution, or the salt crystals may seal it on.

Vinegar is also used effectively to wash away investment when cleaning off castings. (Keep separate from pickling solution so as not to introduce unnecessary dirt into your pickle.)

Disposal Same applies as to the disposal of citric acid.

ANTICLASTIC CUFF – UTE DECKER
This sculptural cuff was created in 100 per cent recycled silver using anticlastic forging; compressing the inner and stretching the outer sections of silver sheet on stakes. After each annealing, the piece was pickled in environmentally friendly, non-toxic citric acid pickle.

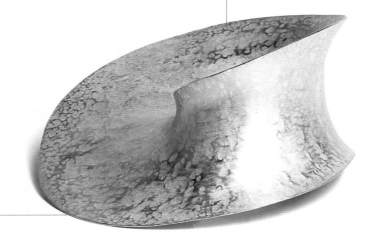

SOLDERING

PRECIOUS METALS ARE USUALLY JOINED TOGETHER BY MEANS OF A SOLDER THAT IS COMPATIBLE WITH THE METAL. SOLDERING IS CARRIED OUT WITH A GAS TORCH, OF WHICH THERE ARE SEVERAL POSSIBLE TYPES AVAILABLE.

GEOMETRIC CUFF LINKS – FAITH TAVENDER
The shapes on these cuff links have all been cut out individually and then sweat-soldered one on top of the other. The edges of each shape are finished before being soldered. The cuffs are then oxidized and polished, leaving the dark areas to emphasize the shapes.

SOLDERING TOOLS I
1 Borax cone for making flux; **2** strips of hard, medium, and easy solder; **3** Argotec, mixed with denatured alcohol and painted onto silver before annealing and/or soldering to prevent fire stain.

SEE ALSO

• Annealing, pages 42–43
• Pickling and quenching, pages 44–47

Before metal is soldered, it must be perfectly clean, and there should be no signs of oxidization or grease on the surface. In addition, the pieces to be joined should fit as closely together as possible, with no visible gap between them. This is because solder flows by capillary action between close-fitting pieces of metal, and if light is visible between the two pieces, soldering will be difficult. When pieces of gold are to be soldered together, the seam must fit as tightly as possible. If there is a gap of any sort, the solder will run on one side of the seam only – gold solder will never 'jump' across a gap, although silver solder may occasionally do so.

FLUXES

Solder needs an agent to help it flow, and this agent is called flux. Different kinds of flux should be used with different types of solder and at different temperatures. It prevents any air that is around the seam being soldered from oxidizing in the heat from the flame, thereby keeping the metal clean enough for the solder to run and make the joint.
Borax The most common, general-purpose borax comes in a cone, which sits in a ceramic dish.
Auflux Also a general-purpose flux, auflux is supplied in liquid form. Use a paintbrush to transfer it to the seam.

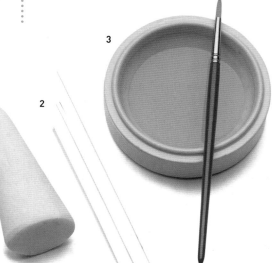

Tenacity no. 5 Like Easy-flo, this flux comes in powder form and is mixed with water to form a paste. It can withstand much higher temperatures, and it is, therefore, used with metals that require high-temperature solders.

TYPES OF SOLDERS

For the projects in this book, silver solder has been used on all the metals, apart from gold and platinum.
Silver solder Silver solder is available in five different grades – enamelling, hard, medium, easy and extra easy – and it is supplied in strips about 46 cm (18 in.) long.
   Enamelling This is the solder with the highest melting point, and it requires a temperature of around 810°C (1490°F), which is close to the melting temperature of standard silver, 960.5°C (1760°F). For this reason, enamelling solder can cause problems. It is, as the name suggests, used on work that is to be enamelled, but not normally for other purposes. Enamel fires at temperatures between 780–980°C (1440–1800°F), so the higher the melting point of the solder, the less likelihood that the seam will come apart in the kiln. In practice, however, hard solder usually withstands lower enamelling temperatures and can be used instead.
   Hard The strips of hard solder are about 6 mm (¼ in.) wide. If a piece is to have more than one soldered seam, hard solder is the grade to use first, and if a piece has several seams, it is possible, if you are careful, to use hard solder four or five times before using medium or easy solder.
   Medium This solder is sold in strips approximately 2 mm (¹⁄₁₆ in.) wide. It can be difficult to use because it sometimes seems 'sticky' and unwilling to flow. It should be used after hard solder but before easy solder.
   Easy Strips of easy solder are about 3 mm (⅛ in.) wide, and the solder melts at about 670°C (1240°F). It is used for soldering findings, attachments, jump rings and so on, and it is sometimes used when there is just a single joint on a piece – on a simple ring, for example.
   Extra easy This kind of solder should be used only as a last resort. It has a very low

melting point, and it has a rather yellowish-grey appearance.

Gold solder There is a separate solder for use with each carat of gold. It is sometimes supplied in small sheets, about 2 × 3 cm (¾ × 1¼ in.) Each separate carat is available as easy, medium and hard solder, and it can be obtained in the same colours as the gold you have used – yellow, red, white and green.

Platinum solder Solder for platinum is available in hard, medium, easy and extra easy forms. Platinum is a very strong metal, which can be worked extremely finely while still retaining a strong structure. Heat is applied only to the area to be soldered. A fine, hot flame is recommended for soldering platinum, and tinted goggles are usually worn because the temperatures are higher than those needed for silver or gold.

OTHER EQUIPMENT

Keep a pair of insulated tweezers or a titanium soldering stick in your free hand as you solder. If a piece moves or if a paillon of solder becomes dislodged, you can carefully push it back into place. Do not immerse your insulated tweezers in acid, however. Use brass tongs or tweezers to take the metal into and out of the pickle.

Binding wire is used to hold pieces together so that they can be soldered. Never quench a piece in acid while the binding wire is still in place. Either quench the article in cold water, remove the wire and then pickle in hot acid, or remove the binding wire with snips while the piece is still hot, and then quench in the pickle.

SOLDERING METALS

Work that is to be soldered is placed either on a charcoal block or on a heat-resistant soldering block. These can be placed directly on the bench, provided they are on some kind of protective metal sheet. A revolving tray, which can be turned around as soldering progresses, is very useful.

When you are soldering, work in a darkened area. In this way you will be able to see the changing colours of the metal as it is heated.

Flux must be applied carefully onto and into

the area to be soldered. For example, if you are soldering a ring, the two sides should be sprung apart slightly so that the flux can be applied to each side before being allowed to spring back into place. The appropriate grade and quantity of solder should be cut into tiny paillons and placed in the flux. If the paillons of solder need to be held at an awkward angle for soldering, a little 'teepol' or detergent can be added to the flux to help hold the solder in position. If you hammer or roll silver solder before use, you will be able to cut even smaller paillons.

The work should be heated gently at first. Always play the flame over the whole piece. When soldering silver, the entire article needs to be at soldering temperature before the solder will begin to flow. When soldering gold, concentrate on the area to be soldered to make the solder flow once the entire piece is hot. If you need to 'un-solder' a piece, tie the article to a charcoal soldering block with binding wire. Apply flux to the joint to be separated and heat the metal until the solder is about to flow. Then use insulated tweezers to pick up or separate the pieces.

COLOUR CHANGES

It is important to be able to recognize the colour changes that occur in different metals so that you will know when the solder is about to flow. The following are guidelines only for the colours of different metals when hard solder will flow:

• Silver – bright cherry red
• 9-carat gold – alarming red
• 18-carat gold – alarmingly bright orange-red

SOLDERING CHAINS

It is possible to solder several sections of a chain that has been connected up at the same time. Lay up to four sections flat across the charcoal block so that none of the joints to be soldered touch any other part of the links. Cut up paillons of the solder you will be using and place them in the borax flux, which should not be too wet. Use fine stainless steel tweezers or a fine paintbrush to pick up the paillons. Paint flux through the four joints and lay a paillon of solder across each joint. Solder one section at

SOLDERING TOOLS II
1 Third hand – tweezers in stand used to hold pieces in place while soldering; **2** binding wire; **3** boxwood sawdust.

a time and allow it to air cool or quench it in water before preparing the next four sections to be soldered. Pickle the whole chain when you have finished soldering.

If you want to solder single jump rings between sections of chain, flux and solder each ring individually. Hold the ring in a pair of insulated tweezers with the rest of the chain hanging down, or lay the ring on a charcoal block. Place the ring so that the joint is uppermost. Flux and lay a paillon of solder across the top. Only heat the ring you are soldering, by starting at the base and bringing the flame to the top and up to the solder. If you just heat the top of the ring around the solder, the solder will melt first and form a ball on one side of the joint – it is then unlikely that the joint will solder successfully. It will need realigning, and you will need to reflux before heating and resoldering.

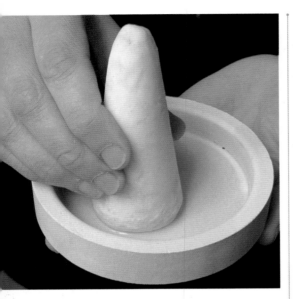

SOLDERING METALS

1 Put a little water in the bottom of the dish and grind the flat end of a borax cone until a whitish paste is produced.

2 Paint the borax paste between the two pieces of metal you want to join.

3 Use a pair of tin snips to cut a strip of solder about 2 cm (¾ in.) lengthwise and then cut across the strips to make paillons. Place the paillons to be used in the borax and keep the others in a dish, clearly marked 'easy', 'hard', and so on as appropriate.

4 Use the tip of a paintbrush to pick up and place a paillon just below or on the joint.

5 Place the piece on a charcoal block and heat it gently, making sure that the paillon of solder stays in position. The heat is likely to make the water in the borax paste bubble, so use a pair of insulated tweezers or a titanium stick to reposition the paillon if necessary.

6 Watch the solder becoming shiny as it melts and runs along the joint. Remove the flame and allow the piece to cool for a few seconds.

7 Quench the piece in pickle and rinse in water.

STICK SOLDERING

1 Instead of paillons, a long strip of solder, painted with flux, is held in insulated pliers so that it can be fed all the way around the area to be joined.

SOLDERING CHAINS

1 You need to isolate each link of a chain before soldering. You can do this either by holding the link to be soldered in a 'third hand' or by laying the chain out flat on a charcoal block and soldering a few links at a time. Always make sure that the areas to be soldered are not in contact with any other metal.

2 When the soldering temperature is reached, feed the stick solder into the work, taking care to remove it when enough has been fed in.

JOINING PIECES

Use a piece of binding wire to hold the two pieces you want to join firmly together and twist the wire with flat-nose pliers to tighten it. Adjust alignment if necessary. Hold the piece in a pair of insulated tweezers and paint the joint with flux before placing the paillons around the area to be joined.

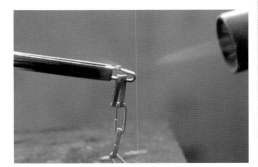

2 Direct a small flame on a single link. It will heat up quickly and allow the solder to flow without affecting the solder on the other links.

THIRD HAND IN ACTION

Here a 'third hand' is being used to hold the ring.

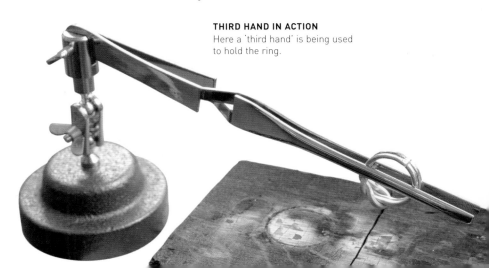

FUSING

METAL CAN BE JOINED WITHOUT SOLDER BY SIMPLY HEATING IT TO THE TEMPERATURE AT WHICH IT STARTS TO MELT. AS THE SURFACE OF THE METAL BEGINS TO MOVE, ANY AREAS THAT ARE TOUCHING WILL FUSE TOGETHER.

Fusing can be a rather haphazard and unpredictable process, or it can be reasonably well controlled. In the example shown opposite, the ring is made from pieces of scrap, and although the fusing process worked, it would be impossible to repeat the procedure to produce an identical piece. The second example is more controlled, and it would be possible to repeat the sequence and produce several similar pieces.

A piece of metal that is thin or a section of metal that stands away from the main area will probably melt before the rest of the piece has heated up adequately to fuse. If one piece of metal is too far away from another, one of them will melt first and become a rather amorphous mass before the other has had an opportunity to fuse to it. It is, however, possible to push and prod small bits of metal into place with a titanium soldering stick.

QUENCHING AND RINSING

A fused seam is as strong as a soldered seam, but because the surface of the metal has started to melt and move, it will have a mottled appearance when it is cool. Also, the surface can be rather porous after fusing, which can cause problems when the metal is immersed in acid because the acid will tend to find its way into the metal. Unless properly neutralized, the acid will seep out and appear as an unattractive green blotch. To overcome this problem, drop the fused metal into hot water after heating and then place it in the acid or pickle bath. When the oxidization has disappeared, boil the piece in a solution of soda crystals and water, which will neutralize any remaining acid. You will still have to give the piece a thorough scrubbing either with pumice powder or with detergent after it has been neutralized, and if any seams are subsequently soldered, you will have to follow the same cleaning procedure.

> **SEE ALSO**
> - Annealing, pages 42–43
> - Pickling and quenching, pages 44–47
> - Doming and swaging, pages 62–65

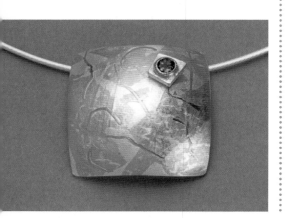

KEUM-BOO PENDANT – FELICITY PETERS
Gold foil is fused onto silver using the Keum-boo method. The foil is laid onto the silver, which is then heated carefully to annealing temperature. As the two surfaces start to fuse together a burnisher is rubbed gently, but firmly, over the gold to secure it to the silver.

FUSING TOOLS
1 Scraps of silver sheet and wire for fusing together; **2** stainless steel tweezers; **3** insulated tweezers to hold pieces in position and for placing metal for fusing; **4** soldering torch and nozzles – this is a hand-operated gas torch which has a small length of rubber hose pipe attached to the smaller terminal for the introduction of blown air. A further rubber hose for the gas is attached to the larger terminal; **5** liquid flux (Auflux), only small amounts are required and the liquid should always be returned to its container after use.

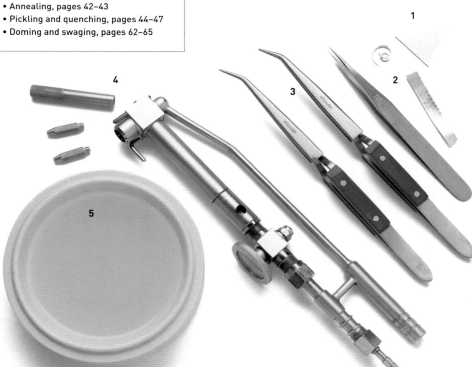

FUSING WIRE

Thin wire, up to about 1 mm (1/32 in.), can be laid on metal as it is fusing. It can be twirled in a fairly long piece or added in little bits as decoration. Thin wire is easy to melt and to fuse, and it can be used in several ways. Hold a length of wire vertically with a pair of insulated tweezers so that one end dangles in front of a charcoal block. Concentrate the heat of the flame on a point just above the end of the wire and watch it carefully as it runs and forms a ball on the end of the wire.

Gold wire, which can be up to 0.7 mm in diameter and in 14 or 18 carat, can be bent and twisted to form a ring or bangle and then joined by fusing. All the parts to be fused should be touching, and the ends of the wire can be left proud so that they will run up into little balls in direct heat. Concentrate the heat of the flame on the areas to be fused and watch the surface of the metal carefully until you can see that fusion has taken place.

GRANULATION

Small metal balls can also be soldered or fused onto jewellery as decoration.

To fuse silver balls to a silver base, you will find that they fuse more easily if there is a layer of copper between them. You can achieve this by pickling the balls in a solution of sulfuric acid and introducing a piece of steel or iron to the pickle. If steel is placed in pickle – as you may have seen if you have accidentally quenched a piece with binding wire still in place – a pinkish copper deposit will appear on the silver. Rinse the balls in water, dry them, and place them with a little flux on the piece. Heat the metal until the balls just fuse to the surface.

To solder the balls to the metal, flux the base of each ball and place it in position. Hold a strip of easy solder over the balls and file the end with a needle file so that tiny solder filings fall all over and between the balls. Keep a stainless steel or a titanium stick in your hand as you solder so that you can reposition any balls that move.

MAKING A RING FROM SCRAP
1 Bend scrap pieces of silver into the approximate shape of a ring.

2 Cover the silver with flux, place it on a soldering block and heat it.

3 When the surface begins to move, hold the flame steady to keep the temperature constant. Allow the scrap pieces to mould to each other. This is the crucial time – if you apply too much heat, the silver simply becomes a mess; and if there is insufficient heat, the piece will not fuse. Take it to the point at which you think that the piece will work as a ring.

4 Rinse, pickle, rinse and clean the ring, then use a piercing saw to cut away any unwanted areas. If you wish, use a file to model it further.

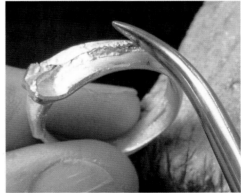

5 Polish the ring or simply burnish the highlights.

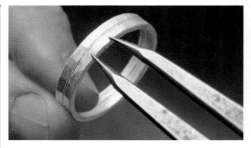

MAKING A FUSED WIRE RING

1 Take two pieces of D-section wire or round wire, approximately 2 mm (¹⁄₁₆ in.) in diameter, that are exactly the same length and form them into rings.

4 Use dividers to mark the section you want to remove.

7 Flux the joints.

2 Fuse the joint together on both rings, place them on a mandrel, and then hammer them until they are round.

5 Cut it out with a piercing saw.

8 Fuse the ring together, this time keeping a careful watch on the amount of heat you apply so that the ring fuses but does not melt.

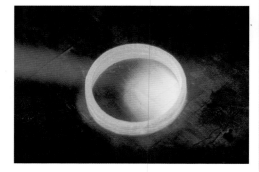

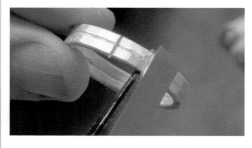

3 Place one ring on top of the other and flux the centre, where they meet. Fuse the two together.

6 Bend the ring so that the ends meet and place the cut-out section over the joint.

FUSED SILVER RINGS
Four silver rings, made by fusing.

FUSING GOLD AND SILVER

1 Paint some flux onto the cut-out gold pattern and place it, flux side down, in the centre of the silver.

4 Dome the circle (see Doming and swaging, pages 62–65) and solder the earring fitting to the back.

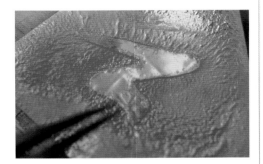

2 Heat the silver until the surface starts to move and press the gold down onto it, using a titanium soldering stick or tweezers.

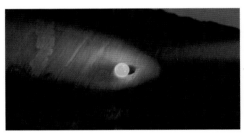

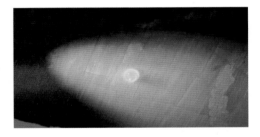

MAKING BALLS FOR GRANULATION

1 Make a small indentation in the charcoal block and place a little piece of wire, about 3 mm (⅛ in.) long, in it. Heat it up.

2 Watch the metal until it starts to shine and forms a spinning ball. Remove the flame, and when it has cooled slightly, pickle the ball until it is shiny.

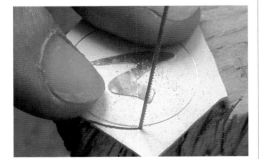

3 After picking, boil the earrings in a solution of soda crystals to neutralize the acid. Use a piercing saw to cut out the silver circle and then rinse thoroughly.

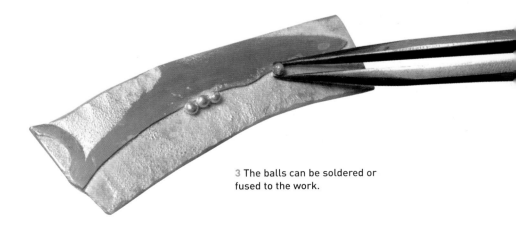

3 The balls can be soldered or fused to the work.

MOVING METAL

In this section we are using different techniques to persuade the metal to move and bend as we want it. Tools such as pliers, stakes, formers, hammers and mallets are used to push and stretch the metal into different shapes. Using the correct tools ensures that any marks left on the metal are intentional.

BENDING TOOLS
1 Coils of gold wire;
2 round-nose pliers;
3 beeswax for bending chenier; 4 small oval mandrel; 5 round ring mandrel.

BENDING

BENDING AND SHAPING METAL CAN BRING AN EXTRA DIMENSION TO YOUR WORK, ALLOWING THE LIGHT TO REFLECT FROM IT IN UNEXPECTED AND INTERESTING WAYS. CURVES, BENDS AND TWISTS CAN BE MADE INTO ATTRACTIVE FEATURES, BUT FOR MAXIMUM EFFECT THEY MUST BE AS SMOOTH AND AS CLEAN AS POSSIBLE SO THAT THE METAL FLOWS FROM ONE SURFACE TO THE NEXT.

MATCHING SET – DANIELA DOBESOVA
Flattened silver strips were wrapped around a tapered stake to achieve the flow of these pieces.

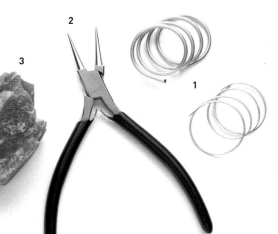

If you are holding metal in a vice, you must cover the serrated edges on the inside of the vice with several layers of masking tape or protect the metal itself with masking tape. Many vices have additional 'safe' jaws, which are made from rubber and which fit neatly over the serrated edges, and some small vices have plastic jaws.

Before you begin, decide exactly where you want the curve to be and how smooth or steep it should be. Your aim must be to get the bend right the first time. Although it is possible to unbend metal, it is much more satisfactory to get it right at the first attempt. Keep your pattern or design close at hand, and after each bend lay your work on the design to check that the curve is correct. A small mistake at this stage can easily make the whole piece wrong. If you want to make two identical curves – in a pair of earrings, for example – make the first bend in one piece, then work on the next before returning to the first. It is much easier to repeat a small step than to have to remember a series of steps.

Always try to make a clean bend rather than an overworked one. Work around a former whenever you can, and always use the correct pliers. Place the curved or rounded nose of your pliers on the inside of the curve, holding the outside with the flat edge of the pliers. If you use the wrong profile – the flat nose on the inside of a curve, for instance – you can create marks in soft metal that are difficult to remove.

Remember that most aids to bending metal are harder than the metal itself and will mark the metal if they are used incorrectly. Try to use them as precisely as possible. Among the most underrated tools are ones that will leave no marks are your fingers and thumbs: they may not always be the right tools, but they can be useful.

It is worth keeping a supply of copper wire and sheets of different thicknesses to hand. Before bending a precious metal, work through the design in copper so that any problems can be identified and solved.

STRAIGHTENING WIRE

It is much easier to bend wire or sheet metal that is straight or flat. Wire is usually supplied in rather loose, large coils, which do not need straightening. Unless you are bending a piece that needs to be springy – a brooch pin, for example – always work with well-annealed metal. Once metal becomes work-hardened, it is much more difficult to bend correctly. You can feel the difference with your fingers between annealed and hard metal. If the wire has kinks in it or has been previously bent, work as shown here or anneal the wire, quench it in water and dry it. Then place one end in the vice and fasten it tightly. Hold the other end in a pair of serrated-edge pliers and pull the wire sharply straight towards you. You will feel the wire lengthen slightly as it straightens.

FLATTENING SHEET METAL

Place the annealed sheet between two smooth steel surfaces, both of which are larger than the sheet to be flattened. Strike the top surface sharply with a hammer. If you are working on a very small piece, you can use the hammer alone, but you must make sure that the head of the hammer completely covers the metal; if it does not, the hammer will leave marks in the soft surface of the metal.

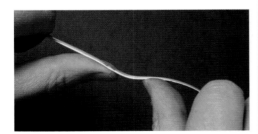

STRAIGHTENING KINKED WIRE

1 Hold the wire gently in both hands and push the bend up until the wire is level. Work along the wire, pushing gently upwards, until it is straight on that side. Turn the wire over and work along the other side in the same way.

2 Use the curved side of half-round pliers on the inside of the bend.

3 Use shaped pliers with one round nose and one flat nose to bend wire into a tight circle.

4 Round-nose pliers can be used to bend wire in a different direction. Take care that you do not mark annealed metal.

USING A FORMER

Short lengths of thick wire – more than 3 mm (⅛ in.) in diameter – can be awkward to bend precisely. Take an over-length piece of wire and bend it around a former, pulling both ends together and crossing them over each other until you have achieved the correct curve. You can then cut away the extra length from each end. This method is useful when you are bending chenier or when you are shaping a neckpiece.

To make repeating sections for a chain, saw off the heads from suitable sized nails. Place a tracing of the pattern on a block of soft wood and hammer in the nails on the inside and outside of the curves of the pattern. Leaving an extra length of wire to start and holding it firmly with a pair of pliers, use the other hand to bend the wire through the nails.

MAKING METAL SPRINGY

To give a sprung bracelet tension, curl it around a mandrel that is smaller than the finished diameter of the bracelet and then hit it with a wooden mallet or a flat-headed steel hammer to increase the diameter gradually while you hit it. Continue to work the bracelet up the mandrel until it is the correct size.

> SEE ALSO
> • Annealing, pages 42–44
> • Hammering, pages 60–61

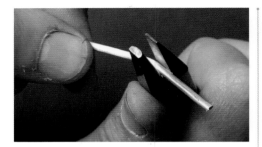

BENDING SECTION WIRE

1 Bend D-section wire with half-round pliers. You can file a groove into the lower end of the pliers, which will give a better grip when you hold the wire. Use flat-nose pliers to keep the D-section flat as it comes from the half-round pliers.

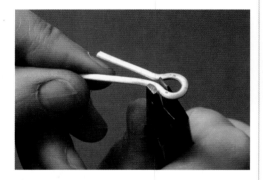

2 To make a 'square knot' ring, bend a loop in D-section wire with half-round pliers.

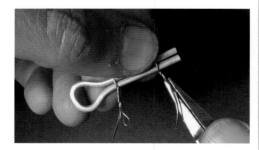

3 Push the two straight edges together and hold them tight with binding wire.

4 Run some hard solder up the middle of two D-section wires.

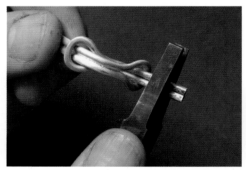

5 Repeat steps 2, 3 and 4 for the other side, then slip the two ends inside the two loops and pull them together. Hold one end in a vice, grip the other end with pliers and pull tight. Cut the ends to length and solder them together with easy solder.

6 Use a mallet to tap the ring into shape around the mandrel.

BENDING CHENIER

1 Before it is bent, the inside of the chenier must be filled so that the sides do not buckle. Warm the chenier by playing a gentle flame along the length of the wire. The heat from the flame will allow the beeswax to drip slowly into the chenier. You can also fill the chenier with fine sand, salt or warm pitch.

2 Use both hands to bend the chenier around a mandrel.

3 Tap the chenier gently around a mandrel with the mallet until it is the correct shape.

BENDING SHEET

1 Scribe along the line you wish to bend – in this case for the base of a box.

2 File along the scribed line with a three- or four-sided file until you have made a groove that is just more than half the thickness of the metal.

3 Protect any part of the metal that may come into contact with the jaws of the vice or use 'safe' jaws.

4 Place the metal in the vice so that the line you wish to bend is parallel to, and just visible above, the jaws of the vice. Tap it down cleanly with your mallet.

5 Alternatively, place the metal on a flat bed and hold the metal along the filed line in a pair of flat-nose pliers. Push it over until the metal is bent at 90 degrees.

6 If you cannot reach the filed line with your pliers, use a steel former, held in a vice, to bend the metal up.

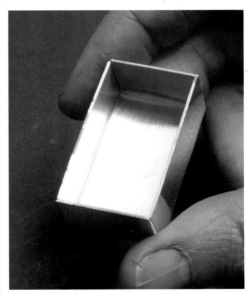

7 When you are bending up the sides of the base of a box, make sure that all the corner edges are filed to an angle of 45 degrees. This makes a neat seam for soldering.

HAMMERING

THE ARRAY OF DIFFERENT HAMMERS USED IN JEWELLERY AND SILVERSMITHING CAN BE RATHER OVERWHELMING AT FIRST, AND IT IS DIFFICULT TO SELECT THE ONE OR TWO THAT WILL BE USEFUL AND VERSATILE. HAMMERS HAVE DIFFERENT HEADS FOR DIFFERENT PURPOSES: A ROUND, FLAT-FACED HEAD ON ONE END WITH A ROUND DOMED OR WEDGE-SHAPED AT THE OTHER IS THE KIND OF HAMMER WITH WHICH MOST OF US ARE FAMILIAR, BUT THERE ARE ALSO ROUNDED RECTANGULAR HEADS, BROAD, FLAT HEADS, WEDGE-SHAPED HEADS, SQUARE BLOCK HEADS, ROUND HEADS AND MANY MORE, ALL MADE FOR SPECIFIC PURPOSES.

One factor that must be considered is the weight of the hammer. A light hammer is used for riveting or hitting a chasing tool, for example. A heavy hammer used for these tasks would be unbalanced and difficult to use evenly. It is important that metal is kept well annealed during all the stages of hammering, except when it is being made springy. If the metal becomes too hard when it is being hammered, it will crack.

OTHER HAMMERS

A **planishing hammer** – that is, one with a flat, highly polished face – is used to smooth out marks made by other hammers. The planishing hammer is worked in the same direction as the ordinary hammer.

A planishing hammer or the polished, flat head of a **ballpien hammer** is used to stretch, strengthen and add springiness to rings, bangles, neckpieces, pins and so on. If a length of wire that is going to be used for a neckpiece needs to be springy, for example, the wire is first annealed and then the whole length is coiled around a section of the mandrel that is a few sizes smaller than the required finished size. It is then hammered around the mandrel as it is gradually pushed down to increase the

diameter. By the time the wire has reached the full diameter, it will be springy.

Mallets are either wooden or are made from rawhide or rubber. They are used to shape metal against a metal stake, but because they are relatively soft, they do not mark it. Used on its own, a mallet will not stretch metal nor harden it to any great degree.

USING HAMMERS

When you use a hammer, the head should always make positive contact with the metal. Use it at an angle so that the face meets the metal squarely and does not leave edge marks. This is just as important for the metal stake on which a piece of metal is supported. Any damage caused by a hammer on a stake will mark the underside of any new piece of metal that is used with that stake. Badly damaged stakes can be professionally reground, and hammers used only for shaping metal should be kept polished and dry.

The action of the hammer comes from the wrist. The weight of head is balanced against the weight of the handle, so that a rhythmic movement can develop, which makes it possible to hit the metal with blows of equal pressure. Hammer marks left during the making process have to be removed so that the piece has a smooth, shiny finish. The more even the marks are, the more easily they can be removed or smoothed out with a planishing hammer.

GOLD RING WITH DIAMONDS – JINKS McGRATH

The 22-carat gold was hammered out from an ingot until the correct length for the ring was achieved. After joining and rounding it, the surface was hammered so that the surface remains uneven.

TYPES OF HAMMER
A range is shown here.

Chasing hammer

Jeweller's hammer

Creasing hammer

Blocking head hammer

Raising hammer

Planishing hammer

Rawhide mallet

Wooden bossing mallet

HOLDING AND USING HAMMERS
A wooden mallet or a rawhide mallet is used to round a ring on a mandrel.

Use a polished hammer head for planishing a surface or enlarging a ring. This can be either a planishing hammer or the clean head of an ordinary hammer.

A creasing hammer is used to curve metal in a swaging block. The hammer hits the centre line of the metal, and this forces it up into a curve. This hammer is also used in anticlastic raising.

You can use a ball head or a blocking head to produce a curved or a rounded effect.

Use a little jeweller's hammer to harden pins, tap down rivets and so on. Harden pins by rolling them along a flat plate or the top of an anvil, tapping along the metal with the hammer as you do so.

A blocking hammer gives a gentle curve to a copper dish. Turn the dish in the wooden block and tap rhythmically, working out from the centre or from the point at which the curve begins.

The underside of the bowl can be planished with a planishing hammer. Place the piece on a metal stake that reflects the curve you have made and work gently around the piece with the hammer to smooth out the hammer marks made earlier.

A chasing hammer, which is balanced for light, continuous hammering, can be used to curve over the edges when you make chenier.

Use the flat face of an ordinary hammer for hitting the head of a doming punch or a punch with a diameter of 15 mm (⅝ in.) that you have made yourself.

SEE ALSO

• Engraving, pages 38–41
• Annealing, pages 42–43
• Chasing and repoussé, pages 70–73

DOMING AND SWAGING

THE BLOCKS USED FOR DOMING AND SWAGING ARE USED TO FORM METALS INTO HALF-SPHERES AND HALF-CYLINDERS. THE BLOCKS, WHICH ARE MADE FROM STEEL OR BRASS, ARE AVAILABLE IN A RANGE OF SIZES, AND THEY ARE USED WITH WOODEN PUNCHES THAT MATCH THE SHAPES OF THE BLOCKS.

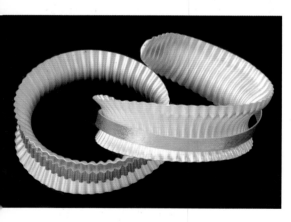

WAVE BANGLES – FELICITY PETERS
Corrugated and formed sterling silver and 24-carat gold bangles.

DOMING AND SWAGING TOOLS
1 Metal doming punches; **2** wooden doming punches; **3** stainless steel swage block – the doming punch handles are used in conjunction with the swage block; **4** stainless steel doming block; **5** leather sandbag used to give a resistant but soft backing.

SHAPING

Cut the metal to be shaped to the appropriate size and anneal it. For example, if you want to form a dome of about 15 mm (⅝ in.) in diameter, cut a circle with a diameter of 20 mm (¾ in.) and place it into a dome that has a diameter of 22 mm (⅞ in.). Find a punch that fits the hollow, but remember to allow for the thickness of the metal being shaped.

Once the dome has been shaped, you can bring up the outside edge of the dome so that it will form a neat half-sphere. Punch the dome through a hole drilled in a steel sheet. The entrance side of the hole should be countersunk, and the punch should be able to pass right through the hole, allowing for the extra thickness of the metal dome.

There will be times when you cannot match the punch to the dome. You may, for example, want to make a large domed piece by forming it in a sandbag or on a lead block, or you may have a doming block but only a limited selection of punches. To overcome this problem, place the circle of metal in the block, on the sandbag, or on the lead cake, position the punch over it, and strike the punch, working first around the outside edge of the metal to begin the shaping process, then gradually working down into the centre in a series of ever-decreasing circles.

When you use lead cake to shape metal, place a piece of cloth or soft leather between the lead and the metal. Any particles of lead that are left on metal during heating melt very quickly and burn holes in the metal, with potentially disastrous results.

CUTTING CIRCLES

When you need to cut out several circles to the same size, it is tedious to do them all by hand. You can either make a tool to do the job for you, or you can buy a tool with a series of different-size holes and matching cutting punches.

SWAGING

A swage block is used in exactly the same way as a doming block, but this time you will need to use the handles of your punches, laid on their sides, to shape the metal into the hollows of the block. Use a wooden mallet to strike the handles so that they are not marked, or place a flat plate on top for protection.

If your punches do not have handles of the correct size, use a small metal rod to push the edge of the metal into the curve, and gradually work the rod into the centre. Work gently, hitting and pushing, and decrease the size of the rod to prevent 'creasing'.

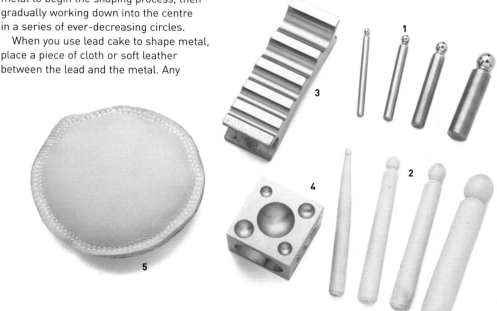

MAKE A CIRCLE-CUTTING TOOL

To make a circle-cutting tool, you will need two square blocks, each about 1 cm (½ in.) thick and large enough to accommodate your circle and leave a margin of about 1 cm (½ in.) around the circumference of the circle. Clamp the blocks together and drill a hole to the desired diameter through both. Drill two or four locating holes with a small diameter into the two inside faces of the blocks. These holes do not need to go right through the blocks. Insert locating pins into the base block (they should fit tightly), place a metal washer over each pin, and position the top half of the block over the bottom half. Make the cutter from a steel rod that will fit snugly into the drilled hole. The rod should be 10–13 cm (4–5 in.) long, and the top and bottom edges must be completely flat. Place the metal to be cut between the two blocks, centring it under the hole, locate the punch in the top half of the hole, and hit it firmly with a hammer.

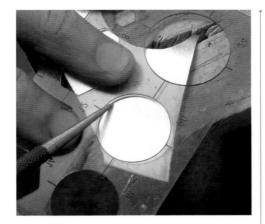

DOMING

1 Scribe a circle with a diameter 2 mm (1/16 in.) larger than the diameter of a finished dome.

2 Use a piercing saw to cut around the scribed line. Anneal the metal before doming.

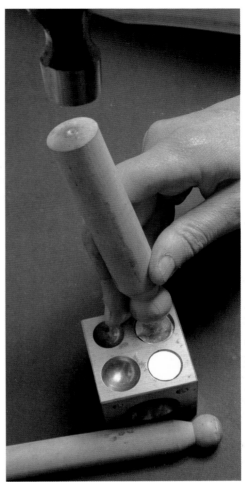

3 Place the circle of metal in the doming block, in a hollow that is slightly larger than the circle. Use a wooden or metal punch that matches the size of the hollow, place the punch over the circle and hit the top of the punch with a hammer or mallet until the dome is formed. This can usually be done with a single blow.

SEE ALSO
• Piercing, pages 20–23
• Annealing, pages 42–43

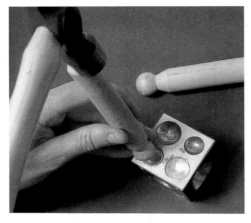

4 Place the domed circle in the next smallest hollow and use a matching punch to make a higher dome.

5 The circle and the domed circle should fit inside the hollow at each stage. If they are larger, the edge of the hollow will mark the metal. Remember that the finished dome will be smaller than the original circle.

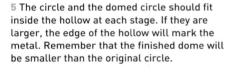

CUTTING CIRCLES

1 Place the sheet of metal in the block of a cutting-out tool, under the appropriately sized hole.

2 Place the cutter squarely into the hole and hit it sharply with a hammer.

3 The circle will fall through the bottom of the cutting-out tool.

MAKING A SILVER SPHERE

1 Make a large silver sphere by soldering a domed circle to a silver or copper ring that has a slightly larger diameter. Flatten the edges of the ring and file the bottom edge of the dome to make a neat edge, and use hard solder to solder the pieces together. Drill a hole in the centre of the dome.

2 File the outside edge so that it is flush with the dome to make it easier to position the second dome correctly.

3 Support the lower section between two charcoal blocks and use medium or easy solder to solder the second dome onto the ring edge. After soldering, drying and cleaning, place the drill through the first hole and drill through to the other side. Drilling the second hole when the bead is assembled means that the holes will line up.

2 Continue to work in ever-decreasing sizes of slot, annealing the metal if it becomes hard, until you have the curve you want. Do not continue if the metal is too large to fit into the slot.

3 When both edges meet, fit the strip into the closest fitting hole in the drawplate. Holding a small blade between the edges just before pulling the strip through the plate will keep the line straight. Continue the process until the correct size is achieved. Anneal after three consecutive pulls.

MAKING CHENIER

1 Cut a thin strip of metal and file one end to a point. Place the strip over a swage block so that it just fits into one size slot. Using the handle of a punch, tap the strip down into the slot and continue until the strip is bent to just over halfway. Anneal when necessary to keep the strip soft.

4 Make a small groove along the seam line with a triangular file. Flux along the groove and place paillons of hard solder along it. Carefully solder it up. Mark where the solder seam is with a saw blade. The soldered side of chenier should be the side which will be soldered to the parent metal.

SWAGING

1 Cut a strip of metal that exactly fits into a semicircular slot in the swage block. Match a wooden or metal punch lengthwise along the block, place it on top of the strip of silver and tap along its length with a mallet or hammer.

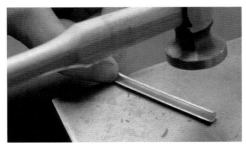

2 Next, place the strip on a flat plate and gently tap down the top edge. Turn the strip over and work along the opposite edge in the same way.

FORGING

FORGING IS A WAY OF STRETCHING, FLATTENING, CURVING AND SHAPING METAL BY APPLYING FORCE FROM DIFFERENT DIRECTIONS BY MEANS OF SPECIALLY SHAPED HAMMERS, WHICH ARE USED FROM THE TOP WHILE THE METAL IS SUPPORTED ON STAKES OF VARIOUS SHAPES OR ON AN ANVIL. HAMMERS AND STAKES USED FOR FORGING SHOULD BE KEPT HIGHLY POLISHED SO THAT NO UNNECESSARY MARKS ARE TRANSFERRED TO THE METAL. CLEAN THE HEAD OF YOUR HAMMER WITH FINE WET AND DRY SANDPAPER AND THEN POLISH IT WITH A MOP OR ON SOME FLAT CHAMOIS LEATHER BEFORE USE.

Metal that has been forged has a wonderfully flowing quality, but if the process is to be successful, you must use a piece of metal that is large enough to shape, curve, twist, file and finish; otherwise, you will end up with a poorly proportioned, over-thin piece. It is easier to take metal away from a forged piece than it is to add it, although 'simulated forging', which involves adding pieces of metal, is also described here.

It is also easier to work to a drawn design. Lay the metal on top of the drawing while you work so that you can check that you have achieved the right curve and know where the next one should start.

Forging stretches and compresses metal. For example, if you take a piece of metal measuring approximately 10 × 65 mm (½ × 2¼ in.) and about 3 mm (⅛ in.) thick and place it on a flat metal plate or anvil, you can lengthen it by hitting it with a rectangular raising or flat-faced hammer. Begin in the centre and bring the hammer, in even strokes, towards you, then, turn it around and repeat the process, so that each end is drawn out from the centre. If you want to spread the ends of the metal out more gradually, work in the same way, but use a flat-faced hammer and increase the strength of the blows as you work along the metal.

The metal can be widened by working across the strip with a rectangular raising hammer, which is used along the line of the strip from one side to the other. If you work the same hammer down the centre of the strip, the edges will begin to curl upwards. If necessary, they can be flattened again by annealing the strip and hitting it flat with a large flat-faced hammer.

FORGING

1 Use the flat head of a heavy hammer to broaden the end of a strip of metal. Work from the centre toward the area that is to be broadened.

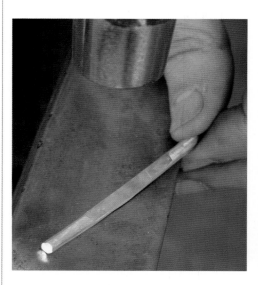

2 Make sure that the area of metal being forged is in direct contact with the anvil or flat plate.

ASSORTED RINGS – JINKS McGRATH
22-carat gold rings with assorted diamonds, emeralds, sapphire ruby and tanzanite. The shanks of all these rings were forged from individual ingots of 22-carat gold. The settings for the stones were fabricated separately and then soldered to the shanks.

FORGED EARRINGS – SUSAN MAY
18-carat yellow D-section wire has been forged to make the twists in these earrings. As well as flattening the wire, the hammer was used to produce the curves.

SEE ALSO
• Filing, pages 24–26
• Annealing, pages 42–43
• Hammering, pages 60–61

3 You can round square edges by gently working down the line with the ball end of a hammer.

5 Reduce the hammer marks by using a planishing hammer.

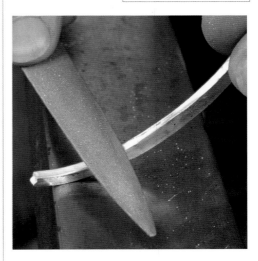

4 Form a curve by hammering the outside edge only. Enlarging the outside edge in this way pushes the inside edge into a curve.

6 Use a flat file to shape uneven edges.

7 An oval file can be used to clean up the inside curve.

SIMULATED FORGING

It is sometimes necessary to add an extra piece of metal to the side or top of a piece of forged metal. You may, for example, be forging a piece of 3-mm (⅛-in.) square wire and want to include a sweeping turn or bend. The wire is not sufficiently deep enough to create a flat area of 6 mm (¼ in.), and you will, therefore, need to solder a similar piece of 3-mm (⅛-in.) wire to the first length on the outside of the curve you intend to make. The bend is forged in the usual way, then the metal is filed into shape.

SIMULATED FORGING
1 Solder a strip of the same width to the area that is to be formed into a wide curve.

2 Forge the soldered piece in the same way as the single piece. When you are satisfied with the curve, remove the ends with a piercing saw and file the top and bottom surfaces to remove the solder joint.

ANTICLASTIC RAISING

This process of anticlastic raising adds an extra dimension to forging. The word 'anticlastic' means that a piece has opposite curvatures at a given point – that is, it is curved convexly along a longitudinal plane and concavely along the perpendicular section.

The technique requires the use of a sinusoidal stake. The stake resembles a tapering, wavy line. Metal can be persuaded into a concave curve along its face while all the opposing curves, necessary to form a bangle, ring or necklace, can be formed at the same time. The stake can be made from steel, wood or plastic, as can the wedge-shaped hammer that is used to form the metal against it. Although a metal hammer used against a metal stake forms the work quickly, the piece may then need planishing to restore a smooth surface to the metal. It is preferable to use a wooden or a plastic hammer against a steel stake, or vice versa. The forming may take a little longer, but it will need less finishing.

An annealed metal sheet is held between the thumb and forefinger on the curve while the hammer, held in the other hand, is used to make small overlapping blows along the top edge of the metal, which is rotated slowly down over the stake. The hammer should strike the metal at 90 degrees and just below the point of contact between the metal and stake.

One continuous line is worked across the top edge before the piece is turned through 180 degrees so that the other edge can be worked in the same way. Working in this way stretches the outside areas of the metal and creates a concave curve, known as an axial curve, while the centre section of the metal is compressed and forced into a convex curve, which is called the generator curve.

Continue to make passes with the crosspien hammer, working into the centre of the metal. Only when the whole piece has been worked will it be necessary to anneal the metal. The compression may cause a ridge to appear along the center of the metal, but after annealing this can be carefully planished flat by another pass over the stake.

You can achieve different degrees of concave curves by working the metal over tighter curves of the stake. When all the concave curves have been made, the piece is placed against an ordinary ring mandrel to bring the somewhat oval shape that has formed into a circle or whatever shape is required. Maintain direct contact between the hammer, the metal and the mandrel, and allow the piece to become hard and springy, which will give it its strength.

COPPER 'COLLAR' BRACELET – SIAN PITTMAN
The copper for this bracelet has been shaped using the anticlastic method of shaping the metal. The small rivet holding it together adds a nice touch to its collar-like appearance.

ANTICLASTIC RAISING: OPEN FORMS

Use 0.6-mm silver sheet for this project. This may seem thin, but the resulting structure of the piece gives the form an integral strength, and helps keep the piece light.

1 Design a template, and pierce around it on silver sheet. Wide areas will cure more slowly than thinner parts, but a greater degree of curvature may be achieved.

2 Bend the sheet around its length so that it is circular. Work on the sinusoidal stake as previously described, starting at one end of the silver piece. Hold the silver tightly to prevent the circle from opening up as it is hit. Work along the full length of one edge, before malletting the other edge.

3 True up the piece on a mandrel, tapping out the ridge if one has formed, and then anneal it. Work through the crooks on the stake as before. Curves can be tightened or closed by malletting the side of the form while it is supported by the stake.

4 The finished piece.

ANTICLASTIC RAISING

1 Place a piece of silver on the sinusoidal stake in the centre of a curve and hold the ends between the finger and thumb of one hand. The silver strip must be laid directly over the curve before you begin – that is, there will be a gap between the silver and the stake. Hold the metal firmly all the time you are working. Use a crosspien hammer to hit along the top edge of the metal. Work along the whole line, in a series of overlapping blows, then return to the beginning to work another line just below the first. Turn the silver through 180 degrees and work along the opposite edge in the same way. Continue to work in this way until the whole strip has passed along the stake.

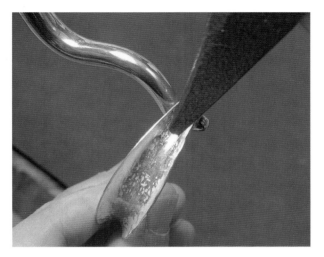

2 After one or two passes on the first curve of the sinusoidal stake, make a tighter curve on one of the smaller curves of the stake, which can be turned around if necessary. Always hold both ends of the strip to keep the generator curve intact.

4 Give the edges an extra-close curve by placing the strip on a flat plate and gently tapping it over with a light jeweller's hammer. Turn it over and tap down the other side.

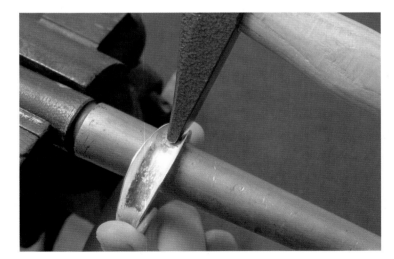

3 The generator curve is defined on an ordinary mandrel. Try to keep the area of silver that is being worked in contact with the mandrel so that the work is as smooth as possible.

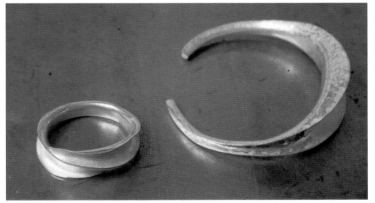

5 The strip after raising but before finishing, together with a ring worked in the same way.

SINUSOIDAL STAKE
This is a curved stainless steel mandrel which is held on its straight length in the vice, used for anticlastic raising.

CHASING AND REPOUSSÉ

CHASING IS THE ART OF CONTROLLING A SMALL STEEL TOOL TO PUSH THE LINES OF A PATTERN ALONG THE SURFACE OF THE METAL. THE METAL ITSELF IS NOT REMOVED, AS IT WOULD BE IF AN ENGRAVING TOOL WERE USED. RATHER, IT IS MOVED SIDEWAYS AND COMPRESSED DOWNWARDS ON THE SURFACE OF THE METAL AS THE TOOL IS PUSHED ALONG THE LINE. CHASING IS USED TO OUTLINE AND DEFINE AREAS OF METAL THAT HAVE BEEN REPOUSSÉD, AND IT IS WORKED FROM THE TOP, OR VISIBLE, SIDE OF THE METAL. REPOUSSÉ IS THE ART OF WORKING WITH PUNCHES FROM THE BACK OF AN ARTICLE TO FORM SHAPES AND LINES THAT GIVE YOUR WORK A THREE-DIMENSIONAL APPEARANCE WHEN IT IS VIEWED FROM THE FRONT.

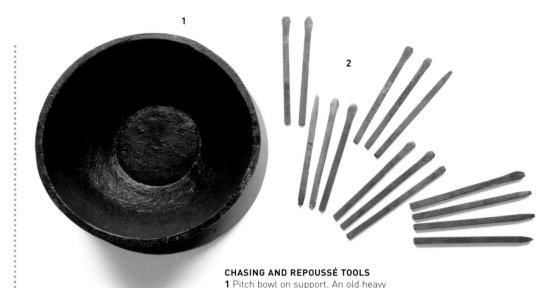

CHASING AND REPOUSSÉ TOOLS
1 Pitch bowl on support. An old heavy saucepan could also be used. It is filled almost to the top with a ready-made pitch mixture; **2** selection of repoussé and matting punches.

TYPE OF PUNCHES

You will need several different punches for chasing. A tracer punch is used to outline the design. It has a rounded, chisel-type head, which can be rectangular, slightly curved, V-shaped, half-round and so on. The head is slightly rounded so that the metal is not cut by a sharp edge as the punch is hammered along.

A **modelling punch** has a flat, rounded head, and it is used to define areas of repousséd work by pushing down the metal around and between the raised areas. Keep the head rounded and shiny so that the metal is not marked when it is being worked.

A **matting punch** has a patterned head and is usually used to punch texture into background areas. Matting punches also vary in shape and size, and the faces of the heads can be criss-cross, striped, lined or dotted, but, like the other punches, the heads should have rounded edges. The patterned faces

are not polished, because this would lead to loss of definition.

A **planishing punch** has a polished, flat face. These punches, which are made in a range of sizes, are used for smoothing over repoussé marks left by the punches used to work the back of the metal.

Circles in relief are made by a **hollow-faced punch**, which can be used on either the front or the back of the metal. The heads of these punches vary in diameter and, as with matting punches, they are not polished so that definition is not lost. The edges are slightly rounded so that the metal is not cut by the punch.

Most repoussé work is done with an **embossing punch**, which is used to push up areas of metal from behind to create the relief on the front. These punches are usually oval, round, square or rectangular, and they have rounded edges and polished faces.

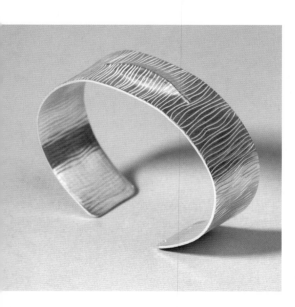

EMERGENCE BANGLE – ANNETTE PETCH
The lines on this silver bracelet were chased while the raised area in the centre was worked from behind and therefore repousséd.

USING PUNCHES

When you use a tracer punch to make a line, the top of the punch is held at a slight angle away from you, while the bottom or face is towards you so that the line being traced is clearly visible. Hold the punch between your thumb and three fingers, while your little finger rests on the metal to steady and support your hand. Hit the top of the punch rhythmically with a chasing hammer – a small hammer with a broad head and a well-balanced handle – which facilitates repetitive hitting. If you are using a tracer punch to outline a curve or a V-shape, hold the punch upright and give it a single hammer blow.

Modelling and planishing punches are held in the same way as the tracer punch and they, too, are hit with the chasing hammer.

Matting and hollow-faced punches are held upright and struck with a single hammer blow. The punch is then lifted and repositioned on the metal so that it slightly overlaps the previously punched area.

Embossing punches are held slightly away from you and hit continuously. The punch is moved across the metal and not lifted from the surface in order to form a smooth indentation in the metal.

HOLDING YOUR WORK

Work that is going to be chased and repousséd has to be held in a firm but 'giving' medium called pitch, which is a mixture of pitch, tallow or linseed oil, and plaster of Paris or pumice powder. You can add tallow or linseed oil to pitch to soften it if it becomes brittle, which sometimes happens in cold weather.

Metal will be held more firmly in the pitch if the corners of a piece are turned down. Allow a good margin around the design so that you can turn down the corners with pliers.

You will have to take the metal from the pitch several times during the chasing and repoussé process. Not only will it need annealing from time to time to keep the metal pliable, but you will have to turn it over when you have to work on the back or the front. When you remove the work, gently heat the pitch around the metal

and lift up one corner with an old pair of insulated tweezers. The metal will be covered in pitch, and you have to remove this before you can continue with your work. Hold the work in the flame of your torch so that the pitch burns off. Allow the pitch to burn until it is dry and forms flakes, which will either fall off or can be blown off. Do not quench the metal until the pitch has burned off. This method also anneals the metal.

When you put the piece back in the pitch, the indentations on the back need to be filled with pitch to provide support. The piece would collapse if a matting, tracing or planishing punch were used on unsupported metal. Keep a small, separate container of pitch and heat it up so that you can pour it into the indentations. Allow it to cool before turning the piece over and replacing it in the pitch.

SEE ALSO
• Annealing, pages 42–43
• Hammering, pages 60–61

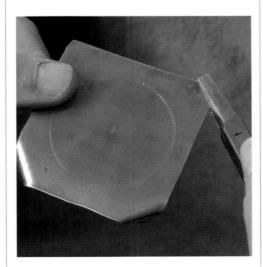

WORKING THE METAL

1 Mark on the metal the area needed for the pattern, making sure that you leave an outside border of 1–2 cm (½–¾ in.), then bend down the corners of the metal with a pair of flat-nose pliers.

2 Heat the pitch until runny and shiny, then place the metal in it. The turned-down corners, or tabs, will help to hold the metal firmly. Wet the ends of your fingers and push the pitch over the edge of the metal.

3 When the pitch is cool, rub the surface of the metal with plasticine or putty and trace the pattern through the tracing paper to the surface of your work.

5 Tap the head of the tool with gentle, rhythmic strokes with a chasing hammer while following the line. When all the lines have been chased, gently heat the piece to remove it from the pitch. Anneal and pickle.

4 Carefully remove the tracing paper and take a small chasing tool. If you are right-handed, hold the tool in your left hand; if you are left-handed, hold it in your right hand. Rest your little finger on the metal to help support and steady your hand, and hold the tool at a slight angle away from the direction of the line to be chased.

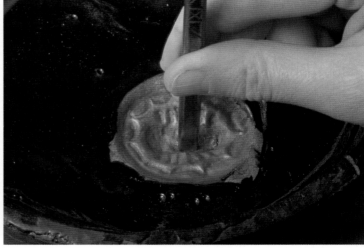

6 Dry the piece. Turn it over and then turn the corners down in the opposite direction. Replace in the pitch so that you are now working on the reverse side. Hold the repoussé punch upright and use an ordinary flat-headed hammer to hit the punch.

7 Choose a repoussé punch that will fit the shape you want to hammer and use the lines made by the chasing tool on the other side as a guide. Continue until you have the depth that you want.

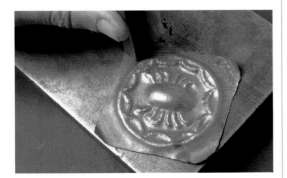

8 Place the work on the flat plate and gently punch down all the areas that should be flat. Work especially around the outside edge of the pattern so that it is level all around.

9 Pierce away the outside edges.

10 Use a file to clean up the edges before polishing the piece.

SILVER NECKLACE SET WITH ROUGH-CUT TOURMALINE – JINKS McGRATH
The smaller back fasteners reflect the shape and character of the large front-piece of this repousséd silver necklace. The rough-cut tourmaline pieces are set in a gold surround.

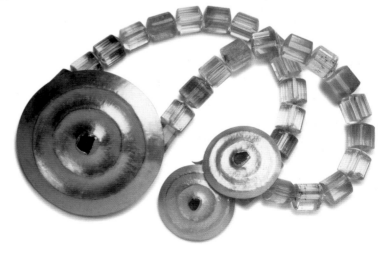

SURFACE DECORATION

Surface decoration here refers to the many ways that the surface of a sheet of metal can be altered to produce a different effect. Some surfaces are applied before the metal is cut and others are applied after most of the work is complete. To get the full benefit of an interesting surface, the way of achieving it should be decided at the design stage.

TEXTURING

THERE ARE MANY MORE WAYS OF FINISHING OFF A PIECE OF WORK THAN BY POLISHING. THIS IS OFTEN AN APPROPRIATE WAY TO COMPLETE A PIECE, BUT THERE ARE LOTS OF INTERESTING WAYS OF TEXTURING THE SURFACE OF THE METAL TO MAKE IT REFLECT THE LIGHT IN DIFFERENT WAYS, TO EMPHASIZE PARTICULAR PARTS OF THE PIECE OR TO GIVE A CRISP, SHARP LOOK TO A PIECE OF MODERN JEWELLERY.

DOUBLE RING WITH MOONSTONES – JINKS McGRATH
The silver around the stone settings on this ring was textured by placing a piece of annealed silver through the rolling mill with a sheet of stainless steel onto which the pattern was pierced.

SEE ALSO
• Annealing, pages 42–43
• Pickling and quenching, pages 44–47
• Polishing, pages 78–79

When you are designing a piece, take the finished appearance into account from the start, because texture and surface finish are often added before the piece is assembled or soldered.

All kinds of interesting shapes and patterns can be imprinted on metal by passing it through a rolling mill with fabric, patterned metal, paper, absorbent cotton or even string. The rollers are made of stainless steel, and you must be careful that you do not use anything that will mark them, or every piece that you subsequently pass through them will be spoiled. Although the rollers can be reground professionally, this is both expensive and inconvenient.

USING A PENDANT MOTOR
Apart from all its other uses, a pendant motor can be fitted with a variety of shaped and graded metal burrs, cutters and grinders.

Before you work on a carefully finished piece, try out the different burrs and cutters on pieces of scrap metal so that you learn to control the tool. You will find that it slips quite easily. When you use a pendant motor to add texture, take as much care as you do when you are polishing. Tie back long hair and fold back loose sleeves. Always wear goggles to protect your eyes.

TEXTURING AFTER POLISHING
Some textures are applied when everything else on a piece has been finished. If a stone has been included, you must take care.

To achieve a successful textured finish, all scratches, file marks, solder marks and so forth must be removed first.

FINISHING A MIXED-METAL SURFACE
When one metal or more has been inlaid or added to another, a highly polished finish can lessen the impact of the colour contrast. A matt surface, on the other hand, may enhance the difference.

One way of highlighting the change in colour is by polishing the piece to a gloss finish. Clean away the excess polish, rinse and dry, then heat the piece with a gentle flame until it begins to oxidize. Quench it when it has cooled a little. Place the piece in a warm solution of sulphuric acid for a minute or two, remove, rinse and dry. Reheat and proceed as before. Repeat the heating, pickling and rinsing processes three or four times, then the piece can be finally reheated. If the contrasting metal looks better oxidized, the piece needs no further treatment. Otherwise, pickle it in warm acid, rinse and dry.

RE-TEXTURING AFTER ASSEMBLY

When a piece of metal has been textured before assembly, part or all of the texture may be accidentally removed when you are cleaning and filing around soldered joints. Clearly, it is best to try to avoid this altogether by using the minimum amount of solder necessary for the job, but if it does happen, try re-creating the texture by placing the texturing material you used originally on the work and tapping a small, flat-headed planishing punch around the affected area. If the texture was originally created by direct hammering, use a small, shaped punch.

A piece of jewellery with a textured finish can be given extra definition by highlighting edges or high spots with a burnisher.

USING A HAMMER
1 Use the round end of a ballpien hammer to give an interesting hammered look. Use regular, smooth blows to keep the metal the same shape, although the method can be used to curve a piece of metal (see Bending, pages 56–59).

2 Use a rusty hammer and place the metal on a rusty anvil. Texture the piece all over, then clean it thoroughly afterwards with pumice paste to remove all particles of iron.

ACHIEVING A MATT FINISH
1 Using steel wool with liquid detergent gives a fine, matt finish.

2 A brass brush, also used with liquid detergent, gives a matt finish. Always use the detergent – if you do not, the brass will leave the silver rather dark and unattractive.

TEXTURING TOOLS
1 Brass brush used with detergent; **2** burrs for use with the pendant motor; **3** graded wet and dry paper; **4** muslin square for use with the rolling mill.

USING A STEEL MOP

A steel mop gives an attractive 'frosted' appearance. Always wear goggles when you use a steel mop because bits of steel can fly off.

THE ROLLING MILL

The rolling mill is an excellent way of achieving an interesting texture on metal. The metal sheet is always prepared first before any construction work begins, which means that careful thought needs to be applied when soldering.

To achieve a strong pattern on silver, anneal and pickle at least three times. When the silver is pickled, the copper on the surface is removed leaving a 'white' fine silver surface. If this process of annealing and pickling is repeated, the fine silver gradually builds up on the surface. As fine silver is softer than standard silver, impressions will be deeper.

Take care of your rolling mill! Any object that goes through the rollers which is harder than the steel they are made from will leave a mark which is almost impossible to remove. If in doubt, always cover any metal you are using to make an impression with a layer of copper.

METAL EARRINGS – SUSAN MAY

The pattern in the top silver section of these earrings was made by printing it on the silver with the rolling mill. They were then bent over the pierced gold, which was soldered and bent to shape.

USING A PENDANT MOTOR

Some of the finishes that can be achieved by using different tools in the pendant motor.

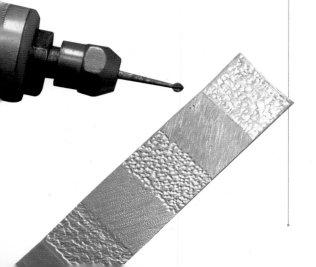

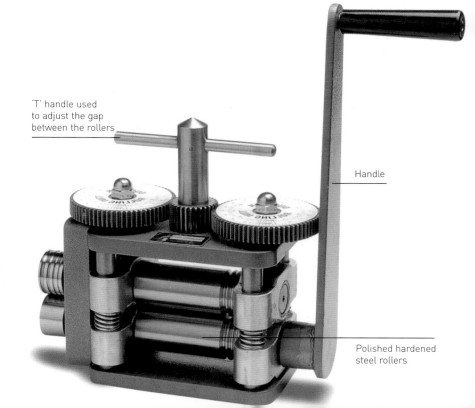

'T' handle used to adjust the gap between the rollers

Handle

Polished hardened steel rollers

ROLLING MILL TEXTURING

Here are just a few examples of the type of textures and patterns that you can achieve with this technique. As you can see, the process can be used for very subtle surface finishes as well as bold, defining imagery. Where appropriate, a patina or oxide has been used to enhance the texture.

USING A ROLLING MILL

Some materials that can be used with the rolling mill. Clockwise from top left: Absorbent cotton, tissue paper, hessian, patterned net and coloured silk. The silver shows the pattern made with binding wire and the hessian.

1 Place the silver to be textured on a charcoal block to anneal it. Charcoal reflects the heat better than a soldering block and is therefore excellent when building up a fine silver surface, but use it sparingly, since it is expensive and disintegrates quickly. After heating, cold water can be trickled over the charcoal to stop too much burning through.

2 To make an impression using any material that is harder than either the steel of the rolling mill or the silver, place the work between two pieces of copper. Otherwise the steel of the rollers could be badly damaged.

COPPER
1 Impression made using coiled and curved pieces of steel-binding wire.
2 Impression made using crocheted linen.

BRASS
3 Impression made using a feather.
4 Impression made using industrial perforated steel sheet.

SILVER
5 Impression made using a pattern cut out of watercolour paper.

3 Open the rollers up so that they just grab the three pieces of metal. They need to be tight enough for the wire or material to make a good impression, but not so tight as to be difficult to pass it through. If the rollers are too tight when using a metal impression, it is likely that the metal will actually cut through the silver.

POLISHING

POLISHING GIVES METAL A REFLECTIVE SHINE AND A SMOOTH FINISH, AND IT IS ACHIEVED EITHER BY SYSTEMATIC HAND FINISHING OR BY THE USE OF AN ELECTRIC MOTOR WITH POLISHING MOPS.

MUSIC AND DANCE NECKLACE – SHELBY FITZPATRICK
The finish on these necklaces complements the simple shapes. The satin look is achieved by using a good polish with no firescale and then applying the fine-scratch finish, by using a very fine wet steel wool with a liquid soap.

POLISHING TOOLS
1 Polishing motor with built-in extractor; **2** lambswool mop on machine for rouge polish; **3** felt cone for polishing inside a ring; **4** felt lap; **5** calico mop; **6** abrasive mops.

HAND POLISHING

When you have finished a piece as far as fine grade wet and dry sandpapers, you have several options. If you want a textured finish, turn to Texturing on pages 74–77. Here we discuss the ways in which you can give a piece a highly polished finish.

You can buy, or make, a **felt polishing stick**. This is a piece of wood, approximately 6 × 25 × 250 mm (¼ × 1 × 10 in.), with a piece of thick felt, measuring about 25 × 130 mm (1 × 5 in.), stuck to one end. Squeeze some lighter fluid onto the felt and rub some **tripoli polish compound** into the fuel. Tripoli is a dark brown, fairly greasy polish, which is supplied in long blocks. Rub the felt briskly over the work. You will need two or three felt sticks, with a different polish on each one.

Spread a soft **chamois leather** over a flat surface, squeeze some lighter fluid on it, and rub in some **fine rouge polish**, in either block or powder form. You can also use paraffin to dissolve rouge powder on the leather. Rub the work vigorously on the leather before cleaning off the polish with a clean cloth.

The inside of awkward areas can be polished with a shank of **fine strings**. Hang the shank over a hook or fasten them into a vice, and take as many of the strings as you will need. Soak these strings with lighter fluid and rub polish into the moist area. Thread the strings through the section that you want to polish and rub the piece holding the strings tight.

Liquid metal cleaners, which can also be used for plastics and acrylics, can be applied with a soft cotton cloth. Take care that you do not use a liquid that is too abrasive. Use an impregnated silver cloth to give a final shine to a piece, but these cloths alone will not polish metal.

USING A PENDANT MOTOR

A pendant motor with small mop attachments is ideal for polishing small or difficult areas. Polishing is a dirty and dusty job, and when you are working at your bench with a pendant motor, you can prevent the polish from flying everywhere by dipping the mop in paraffin before you apply the polish. As with hand-held polishing sticks, keep separate mops for each polish. Hold your work firmly in one hand, using the bench pin for support, and hold the shaft of the pendant motor in the other hand.

USING A POLISHING MOTOR

A polishing motor has one or two arms to which different mops can be attached. You should try to make sure that the motor sits in some kind of box, with enough clear area around it for the spindle arm, in which all the polishing dust can be caught. Keep separate mops for the different kinds of polish.

When you use a polishing motor, always wear safety glasses, tie back any loose or long hair and do not wear any loose clothing or jewellery that might get caught in the revolving wheel. Screw the appropriate mop to the spindle and stand in line with your work so that you can see clearly what you are doing. Switch on the machine, then hold the polish against the mop for 2–3 seconds before holding your work firmly and squarely against the mop. Turn the work between polishing strokes, but remember that the mop has a very fast action, and it is easy to lose the crisp edges and corners by over-polishing. Place the sides of the piece directly on the mop, and any difficult angles can be worked by using the edge of the mop.

After the first polish with tripoli compound, clean and dry the work before using another polish on another mop. At this point, you can go straight to a soft calico or lambswool mop, used with a rouge polish.

CLEANING

When you have polished the articles, clean them by placing them in an ovenproof dish of hot water and either a liquid cleaning agent or a household detergent to which you have added a teaspoon of ammonia.

POLISHING A RING ON A POLISHING MOTOR

1 Hold a ring in both hands so that it is just below the horizontal axis of the mop. (If you imagine that the vertical axis runs from 12 o'clock to 6 o'clock and the horizontal axis runs from 9 o'clock to 3 o'clock, you should hold the work at about 4 o'clock.)

2 Polish the inside of a ring on a felt cone, which should be screwed to the shaft of the polishing motor. Hold the ring with both hands and press the sides against the cone while you rotate the ring.

POLISHING A CHAIN ON A POLISHING MOTOR

1 When you are polishing a chain, wrap it around the handle of an emery stick so that there are no loops that might get caught up in the mop. Hold each section against the polishing mop, moving the chain around the stick, section by section.

2 If you want to polish a chain without a stick, hold the whole chain in one hand and pass it, one section at a time, to the other hand when it has been polished. Never try to polish more than one section at a time and make sure that the sections of chain not being polished are covered by one or other of your hands.

USING A PENDANT MOTOR

1 Use a brass mop and detergent to give silver a matt finish. Always use a detergent with a brass mop; if you do not, the finish will look rather harsh.

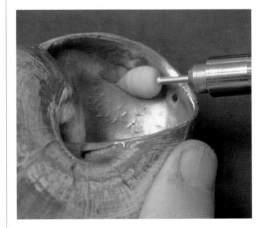

2 A felt mop is mounted onto a pendant motor to polish difficult areas. Work on your bench pin, hold the mop on a block of polish while it is rotating, and then carefully polish inside the piece. Take care that the metal shaft does not mark the silver edges.

SEE ALSO
• Basic tools, pages 8–11

RETICULATION

THE DICTIONARY DEFINITION OF RETICULAR IS 'IN THE FORM OF A NETWORK' AND THE DEFINITION OF RETICULATED IS 'HAVING VEINS, FIBRES OR LINES CROSSING LIKE A NETWORK, AS IN A LEAF'. THESE DEFINITIONS ACCURATELY DESCRIBE THE APPEARANCE OF METAL AFTER A PARTICULAR TYPE OF HEAT TREATMENT HAS BEEN APPLIED, A PROCESS THAT IS KNOWN AS RETICULATION.

SEE ALSO
• Annealing, pages 42–43
• Pickling and quenching, pages 44–47

GOLD KEEPSAKE EARRINGS – ALISON MACLEOD
The gold wire on these earrings is heated and, while melting, is pushed into itself to create balls along its length.

For reticulation to work, the surface of a piece of silver must have a higher melting point than the interior of the piece. This is because the effect is achieved by the silver's surface creasing as the piece is heated: the heat melts the inside of the silver, which flows as a liquid and causes the thin, but unmelted, surface to ripple.

The pure silver content of standard silver is 92.5 per cent. The remaining 7.5 per cent is copper, and reticulation relies on this 'impurity'. When standard silver is heated, the copper content oxidizes, turning the surface black when it is cooled in air. When pure silver is heated, no oxides appear and the piece remains a whitish-silver colour.

It is also possible to bring the pure silver to the surface of standard silver. This creates a 'sandwich' of two layers of pure silver, with an exterior melting point of 960.5°C (1760°F), and an inside layer of standard silver, which has a melting point of 890°C (1635°F). This is done by heating the piece of silver to annealing temperature and then either pickling it in a solution of 1 part sulphuric acid to 10 parts water and rinsing it, or pickling it in a warm solution of alum.

This process is repeated six or seven times to bring the fine silver to the surface. It is important that the temperature does not exceed the point at which annealing takes place, or the copper will break through the surface of pure silver that has begun to build up.

As the annealing and quenching process is continued, a layer of fine silver will build up until no oxidization appears on the metal's surface. It is now time to begin reticulation.

If you do not have two sources of heat, work on the whole piece of silver, heating it just past annealing temperature, and then concentrate your flame hard on one area until the surface begins to move. Then move the flame slowly over the silver, and the surface behind the flame will 'ripple' until you have covered the whole piece. It is important that the temperature of the silver is maintained throughout the procedure and that concentrating the flame on one area does

not allow the rest of the piece to cool down. If you are working with a single flame, it is probably best to reticulate one small piece at a time, probably no more than about 3 × 5 cm (1¼ × 2 in.).

Throughout the reticulation process, the metal is on the point of melting, and there will be times when the silver will actually melt and collapse into holes. This need not necessarily be a disaster, and the holes can often be incorporated into the design. In fact, if you are aiming for a rippled, haphazard effect, a few holes can enhance the appearance of the piece.

STARTING THE RETICULATION
1 Place the seven-times-annealed silver on the charcoal block and begin to heat it up with a soft flame, gradually increasing the heat.

2 Once the silver is hot enough – that is, once it is a deep red – watch the surface carefully until you see that it is beginning to move.

3 Introduce a smaller flame, directing it at one small area and moving it along the length of the silver.

4 Continue to watch as you draw the smaller flame along the surface of the silver and keep the larger flame steady because it keeps the whole piece at the same temperature.

5 Withdraw the flame when the surface is stippled, and allow the piece to cool for a while before quenching it in water.

6 Clean the piece thoroughly with pumice powder paste and, if necessary, place it in the pickle until the firestain has disappeared.

7 Place some soda crystals in an oven-proof dish and cover them with boiling water to make an alkaline solution. Place the piece in this solution, which you can keep warm by placing the dish in a pan of hot or boiling water.

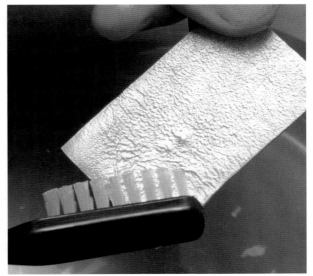

8 Clean thoroughly with pumice powder paste.

STAMPING AND EMBOSSING

IMPRESSIONS CAN BE MADE IN METAL IN SEVERAL WAYS, BUT ALL INVOLVE THE USE OF SOME SORT OF PUNCH THAT HAS BEEN FASHIONED INTO THE PATTERN REQUIRED IN THE METAL. THE TIME TAKEN TO MAKE A TOOL IS WELL SPENT WHEN YOU WANT TO PRODUCE SEVERAL IDENTICAL PIECES. STAMPED METAL HAS AN APPEARANCE THAT CANNOT BE ACHIEVED IN ANY OTHER WAY.

FLOWER BROOCHES – BIRGIT LAKEN
The shape for these stamps was made first and the pattern then engraved in each one. In the first brooch, the surround has been left as part of the design and in the second, part of the surround is used in the top edge.

Keep some tool steel stock on hand so that you can make a punch when you need it rather than having to buy a little bit every time. You may need to have access to a grinder or you can fit a round carborundum stone to your polishing motor. Alternatively, use a file to model the steel and round off the edges, while the inside edges can be filed away with a burr attachment on the pendant motor. Punches are made from round, square or six-sided stock up to about 2 cm (¾ in.) in diameter. Larger stock is difficult to heat properly without special equipment, and you should not, in any case, use stock that is too large for your needs. Punches are normally 8–10 cm (3½–4 in.) long.

Keep your punches wrapped in a cloth or in a dry plastic bag so that they do not rust, and keep the ends polished.

Metal that is to be stamped should be annealed and should not be too thick, because the thicker the metal, the greater the force that is needed to make the depression. Metal that is 0.5–1 mm (¹⁄₆₄–¹⁄₃₂ in.) thick is suitable.

SUPPORTS

Lead cake Small amounts of lead sheet can be bought from plumbing and building suppliers. Find an old rectangular tin, measuring about 14 × 8 × 5 cm (5½ × 3½ × 2 in.), cut up the lead into small pieces, and place them in the tin. Heat the lead with a large flame until it melts and leave it to settle and cool. Use a strip of wood to scrape away any impurities that may gather while the lead is molten. When the lead is cold, it is ready for use. Impressions made by punching into the lead can be easily erased by heating it once more.

Pitch Although it can be a little soft, pitch can be used as a backing for a punch.

Anvil or flat bed A stamped impression can be made into metal by placing it on a flat metal surface. Hold the punch on the metal and give it a sharp blow with a hammer. This will not form the pattern or design on the other side, although it may leave a mark, even though it does leave a fairly deep impression of the stamp on the top surface of the metal. Hallmarking is a classic example of this kind of stamping. If you are making a tool to use to impress a mark, remember that the edge of the tool will leave a mark unless it has been filed away or unless the impression of the pattern itself stands above the punch by 1–2 mm (¹⁄₃₂–¹⁄₁₆ in.).

Casting sand This very fine, cohesive material can be packed into a container and used to back metal that is to be embossed. The metal is placed face down in the sand, the punch is placed on the back of the metal and then hit with a hammer. The metal will be depressed into the sand as the punch is hit, pushing the pattern through to the front. You can make a metal block to locate the punch so that a second blow can be struck without moving the punch out of line.

Leather pouch or sandbag A round leather pouch, filled with sand, gives a firm but malleable backing into which metal can be hit. It is used more for general shaping than for making punched impressions or embossing.

PUNCHES

Wooden moulds Metal can be punched into a turned or carved wooden mould. Alternatively, a male wooden mould can be made in conjunction with a female one, so that the metal can be put between the two pieces and the whole thing squeezed slowly in a vice.

Metal stamps and dies Because they must be very precise, metal stamps and dies are produced by professional companies. If you are going to be making a large number of pieces with a single pattern, it is worth considering having a stamp made for you.

SEE ALSO
• Annealing, pages 42–43
• Soldering, pages 48–51

MAKING A PUNCH

1 Heat a piece of tool steel about 10 cm (4 in.) long and with a diameter of about 1.5 cm (⅝ in.). Pack charcoal blocks around it and use a large torch. Heat the steel until it is cherry red, hold it at that colour for a few seconds, and then allow it to cool naturally.

2 File or grind the pattern of your choice into the end of the steel bar.

3 Reheat the whole piece until it is bright red, then quench it in water to harden it.

4 Hammer the punch lightly into a lead block to check the appearance and make any refinements you wish – filing away sharp edges, for example – then clean the end with wet and dry papers before polishing it on the mop. Rub some soap over the polished end to protect it while it is being 'tempered'.

5 Reheat the end one-third of the steel bar until it becomes a deep yellow. This tempers or just softens the pattern on the punch, which might otherwise become too brittle and liable to chip.

6 Place the silver on the lead block, protecting the underside of the silver with muslin, leather, calico or soft paper so that lead particles are not left in the metal (these would burn into the metal during annealing). Hold the punch upright and give it a sharp blow with a heavy hammer.

7 Build up a stock of individual punches so that you can make repeating patterns on earrings, cuff links, badges and so forth.

EMBOSSING

1 Pierce the pattern you want to emboss in a sheet of stainless steel. Place the pierced pattern, your template, on a piece of annealed silver about 0.5 mm (1/48 in.) thick. If you have used a piece of stainless steel that is more than 1 mm (1/32 in.) thick, use a thicker piece of silver. Pass the two through the rolling mill so that the steel presses into the silver.

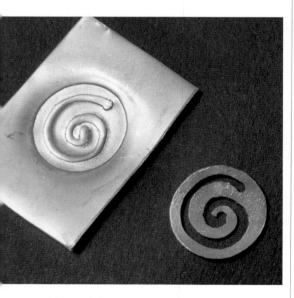

2 The stainless steel template can be used again and again.

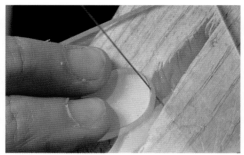

3 To make the border, pierce the desired shape out of a sheet of perspex that is the same thickness as the depth of the finished piece of silver.

4 Use an oval file to clean up the inside of the 'male' side of the block.

5 File the 'female' part of the block to the shape required for the piece of silver. This is a gently domed, oval shape. Make sure that you leave a clearance that is the same as the width of the metal – 0.5 mm (1/48 in.) in this instance – between the 'male' and 'female' parts.

6 Place the 'female' oval on the back of the silver that is to be embossed and use either a fly press to push the 'female' part into the silver, using a rubber block as backing, or use the 'safe' jaws of your vice, with a rubber block on one side so that the silver and the 'female' dye behind it can be pushed into it. Tighten the vice carefully so that the perspex is pushed into the silver and the silver is slightly domed.

7 Now place the silver into the 'male' part of the block and place the 'female' part on top. Place it in the fly press as before or press them carefully together in the 'safe' jaws of your vice.

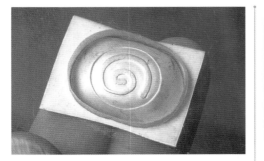

8 The dome will be clearly defined.

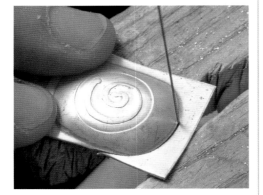

9 Use your piercing saw to remove the spare silver from the outside edge of the dome.

10 This bracelet by Naomi James was made by a series of domed pieces, soldered together, with simple stamped pieces between them.

FORMING WITH A PUNCH

1 Solder the model of the shape – in this case, a fish – to some tool steel and file it to shape. Smooth and polish the surface.

2 It can then either be hammered into a cold lead cake, or the lead can be heated until it is soft and the punch then carefully placed in it and left to cool with the lead.

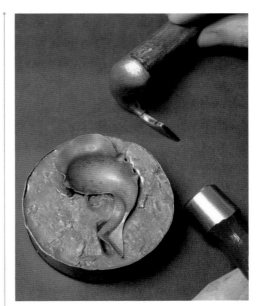

3 Push the annealed copper sheet into the depression in the lead with the punch. Repeat this, using a sheet of silver.

FINISHED BROOCH
The two pieces can be soldered together to create a brooch.

WORKING WITH WIRE

The design possibilities of working with wire are many and varied. It is a medium for your own creativity. This section demonstrates the techniques of working with wire and chain making, as well as covering catches, joints, fittings and findings, since wire of all shapes and sizes is used in the majority of these techniques.

DOODLE PANEL NECKLACE – CHRISTINE KALTOFT
As the name suggests, the design for this necklace came from a doodle made in a sketchbook. Gold wire has been bent, twisted and forged to create the doodle around the wire for the necklace.

USING WIRE

SILVER AND GOLD WIRE ARE AVAILABLE IN ALMOST ANY THICKNESS YOU WANT. YOU CAN GET COPPER WIRE SIMPLY BY REMOVING IT FROM OLD ELECTRIC CORDS OR BY REMOVING THE RUBBER CASING FROM LENGTHS OF ELECTRICAL WIRE. YOU CAN ALSO BUY COPPER WIRE IN COILS, BUT IT OFTEN HAS A COAT OF LACQUER, WHICH IS NOT DESIRABLE WHEN IT IS USED FOR JEWELLERY MAKING. COPPER WIRE IS USEFUL FOR WORKING OUT THE EXACT DIMENSIONS OF A PIECE, AND TO SHOW HOW THE DESIGN WILL BEND UP, HOW MUCH WIRE WILL BE NEEDED AND HOW THICK IT SHOULD BE.

> **SEE ALSO**
> - Annealing, pages 42–43
> - Bending, pages 56–59
> - Chain making, pages 92–97

To make working with wire easy, it should be kept annealed. Always use the correct pliers so that the wire is not marked by accident, and make jigs if necessary to bend the wire uniformly (see Bending, pages 56–59).

You can obtain wire of any section – square, round, oval, triangular, D-section or rectangular – and the shapes are made by drawing the wire through heavy industrial rollers. However, you can create your own shaped wire by pulling it through a draw plate. This is a steel plate, measuring 2 × 23 cm (¾ × 9 in.) and approximately 6 mm (¼ in.) thick, which has a series of holes in decreasing holes, squares, rectangles and so on on one side. On the other side of the plate, the holes are slightly opened to allow the larger wire to be inserted in the hole.

The plate should be held in a vice. Make sure that the jaws of the vice do not overlap any of the holes. By drawing down wire and chenier to widths of your own choice, you can make jump rings to specific sizes, and once you have a selection of jump rings, all kinds of ideas for chains will occur to you (see Chain making, pages 92–97).

If you need to straighten out a length of wire that has been bent or wound, make sure it is annealed, fasten one end tightly in the vice, hold the other end with a pair of serrated-edge pliers and pull tightly until you feel it stretch, which means that it is completely straight.

DRAWING DOWN WIRE

1 File the end of the wire into a longish point.

2 Hold the draw plate in a vice, making sure that the jaws do not cover any of the holes in the draw plate, and push the pointed end of the wire through a hole that is just too small to take the rest of the wire.

TOOLS FOR USE WITH WIRE
1 Triangular draw plate; 2 round draw plate; 3 square-section draw plate.

3 Grip the filed end of the wire with a pair of serrated-edge pliers and pull the wire straight through the hole. Repeat this for each decreasing size of hole until the wire is the correct diameter. It will need annealing after three or four pulls.

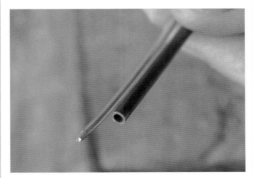

DRAWING DOWN CHENIER
1 Find a piece of wire that will fit snugly inside the chenier that is to be made narrower.

2 Melt a little beeswax on the wire and thread it down the chenier. Although the beeswax is not essential, it makes it easier to remove the wire, especially if the chenier is later bent or curved. Push the wire through the chenier until only about 5 mm (¼ in.) is visible. File the wire and chenier to a point.

3 Place both wire and chenier through a hole in the draw plate that is just smaller than the chenier. Grip both the chenier and the wire with serrated-edge pliers and pull them both through the draw plate. Continue until the chenier is the correct size. You will have to anneal the wire and chenier after three or four pulls.

4 Remove the wire by pushing the point through the smooth side of the draw plate. The chenier will not pass through the draw plate as the wire is removed.

MAKING JUMP RINGS

1 Place a metal former in the vice – the smooth end of a drill bit is suitable for this, but make sure that the drilling end is either protected with masking tape or is held in the 'safe' jaws of a vice. Fasten one end of a piece of annealed wire against the former in the vice.

3 Wrap adhesive tape around the wire and the former.

5 The rings will be cut at the right angle, which means that you will not have to tidy the ends with a file. They should sit neatly and close to each other.

2 Wind the wire up the former, keeping each turn as close as possible to the preceding one.

4 Place the piercing saw at an angle across the tape and pierce through both the tape and the wire.

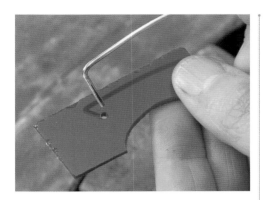

MAKING A SPIRAL

1 When you make a spiral from wire that is too thick to wind easily in a pair of pliers, bend the end of the wire to a right angle and place it through a hole that has been drilled either in a sheet of metal or in thick perspex. The wire should just fit the hole.

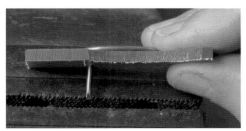

2 Fasten the end of the wire tightly in the vice.

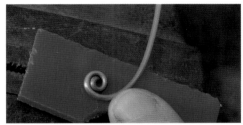

3 Use the metal or perspex as a flat plate to start winding the spiral.

4 Remove the spiral from the perspex and cut away the piece that was held in the vice.

MAKING A HELIX

You can make the spiral into a helix by pushing through from the back with a tapered punch.

TWISTING WIRE

Round wires twisted together can be used as a decorative border around a setting for a cabochon stone or around the top and bottom edges of rings and bangles. Square, rectangular and triangular section wires can be twisted by themselves to create effective edging, although round and oval wires must be twisted with another wire to look effective. You can also use different sections together, either twisting them separately before twisting them together or twisting them all together.

Before bending wire to shape, run solder along the length. If you do not, the twists will open out and loosen. Flux needs to be applied along the whole length of twisted wire, and paillons of solder should be positioned every few millimeters so that the whole piece is evenly soldered. Try not to use too much solder, or the twisted wire will look heavy and overworked.

HOW TO TWIST WIRE

1 Make a metal hook and fasten it into a hand drill. Take a long piece of annealed wire and bend it in half. Anchor the two ends into a vice – it doesn't matter if they are flattened, but they must be held securely. Hook the loop end over the hook in the drill.

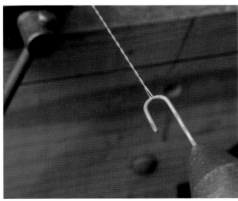

2 Hold the wire straight and wind the handle of the drill smoothly until you are happy with the amount of twist in the wire.

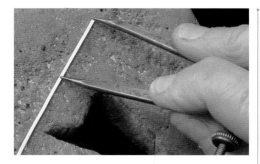

TWISTING SECTIONS IN A LENGTH OF WIRE

1 Use dividers to mark on square or rectangular section wire where the twists are to be.

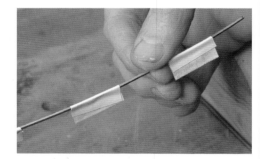

2 Use tape to mask the areas of wire that are not going to be twisted, then place the first section in the vice.

3 Hold the second, protected section with serrated-edge pliers and twist the wire four or five times.

4 This piece of silver wire has separate twisted sections along its length.

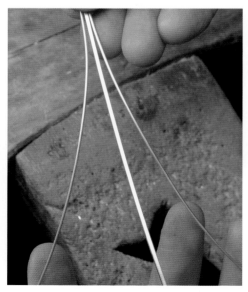

TWISTING MORE THAN ONE WIRE

1 A length of square section wire is being twisted with two lengths of round wire. Solder all three together at one end.

2 Hold the soldered end in the chuck of the hand drill and fasten the other ends in a vice. Wind the handle of the drill until you have the correct twist.

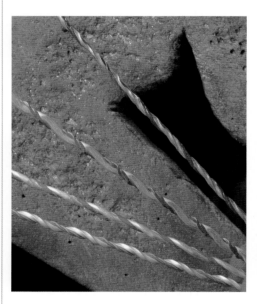

3 Copper and silver wire can be twisted together as shown here (from the top): the copper wire was twisted first, then twisted with silver; after twisting, the wires were pulled through a round draw plate; the copper was twisted first, but less twist was put on the wire, and the whole piece was slightly flattened with a hammer; the twisted wires were pulled through a square section draw plate.

WORKING WITH FINE OR CLOISONNÉ WIRE

This fine 0.25–0.35 mm wire is made specifically for enamelled cloisonné work (see Enamelling, pages 114–119). It is supplied on spools in lengths of about 20 m (65 ft).

It can be difficult to anneal cloisonné wire with a torch, because the wire nearest the flame is liable to melt while the rest of the coil is heated. The best method is to cut off the required length from the reel and coil it loosely into a clean shoe polish or tobacco can. You can then place the can in a kiln, heated to about 600°C (1110°F), for a minute or two. Only anneal fine wire if it is to be used as shown below. It is not necessary to anneal wire that is to be used for enamelling.

This kind of wire can also be used to make fine 'lace-type' and knitted work, and there are some beautiful examples of jewellery made primarily from knitted or crocheted wire, including pieces made by Mary Lee Hue.

KNITTING WITH WIRE

1 Use annealed 0.25–0.35 mm cloisonné wire. Cut a circle out of the centre of a piece of medium density fibreboard (MDF) and cut a further circle about 3 cm (1¼ in.) wide. Mark the positions for eight loops, and at these points drill holes slightly smaller than the diameter of the wire to be used for the loops.

2 Use half-round pliers to form eight loops. Hammer each loop into place and bend over the tops slightly with the half-round pliers.

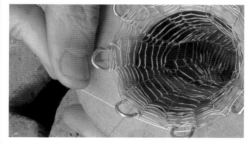

3 Make a double turn of fine wire around one side of a loop to start off. Take the wire around the back of each loop until you are back at the first loop.

4 Use a smooth crochet hook or a curved burnisher to lift the first wire up and over the second and then over the top of the loop so that it drops into the centre hole.

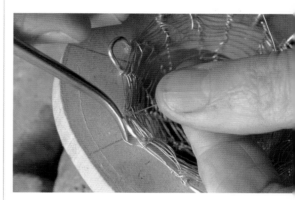

5 Continue to work around the circle, placing one wire over the next, and pushing the inside down as necessary.

6 To finish, remove the piece from the frame and fit jump rings through the loops so that you can attach magnetic ends. Wrap the ends neatly around each other and snip them off.

CHAIN MAKING

WITH SO MANY VARIATIONS IN THE KINDS OF MATERIALS, LINKING SYSTEMS, COLOURS, LENGTHS, WEIGHTS AND FASTENINGS, CHAIN MAKING CAN BE AN OPPORTUNITY TO LET YOUR IMAGINATION HAVE FREE REIN. THERE IS ALSO GREAT SATISFACTION IN MAKING AN OBJECT THAT IS COMPLETE IN ITSELF.

The decorative aspects of chains follow from their functional aspects. If two sections of a chain are linked together with a single wire ring, the piece will be flexible because the sections will be able to move around the ring to form a curve as well as being able to move back and forth to curve in the opposite direction. A simple jump ring, although ideally suited to this purpose, does not always suit the design and may look ill-considered or simply boring. Therefore, while aiming to accommodate the principle of the jump ring, the challenge of chain making lies in the ways in which the simple jump ring's function can be translated into a decorative form.

PLANNING THE CHAIN

Before you make a chain, there are several points to consider. First, you must determine the length. If it is to be an exact length; you will need to work out the number and size of each section. This may not be critical on a long chain, but if you are making a shorter one (about 40 cm/16 in. long), you should draw a circle with this circumference and divide it up until you have the correct number and length of sections.

Remember that the fastening is important, too. If it is made to be an integral part of the design, it will bring the whole thing together. Although bolt rings are useful, they can look rather like afterthoughts and spoil the effect of a well-designed necklace or chain.

You must also take the weight of the chain into consideration, and think about the weight of each link in terms of the sections it will be joining. A heavy chain will need a sturdy link; a light chain will need a proportionately delicate link.

SOLDERING CHAINS

It is not always necessary to solder the links of a chain, but if they are not soldered, the links should be strong enough that they cannot be pulled apart by hand. For information on soldering chains, see pages 48–51.

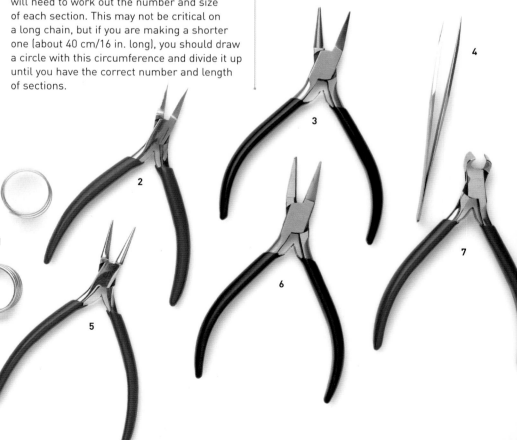

EGG PENTAGON NECKLACE – BABETTE VON DOHNANYI
The sections for this silver necklace have an egg shape on the inside and a pentagon on the outside. Each one was cast, and then every other one pierced open, linked into the next and soldered.

CHAIN-MAKING TOOLS
1 Coils of silver; **2** flat-nose pliers; **3** round flat pliers; **4** stainless steel tweezers; **5** round-nose pliers; **6** half-round pliers; **7** oblique cutters.

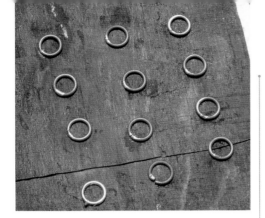

SIMPLE LINKED CHAIN

1 Solder the joints in a sufficient number of 6-mm (⅓-in.) jump rings to make the length of chain you require. Quench, rinse and dry.

4 Open the rings by holding them in two pairs of flat-nose pliers and twisting one pair of pliers away from you and the other pair toward you.

5 Link the rings so that they lie in the same direction. Flux the joint and resolder it. You may not need to add more solder, but try one ring first to check. When you are resoldering, work on one link at a time and make sure that the joint is not resting on the next link; hold the ring upright in a pair of insulated tweezers.

2 File away all excess solder, then hammer the rings flat on an anvil or flat plate.

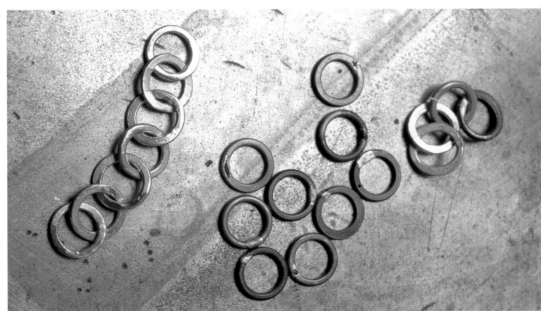

3 Pierce through the solder joint of every other ring.

HAMMERED CHAIN

This method makes an attractive hammered chain, which can be thoroughly pickled and cleaned when it is finished (see Polishing, pages 78–79).

SEE ALSO

- Drilling, pages 27–28
- Soldering, pages 48–51
- Bending, pages 56–59
- Polishing, pages 78–79
- Using wire, pages 86–91

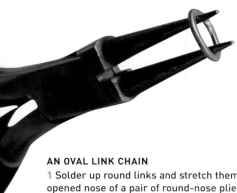

 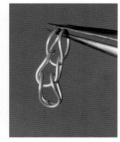

AN OVAL LINK CHAIN

1 Solder up round links and stretch them over the opened nose of a pair of round-nose pliers.

A DOUBLE-LOOP CHAIN

1 Solder up lots of 0.5 mm rings.

3 Bring the two ends of each loop together, loop one link into the next and continue to make a chain, closing up each link as you work.

2 Twist half the links through 360 degrees and cut the remaining links open at the solder joint in the long side. Slip the twisted links in then resolder the joints.

2 Stretch the rings into ovals, then fasten an old drill bit securely in a vice and use the straight end as a former around which the loops can be bent.

4 This makes a flexible, lightweight chain.

SIMPLE TWISTED CHAIN

Make a simple twisted chain by cutting sheet metal into pieces about 6 × 25 mm (¼ × 1 in.), filing the ends to round them and drilling a hole in each end. Twist the piece by holding each end in flat-nose pliers and twisting one pair away from you by 90 degrees and the other pair toward you by 90 degrees. Join the lengths together with jump rings, soldering each ring at the joint.

LINKING SQUARE WIRE

1 Use your dividers to measure and mark a length of about 5 × 5 mm (³/₁₆ × ³/₁₆ in.) silver wire into equal pieces, each about 3 cm (1¼ in.) long. Cut out.

2 Mentally number the sides of each length from 1 to 4 and cut into sides 1 and 3 for about 5 mm (³/₁₆ in.) at one end. Cut away the outside edges. Repeat this step at the other end, but on sides 2 and 4.

3 Drill a hole in the centre of each end tab.

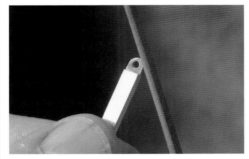

4 Use a file to make the square ends round.

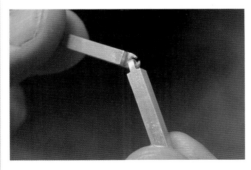

5 Pierce through one end loop and open it just wide enough to slip through the opposite end loop of the next section. Carefully solder the join. Continue like this with each section until you have the right length chain.

USING WIRE AND CHENIER

1 Cut equal lengths of round wire, approximately 2 mm (¹/₁₆ in.) in diameter. Spread the ends of the wire by hammering them out on a flat metal plate. Use a half-round file to shape the end into a gentle curve.

2 Bend some fine chenier so that it follows the same curve and cut it into pieces that will fit into the centre of each curve. Use hard solder to solder a chenier piece to each end of each section.

3 Slip a small jump ring through the chenier link and join the jump ring with soft solder.

LINKING CHENIER

1 Bend chenier to the correct curve for a short necklace (see Bending, pages 56–59) and cut it into sections. Use dividers to mark the four quarters of the diameter at each end of every piece.

2 Drill a hole through two opposite end sections of the chenier.

3 Place the chenier in a chenier holder and pierce out the top and bottom quarters.

4 At the other end, drill a hole through two opposite end sections of the chenier, making sure that they are at the opposite side from the holes at the top end. Pierce out the two remaining side quarters. File the protruding ends to a curve and use a round needle file to clean up the inside area.

5 Try each end section out on each other and file to fit. This chain is joined by means of a universal joint (see page 104).

LOOP-IN-LOOP CHAIN

1 Use wire, approximately 0.7–0.6 mm, to make rings with a diameter of 15 mm (⅝ in.). Lay them on a charcoal block and solder them one at a time.

2 Form each ring into an oval by stretching it over the ends of a pair of round-nose pliers. Place three loops together into a star-shape and solder them together.

3 Solder a sprue of silver or brass firmly in the centre of the three loops. Each loop must make firm contact with the sprue stick.

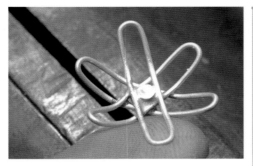

4 Hold the sprue in a vice and, with the ends of your fingers, gently curve each loop up.

7 Bend up the first layer of loops, then the second layer of loops before inserting, in the same order as before, three more loops.

10 Use a smooth hook – a curved burnisher, for example – to ease the loops so that additional sets of loops can be inserted. Carry on inserting three new loops through the two previous sets of loops, curving them with your fingers as you work.

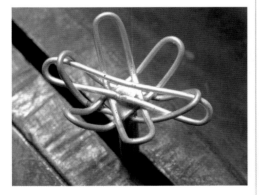

5 Thread a single oval loop through the lowest fixed loop in the group.

8 Thread the third group of loops through both the first and second sets of loops.

11 When the chain is 3–4 cm (1¼–1½ in.) long, remove it from the vice and use a wooden mallet to shape it gently while it is rolled along a flat plate. Keep working in this manner until the chain is as long as you want it. When you have finished all the construction, it will need to be pulled through a large draw plate to straighten it. Place it in the vice, push the sprue end through the hole you have drilled to size and pull the chain through. Alternatively, place the length of chain between two flat pieces of wood and roll back and forward.

6 Place a second loop through the next loop of the group, and then thread a third loop through the third loop in the sprued group.

9 Push the inner loops upwards so that they are close together.

CATCHES AND JOINTS

AS YOU WORK THROUGH THE STEPS ILLUSTRATED HERE, MOST OF THE TECHNIQUES WILL BECOME SELF-EVIDENT. HOWEVER, THERE ARE SOME POINTS TO BEAR IN MIND WHEN YOU MAKE CATCHES AND JOINTS FOR PIECES OF JEWELLERY.

CATCHES

Several types of catch are available ready-made, so when you are designing a piece you should consider whether a hand-made catch will help to create the effect you want to achieve better than a bought one. For example, you might want to consider the time you will have to spend in fashioning a tiny box catch for a small chain when a ready-made one will look just as good.

Standard silver, which is a comparatively soft metal, is not always suitable for use on a spring-type catch. Silver can, of course, be made hard and springy by hitting it with a hammer on a steel support, but even this will not necessarily make it strong enough for your purposes. Steel could be used to make the spring, but it should not be soldered to precious metal if you want the work to be hallmarked. This could be riveted on or held in place under tension.

Remember that catches are put on when all other work has been finished, and usually soft or easy solder is used to attach them. Some bought catches – the bolt rings, for example, which are widely used to close chains – have a little steel spring within them. It is better to buy a catch to which the attachment ring has already been soldered so that any additional soldering will be done on the adjoining jump ring. Try to keep the heat of your torch away from the bolt ring as much as you can when you are soldering, perhaps by placing a small sheet of mica over the ring while you work. Do not quench after soldering, because if the bolt ring is immersed in acid, it may be difficult to remove all traces of acid and the steel may contaminate the metal around it. Also, if it is quenched while hot, the steel will be softened.

Spring T-bars on cuff link findings should be removed before the back findings are soldered to the front, because they contain a piece of steel that acts as a spring within the bar. They should be replaced and riveted in place when all other work is complete.

LADYBUG BRACELET – CATHERINE HILLS
This oxidized silver bracelet has a simple T-bar catch that fastens through the silver ring to hold the bracelet together. The T-bar has to be just long enough to go through the ring and stay in place.

SEE ALSO
• Soldering, pages 48–51
• Bending, pages 56–59
• Riveting, pages 111–113

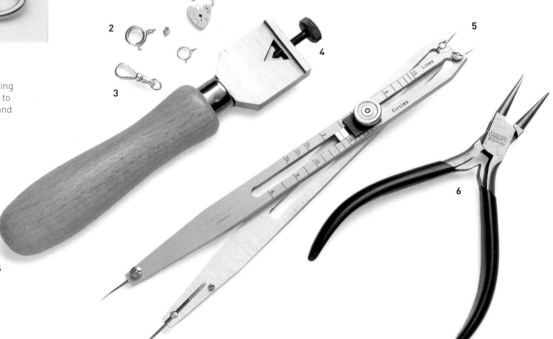

TOOLS FOR MAKING CATCHES AND JOINTS
1 Gold padlock catch; **2** silver bolt rings of different sizes; **3** silver swivel catch; **4** jointing tool for holding chenier and wire while cutting a straight edge; **5** pair of dividers; **6** round-nose pliers.

MAKING A FIGURE-OF-EIGHT CATCH

1 Use tweezers to hold the end of a piece of wire against the side of a charcoal block. Concentrate the flame just above the end until the metal begins to run into a ball. Withdraw the flame when the ball is the size you want.

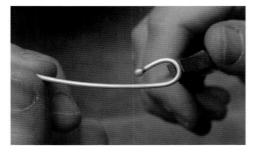

2 Use half-round pliers to make the first curve.

3 Cut the other end to length and form another ball as in step 1. Shape the figure-of-eight and solder one end to close the loop.

4 Place each loop in turn on the anvil and tap it lightly to flatten and harden it.

5 Open out the free loop slightly to make it easier to slip it into the ring on the necklace. Place a jump ring through the soldered loop and attach it to one end of the necklace.

SOLDERED CATCH

1 Solder a length of wire to a small section of wire that is approximately twice the diameter of the first. Cut the wire to length.

2 Solder the smaller end of the wire to the last section of the necklace.

3 Take the last section of the other end of the necklace and pierce a hole in the centre that is large enough to push the larger end of the wire through. Cut a channel to within a scant 6 mm (¼ in.) of the end of the section. The channel should be just wide enough to accommodate the thinner wire.

4 Place the head through the hole and pull the two ends away from each other.

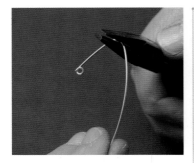

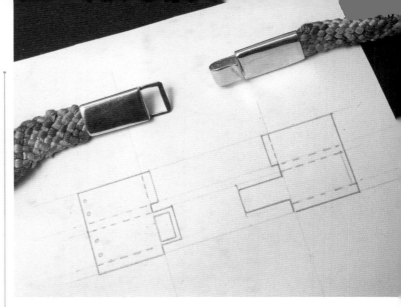

SIMPLE CATCH

1 Curl a small loop in one end of a length of wire. Leave about 2 cm (¾ in.) before bending a right angle.

3 Use half-round pliers to make a slight outward curve on the top end of the loop. Place the two sides around a former, such as the short end of a drill bit held in a vice, and pull the sides together.

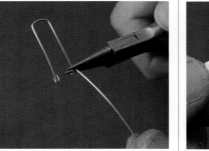

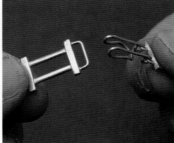

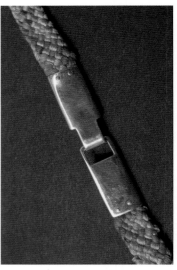

2 Bend a second right angle in the wire. This defines the width of the catch. Make another small loop in the other end of the wire and cut away the excess wire.

4 Attach the two loops of the catch to the last section of a chain and solder on a wire loop, which should be just wider than the catch, to the other end of the chain.

MAKING CATCHES FOR FABRIC

The catches shown in this and the next sequence can be used with fabric. The ones shown here are used to fasten a necklace made from plaited silk.

1 The two halves of this silver catch are made from a single sheet of silver. Calculate the left-hand pattern by doubling the width of the plait and adding to that measurement twice the depth of the plait. The loop for the catch goes on one of the longer sides, and the tab, equal to the depth, goes on the other long side. Draw dotted lines to indicate where the metal will be bent. Draw the right-hand pattern in the same way, but instead of a loop on one side, allow enough metal to fold back on itself to make a catch. This section must be narrower than the loop so that it will fit into it.

2 Cut the pattern from the metal and use a four-sided file to make grooves along the dotted lines. Bend up the pattern and solder them down the inside edges. Clean and polish before attaching it to the plait. Either insert two rivets through the layers of silver and plait or make two silver screws using the tap and die set. The ends of the screws will need to be filed flush with the metal.

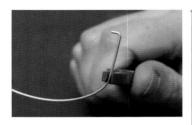

MAKING AN INTERLOCKING CATCH

1 Bend a loop with one straight end and a U-shaped curve at the other. Solder together the ends at the straight end.

2 Use round-nose pliers to make a 'waist' in the loop.

3 Harden the loop by hammering it on an anvil. Make a second loop in the same way.

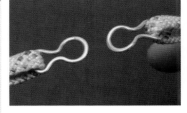

4 Slip one end of the necklace through the straight end section of the loop; repeat at the other end. Check the length before sewing the fabric to itself to hold the loops in place.

5 Turn one loop sideways so it slips through the other loop. Straighten so the catch holds. Use half-round pliers to bend the end of one loop up and the end of the other loop down so that they sit comfortably together.

CATCHES FOR CHAINS

1 Make a small wire loop and thread about 2.5 cm (1 in.) of chain onto it. Place the loop in the middle of a wire bar that has a diameter of about 2 mm (1/16 in.). Flux the joint carefully so that no flux gets onto the chain. Place a paillon of easy solder to the joint and solder the loop to the bar. Paint a little rouge on the chain to protect it against the solder.

2 Solder up a ring that is large enough for the bar to pass through it. Use a smaller jump ring, which can be soldered with easy solder, to attach this to one end of the necklace.

3 Join the short length of chain to the other end of the main chain using a jump ring, which should be isolated and soldered with easy solder. The bar is threaded through the large ring to hold the necklace together.

MAKING A SPRING CATCH

1 To make a catch about 2 cm (3/4 in.) long, take a length of D-section wire about 3 cm (1 1/4 in.) long. Drill a hole in one end and file the end to make it round. Halfway along the flat side of the wire, file a groove that is just over half the depth of the wire.

2 Carefully bend the D-section wire back on itself, flat sides together, at the groove. File another little groove all around the ends, about 6 mm (1/4 in.) from the end.

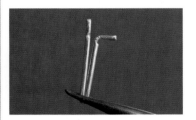

3 Bend what will be the top end of the catch up by 90 degrees.

4 Place the folded end of the catch on the anvil and tap it gently with a hammer, turning it around as you hit it so that it keeps its shape. Check that the catch will fit into a piece of chenier, which should have an inside diameter that is slightly larger than the width of the flat side of the D-section wire. If the catch will not fit, file carefully all around until it does.

5 Cut a piece of chenier approximately 2 cm (¾ in.) long. Solder a ring to one end. The inside diameter of the ring should be slightly smaller than the inside of the chenier.

6 Solder a flat piece of silver to the other end of the chenier. Trim it with a piercing saw and finish the edge with a file. Solder a ring or loop to this flat end. The chain will be attached to this loop.

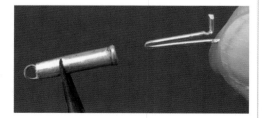

7 Fit the spring end into the chenier catch. If it does not click into place, you will have to make sure that the groove filed at the point where the end turns up is deep enough to fit under the wire ring soldered around the chenier. File two or three small grooves in the top of the tab to make it easier to push down.

HINGES

Hinges are used whenever full movement in a single plane is required. The hinge described here would be appropriate for a small box. On a small object, the hinge needs to be made of only three sections, and the wire used for the pin should fit closely through the chenier.

If the hinge needs to be set slightly away from the piece – as may be the case on a large, round locket or a pocket watch, for example – the sections of the chenier for the hinge must be held in a bracket made to fit the side of the circle. You will need two sizes of chenier for this – the size required for the hinge itself and a larger size into which the smaller piece will fit. Determine the length of the hinge. Cut off a section to the requisite length from the larger chenier and then cut it through the centre lengthwise to make two semicircular sections.

Hard-solder a strip of silver, about 1 cm (½ in.) wide, along the length of one semicircular section of chenier so that it is flush with the top edge. Do the same with the other semicircular section. File or cut away the top quarter on the side length of the chenier not soldered to the silver strip. Repeat on the other piece. The chenier for the hinge is placed in the semicircular curved part of the bracket.

An alternative way of making the hinge is to divide the length required into three or five equal sections and to cut three or five lengths of chenier to fit. File a little edge back from both ends of each section to allow freer movement, then line up the sections of chenier, side by side, in one half of the semicircular strips you have just made. Dab a tiny amount of flux between the first, third and fifth sections and the semicircle they are sitting in and place a paillon of solder in the same place. Place the other half of the bracket on top, dab a little flux between the second and fourth sections, and position a paillon of solder. Heat the whole hinge until the solder just tacks the pieces together, but take care that one piece of solder does not run onto the adjoining piece of chenier. Quench, pickle and rinse the two halves before soldering the chenier to each side more thoroughly.

To fit the bracket to the locket or watch, place the flat strip section of the bracket under the circular locket or watch at the point of attachment and use a scribe to mark around the curved edge. Pierce away the scribed line and file it smooth so that the bracket can be neatly soldered to the top section of the locket or watch. Scribe a similar line on the other bracket and pierce it out as before so that it can be neatly soldered to the bottom half of the locket or watch. The hinge can then be assembled with a rivet.

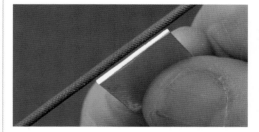

MAKING A HINGE

1 File a groove in the sides of the pieces that are to be hinged. Use either a parallel round file or the side of a joint round-edge file. The groove must be deep enough to allow the chenier that is used as the hinge to sit snugly inside.

2 Place a length of chenier against the groove and use dividers to mark the exact length of the groove.

3 Divide and mark the length of chenier into five equal sections. Use a piercing saw to cut halfway through the chenier at these four points.

6 Remove the remainder of the second and fourth sections with your piercing saw.

9 Solder the two pieces of chenier into the groove on the metal.

4 File away the second and fourth sections to just over halfway through the chenier. Cut the fifth section from the chenier length.

7 Use dividers to measure the gaps left and mark these points on a piece of chenier. Cut off two pieces and file them until they fit perfectly into the gaps left by the second and fourth sections. Check again that they fit.

10 Carefully file around the edges of all the chenier pieces to allow them to move freely against each other.

5 Place the shaped chenier in the groove in the side of one piece of metal, with the filed away areas facing into the groove. Place a small amount of flux and a paillon of solder at the points where the first, third and fifth sections fit into the groove and solder them in place.

8 Place the two pieces of metal side by side and use dividers to mark on the second piece the points at which the gaps occur. These measurements must be very precisely measured and marked. Place the two pieces of chenier between these marks.

11 Thread a length of wire through all the chenier sections. Cut it to length and rivet over the ends.

UNIVERSAL JOINTS

Universal joints are used when full movement in two planes is required. A simple jump ring is a kind of universal joint, but as we have seen, it is not always appropriate for a well-designed piece. A universal joint can be hidden within a tube, or it can be made into a separate entity.

The joint is made by attaching a piece of wire to one side of the chain, pivoting it on another piece, which is attached to the other side of the chain. The design must always take into account the fact that the wire must be strong enough to have a hole drilled through it to take the smaller wire. Both wires have to pass through a central pin, which can be shaped to match your design.

The principle of the universal joint can be applied by placing the joints of a chain or necklace on different planes. For example, a chain could be made extremely flexible if small rectangular sections were twisted through 90 degrees in the centre and hinges soldered to each end.

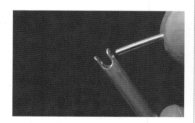

MAKING A UNIVERSAL JOINT

1 Drill a hole through the tabs at one end at a chenier section through which a wire approximately 1 mm (1/32 in.) in diameter will pass.

2 The second wire for the joint must be small enough to pass through the first wire – wire about 0.5 mm should be suitable. Copper wire has been used here for clarity. Drill a hole for this finer wire through the tabs at the other end of the chenier section.

3 Take a piece of chenier that will fit inside the chenier used for the chain and drill a hole through it that is the same size as the hole for the fine wire, positioning the hole about 3 mm (1/8 in.) from the edge. Cut off the chenier so that it is about 6 mm (1/4 in.) long and round off the edges with a file.

4. Try out the smaller chenier on the chenier used for the chain to make certain that it will move freely inside it.

5 Take the thicker wire and thread it through the tabs in the chenier and through the centre of the small piece of chenier so that the small piece is held between the tabs. Hold the wire steady while you drill through it a hole that will take the 0.5 mm wire. Locate the drill by placing it through the hole made in step 3.

6 Place the section of chain over the next section so that the small holes line up.

7 Thread the finer wire through the tabs in the chenier, through the smaller hole of the piece within and through the wire within that piece. Cut the wires to length and rivet the fine wire in place. This holds the larger one, which does not need riveting as well. The smaller holes in the chenier will need to be countersunk for the rivet.

MAKING A BOX CATCH

Box catches are used when a secure finding is needed on a fairly heavy article of jewellery such as a necklace or a bracelet. Make the width of the box suit the overall dimensions of the piece with which it is used.

1 Mark four lines on a piece of silver to show the width and the height. File grooves along each of these lines and cut the silver to length. File the sides that meet when the box is folded to 45 degrees.

2 Fold the silver along the grooves to form a box and solder together (see Bending, pages 56–59). At the same time, apply flux along all the inside corners of the box and run some hard solder along these points. This strengthens the area you have filed to facilitate bending.

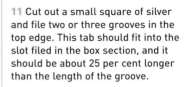

11 Cut out a small square of silver and file two or three grooves in the top edge. This tab should fit into the slot filed in the box section, and it should be about 25 per cent longer than the length of the groove.

3 Solder a plate of silver to one end of the box. Pickle, rinse and dry, and then pierce away the excess metal.

6 Place a small piece of silver across the area you have just removed and solder it in place. Trim away excess with a piercing saw.

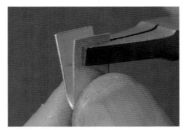

9 Make the snap fastener from a piece of silver that will, when folded over, fit into the box. The silver should be slightly less than the internal width of the box and about twice as long, although it is not crucial if the catch does not reach to the end of the box. You also need a strip at one end that is the same thickness as the metal used to make the slotted front of the box. Mark the appropriate lines on the silver and file a groove at the halfway point. Do not file the line indicating the thickness of the metal. Carefully bend over the silver along the filed line.

12 Use easy solder to attach the tab to the top part of the snap section, leaving the last quarter of its length overhanging the edge. Tap the snap end down on an anvil to make it springy. If you alter the shape while you are doing this, file it to size so that it will fit the box.

4 At the open end of the box, mark a line that is the same thickness as the metal used for the plate at the other end.

7 Mark the centre of the box on the side you have just soldered and file a groove through the soldered strip and about a quarter of the way into the box.

5 Use a piercing saw to cut into the box along the marked line, halfway down the sides of the box. Cut away this fillet and file the edges smooth.

8 Use easy solder to fit a ring to the solid end of the box. Clean the box and finish it with wet and dry sandpapers.

10 Solder a piece of silver at 90 degrees to the longer section of the snap fastener and solder an attachment ring to the back of it.

13 Fit the two sections together. You should be able to hear a click as the snap locates behind the front of the box. Mark on the back plate of the snap where it needs filing. Finish off all edges. Clean and polish.

FITTINGS AND FINDINGS

MOST PIECES OF JEWELLERY NEED AN ATTACHMENT OF SOME KIND THAT ALLOWS THEM TO BE WORN. WHEN MADE BY HAND, THEY ARE CALLED FITTINGS; WHEN BOUGHT READY-MADE, THEY ARE CALLED FINDINGS. FITTINGS CAN BE MADE AS AN INTEGRAL PART OF A PIECE OF JEWELLERY. FOR EXAMPLE, A PENDANT CAN BE MADE WITH AN AREA FOR HANGING AROUND THE NECK AS PART OF THE OVERALL PATTERN OR A PIN CAN BE MADE AS AN EXTENSION OF A BROOCH.

GOLD DIPPED DAISY EARRINGS – FAITH TAVENDER
The fittings on these earrings show how a simple turn at the front allows several different pieces that make up the design to be hung at different levels.

SOLDERING

If a fitting or finding is an extra piece that needs to be soldered to the article, this is usually done after all the main work has been completed.

Carefully mark the position of the fitting or finding, then position yourself in such a way that you can clearly see your mark and that you are placing the fitting or finding correctly. Paint a little flux on the spot on which the finding will sit and place a paillon of solder in the flux. Paint the base of the fitting with flux and, if you think it will be necessary, run a little solder on the base of the fitting before you begin.

ATTACHING FITTINGS

A pendant attachment is placed on the charcoal block, close to the pendant. Flux the joint, making sure the contact is good, and if it moves while you are heating it, push it back into position with insulated tweezers before the solder flows.

ASSEMBLY

Riveted parts of a fitting should always be assembled after all soldering is completed. For example, the pin of a brooch should not be attached until all the other parts of the brooch have been completed; the T-bars of a pair of cuff links should be riveted only when all other work has been completed, and the clips on clip-on earrings should be riveted or sprung into place only when the rest of the work is finished. If these findings are assembled before the soldering is completed, they would become annealed and lose their springiness.

POSITIONING

The balance of a piece depends on the position of the fitting. On a brooch, for instance, the sitting of the fichu joint and catch is crucial. You also need to consider the way in which a brooch will hang when it is pinned to a garment – will it sit comfortably or flop forwards or sideways? The brooch pin will grip more firmly if the catch is set off line from the fichu joint.

If you are making cuff links with a T-bar, check that the alignment is correct before soldering. When you make a chain link, make sure that it is long enough to wear comfortably but not so long that it does not do its job. Use an odd number of links between the two back faces so that they sit properly.

Earring fittings also need careful positioning. The weight of a piece will affect the position of the post on the back of an ear stud. A heavy stud will flop forwards; to avoid this, the post should be placed close to the top of the stud.

SEE ALSO

• Piercing, pages 20–23
• Drilling, pages 27–28
• Soldering, pages 48–51
• Riveting, pages 111–113

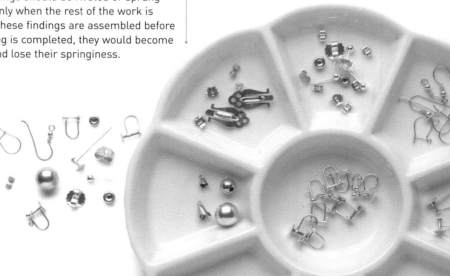

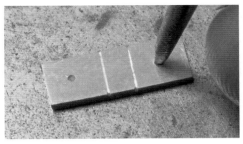

ATTACHING EARRING FITTINGS

1 Use a pair of insulated tweezers to hold the post steady when you solder it to the back of the earring. Allow the solder to begin to flow before placing the post in it, then take away the flame and hold the post in place until the solder is completely hard. Quench, pickle, rinse and dry.

MAKING BROOCH FITTINGS

1 Cut a strip of metal approximately 5 × 10 mm (³⁄₁₆ × ½ in.) and score a line about 5 mm (³⁄₁₆ in.) in from each short end. File along the lines until the grooves are just deeper than half the thickness of the metal. Mark the centre of the end sections.

4 With the flat side of the wire on the inside of the curve, bend a strip of D-section wire into the shape of a small 'e'. Cut the end of the wire with a piercing saw and file the bottom flat so that it will stand on the back of the brooch before it is soldered in place.

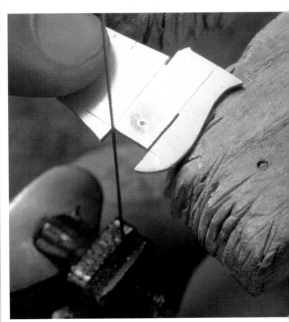

2 Hold the base of the earring steady and allow the solder to begin to flow before placing the fitting onto it. Make sure the clip is correctly positioned before you remove the flame. Hold the clip steady for a few seconds before quenching. Solder a screw fitting to the earring before you bend it up. After cleaning and polishing the earring, use a pair of half-round pliers to bend the screw fitting into a smooth curve.

2 Drill a hole in the centre of each of the end sections and bend up the strip along the grooves until the sides are parallel.

3 Use a three-sided needle file to make a small groove in the top of the joint in which the pin will sit.

5 Make the tab for the pin by marking the centre of a square about 5 × 5 mm (³⁄₁₆ × ³⁄₁₆ in.) and drilling a hole at this point. Use a piercing saw to cut out the square.

FINDINGS
A selection of ready-made silver findings.

6 File a small groove in the top of the tab into which the pin will fit, and solder the two pieces together with easy solder. At this stage the pin should extend beyond the end of the tab; it can be neatened up later. Solder the pin and tab together.

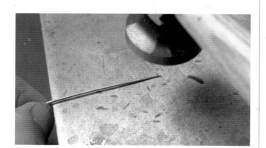

7 After soldering, make the pin springy by rolling it along the steel flat bed, tapping it with a flat hammer as you do so.

8 The fichu joint and catch should not be directly in line with each other. File the tab of the pin so that it fits neatly into the fichu joint and can move easily.

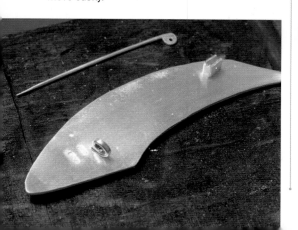

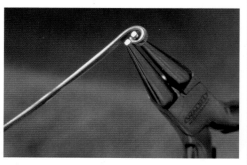

9 Make a simple pin by bending around the end of a piece of wire that is thick enough to fit snugly into the fichu joint. The rivet pin passes through the joint, through the bent wire, and out at the other side.

MAKING A HINGED PIN JOINT

1 A hinge joint is used for the pin on a larger brooch. Cut out a square approximately 9 × 9 mm (³⁄₈ × ³⁄₈ in.), file a groove 2 mm (¹⁄₁₆ in.) in from one edge and bend the edge at a right angle. Cut two pieces of chenier with an outside diameter of 1 mm (¹⁄₃₂ in.), which will sit in the angle. Solder them in place and clean the edges with a flat file.

2 File a groove in the centre of the top edge to accommodate the pin.

3 Flatten the end of a piece of wire for the hinge end of the pin.

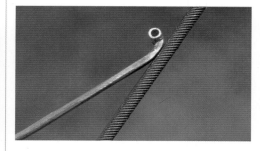

4 Cut a piece of chenier to fit snugly between the two pieces already soldered into position and solder it to the flattened end of the pin. Neaten up the edges with a file.

5 Thread a length of wire that will fit through the chenier through the three hinge sections and rivet the ends to hold the pin in place.

ATTACHING CUFF LINK FITTINGS

Run solder onto the back of the cuff link. Hold the fitting in insulated tweezers and hold it squarely in place as the solder flows. Remove the flame and hold the fitting steady for a few seconds before quenching. Clean and finish the cuff link before riveting the T-bar in place.

FINISHING OFF TIE PINS

Use hard solder to attach the pin to the main part of the piece.

MAKING CHAIN LINK FITTINGS

1 Drill a hole about 2 mm (1/16 in.) from the straight edge of a piece of silver. Scribe a line around the outside of the hole, leaving the bottom edge flat and pierce around the line. Place the flat edge of the fitting on the back of the cuff link.

2 Attach the fitting to the back of the cuff link, using hard or medium solder.

3 Take five or seven sections of chain and pierce open the two end sections. Attach the link to the fitting and isolate it before closing the joint with easy solder.

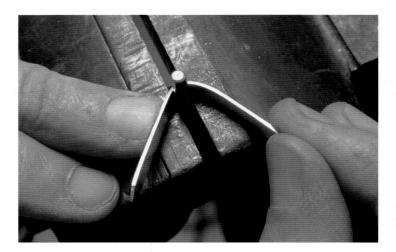

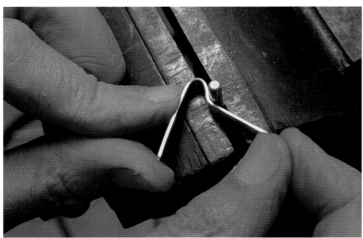

MAKING A TIE CLIP

1 Take a strip of metal about 6 × 55 mm (¼ × 2¼ in.). Do not anneal the metal so that it retains its springiness. Place a former, such as the top end of a drill bit, in a vice. If you are using a drill bit, protect it by wrapping masking tape around it before you place it in the vice. Use your fingers to bend the metal tightly around the former so that the curve is a little less than halfway along its length.

2 Bend a curve in the opposite direction around the same former.

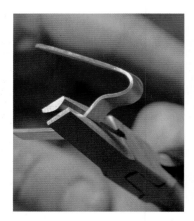

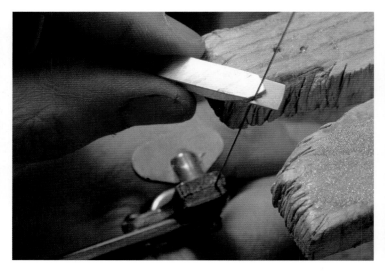

3 Use half-round pliers to bend the second curve back toward the front again. Make another curve away again, using the former. It does not matter that the piece is too long at this stage.

4 Use flat-nose pliers to pull the back past the front and to push it past the front to form a spring.

5 Use a piercing saw to cut the back section to match the front.

RIVETING

RIVETING IS A USEFUL WAY OF JOINING PIECES OF METAL WITH ANOTHER PIECE OF METAL, WOOD OR PLASTIC. IF A RIVETED JOINT IS TO BE TIGHT, THE RIVET SHOULD BE PLACED DIRECTLY THROUGH THE PIECES AND SPREAD AT EACH END TO GIVE IT A TIGHT FIT. IF YOU WANT THE JOINT TO HAVE A DEGREE OF FLEXIBILITY, YOU CAN FIT WASHERS BETWEEN EACH LAYER BEFORE THE RIVET IS SPREAD.

The wire used to make a rivet should fit neatly into the hole. If the diameter of a rivet is too small, the ends cannot be spread enough to hold it in the hole. In addition, the wire will be able to bend slightly inside the hole and will not, therefore, hold it properly.

A rivet should always be spread into a countersunk area around the top of a hole. If it is appropriate, the rivet can be soldered to the bottom piece and the other pieces placed over it, finishing with the top piece, which has a countersunk hole.

To make a rivet, the wire is pushed through all the pieces. The wire should protrude by approximately 1 mm ($\frac{1}{32}$ in.) from the metal, and both ends should be filed straight. A pointed punch is then placed in the centre of one end of the wire and hammered slightly, while the base is supported either on a small anvil or on the end of a flat punch, which is held in a vice. The piece is then turned over, and the other end hammered with a pointed punch.

If you need to remove a rivet, file off the head, place the other end over a hole or hold the piece in a vice, so that the rivet can be pushed through. Place the pointed punch in the centre of the rivet and tap it gently until it comes through on the other side.

USING TAPS AND DIES

Very small taps and dies, similar to those used for fine jewellery work, need careful handling. A hole slightly smaller than the hole you wish to screw into should be drilled through the metal. The tap should be placed in a small hand drill and worked very slowly through the hole. Ideally, it should be given a quarter – or at most a half – turn and then reversed to remove the swarf that

the cut has made. If the tap is forced through the metal, it is likely to break and get stuck in the hole.

The wire to make the hole should be fractionally larger than the first hole that was drilled in the metal. It should be placed squarely in the die and then the die turned around the wire, taking it as far up as necessary. Either undo the die to remove the wire or the other way and unscrew the wire. If you need a head on the screw, it must be soldered on. This can be done before the wire is put in the die, with any excess solder around the head being filed away first. This does, however, mean that it will not be possible to take the thread all the way up the wire. To put a head on a screw that has a thread all the way up, paint a paste of rouge powder to within 1 mm ($\frac{1}{32}$ in.) of one end of the screw and allow it to dry completely. Use a tiny paillon of easy solder to solder the head and screw together and file a groove across the head after it has been soldered.

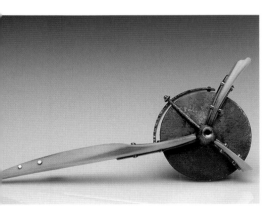

'PROP' BROOCH – ANDY COOPERMAN
Decorative rivets have been used in this bronze, silver, plastic and gold brooch. Rivets are a perfect way of joining different materials together as they eliminate the need to solder while adding a feature to the design.

SEE ALSO
• Drilling, pages 27–28
• Hammering, pages 60–61

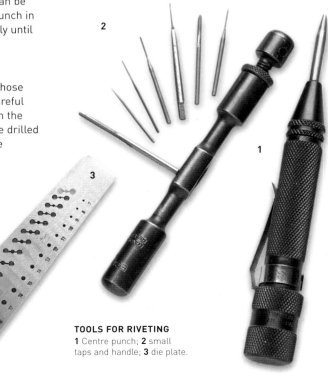

TOOLS FOR RIVETING
1 Centre punch; **2** small taps and handle; **3** die plate.

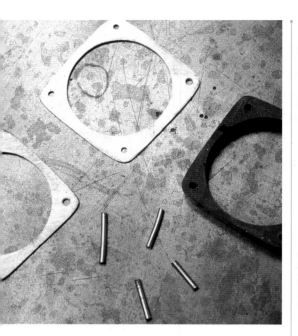

RIVETING SECTIONS TOGETHER

1 Assemble all the parts to be riveted, then line them all up correctly before drilling the holes for the rivets. Use wire that fits the drilled holes exactly.

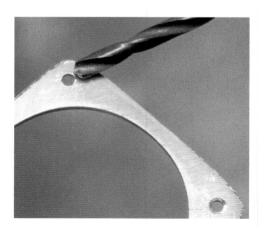

2 Countersink the outside edges of the holes so that the head of the rivet has somewhere to sit. You can do this with a drill bit that is a few sizes larger than the original hole.

3 Place the wire rivet through the piece and cut or file the ends so that they protrude by approximately 1 mm ($\frac{1}{32}$ in.) above the surface of the metal. Use a pointed punch to mark the centre of the rivet and spread it slightly by hitting the punch gently with a jeweller's hammer or a small ballpien hammer.

4 Use a flat-nose punch to spread the head of the rivet on both sides.

5 You can use the flat head of a small hammer to spread the rivet, but be careful that you do not mark the metal with it.

6 Carefully file away any excess rivet.

7 The rivet will seem to disappear completely if the head is spread sufficiently for it to fill the countersunk area.

RIVETING LINKS OF A CHAIN

1 Drill holes in the links for the rivets and countersink the holes at the top and bottom of the chain.

2 You will need to insert a small washer between the two links to allow some movement. Cut a small piece of chenier that will fit snugly over the rivet.

3 Place the two pieces together and cut the rivet to size. As in the previous procedure, the rivet should protrude by about 1 mm ($^1/_{32}$ in.) both above and below. Spread the head of the rivet with a punch.

4 Alternatively, spread the rivet head by tapping it gently with a jeweller's hammer.

RIVETING A PIN TO A BROOCH

Cut a piece of wire to fit snugly through the fichu joint and support the lower half of the rivet on the side of a small anvil. Use a punch to spread the head, turn it over and spread the head of the other side.

TAPS AND DIES

1 Choose a drill bit that is fractionally smaller than the hole you want to tap and drill through all the pieces that are to be screwed together.

2 Place the tap in a hand-held drill and very slowly drill the hole. Work a quarter of a turn at a time and turn the drill back counterclockwise each time to get rid of any swarf that is produced by the cut. Tiny taps such as this break easily if they are forced.

3 Place the corresponding die piece in the handle. The wire for the screw should just fit the hole in the die as it is tightened. Slowly push the whole handle around the wire, hold the wire firmly in your other hand and allow the die to do the work.

4 Screw the pieces together. Cut and file the head of the screw.

SPECIALIST TECHNIQUES

In this section we look at more specialized techniques, which do not necessarily fit with the other categories in this book. You may find an occasional use for them, so the basic information is included. Further reading would be a good idea if you find that you want to further your knowledge in one or all of these subjects.

ENAMELLING

ENAMELLING IS A UNIQUE AND HISTORICAL WAY OF USING COLOUR TO ENHANCE YOUR WORK. ENAMELS ARE A MIXTURE OF SILICA, LEAD OXIDES, SALTS OF SODA, POTASSIUM AND BORIC ACIDS, WHICH FUSE TO A COPPER, STEEL, SILVER OR GOLD SURFACE WHEN THEY ARE FIRED IN A KILN.

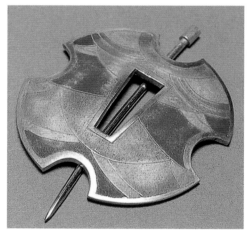

CLOISONNÉ BROOCH – KYOKO URINO
Cloisonné enamelling with subtle colours has been applied over a ground of traditional Japanese wave patterns. The form of the brooch has been inspired by the *tuba*, a Japanese sword.

ENAMELING EQUIPMENT
1 Porcelain mortar and pestle with lump enamel; **2** powdered or ground enamels; **3** transparent lump or frit enamel; **4** unusual Russian lump enamel – the number indicates the colour.

Enamelling is time-consuming. Each stage of the making of the piece has to be related to the enamelling process, and the correct preparation of a piece that is to be enamelled is essential if the results are not to be disappointing.

TYPE OF ENAMELS
Enamels are usually supplied in lump or powder form; they are occasionally found wet mixed. All enamels should be stored in airtight jars. Lump enamels have a longer shelf life than the powdered form, but powdered enamels take less preparation before they are applied to the metal. Enamels supplied in wet mixed form are painted directly onto the metal; they can also be screenprinted onto larger areas.

There are three types of enamel: transparent, opaque and opalescent. Transparent enamels depend on the texture or brilliance of the background metal, which is clearly visible, for their own reflective brilliance. Opaque enamels hide the underlying metal, but they have a brilliance of their own. Opalescent enamels have a slightly milky appearance, and some of the background metal is reflected through them. Opalescent enamels have to be fired at very precise temperatures if they are to look their best.

A material known as flux enamel, which can be in either lump or powder form, is frequently used as a first coat or undercoat on standard silver and copper. A transparent flux coat helps the subsequent enamel to retain its colour and brightness in further firings. Fluxes can also be used as an 'over-flux' – that is, as the last, clear transparent coat on top of either a transparent or an opaque enamel – to give additional depth to a piece or to 'hold' a particular colour that might darken if a further coat of colour were added.

Painting enamels are very finely ground and mixed to a smooth paste with a medium such as lavender oil. They can be painted directly on a metal surface and then covered with a clear flux for firing or, more often, they are painted onto a background of opaque enamels, with the colours being built up slowly over many firings. The final result is similar to a miniature oil or watercolour painting.

PREPARING ENAMELS

Before use, enamels must be finely ground, and the water used to wash the grounds must be completely clear before the enamel is transferred to the palette. Any remaining cloudiness will result in a cloudy enamel. Distilled water should be used for the final rinse.

PREPARING LUMP ENAMELS

1 Place lump enamel in the mortar and cover it with water. Hold the pestle directly above the enamel and start to break up the lumps by hitting the top of the pestle with a hammer. Do this until the lumps are small enough to grind.

2 Hold the pestle firmly and use a rotating movement to grind the enamel. Push down as you work and continue until the enamel is really fine.

3 The water will be cloudy at this stage. Pour it away carefully, making sure that no ground enamel is lost down the drain.

4 Run more water into the mortar and swill it around with the enamel. Tap the side of the mortar with the pestle to encourage the enamel to settle. Continue to wash the enamel, pouring away and replacing the cloudy water until the water remains clear.

5 Use distilled water for the final rinse because tap water contains impurities that can affect enamel.

6 Scrape the enamel into a palette or petri dish. It is ready for use.

PLACING WET ENAMELS

Because the metal onto which you will be laying the enamels has been thoroughly cleaned, you must take care that it does not become dirty again. Hold the edge between your thumb and index finger, and use a small spatula or the quill end of a feather to scrape a small amount of enamel out of the palette into or on the metal. Spread it out as smoothly as possible so that no metal is visible and the enamel forms an even, fine layer. Gently tap the edge of the piece with the handle of the spatula to help the enamel spread and settle.

If you want to lay a second colour close up against another, dry the first colour by holding the corner of a piece of absorbent tissue to it to draw off the water. When you lay the second colour, you may have to let a little water transfer to the first colour, but this will help in the laying. When you have applied a thin coat, the piece must be allowed to dry completely before it is fired. Place it on a wire mesh support on top of the kiln to dry.

If you are placing colours without a flux base, it is better to fire the different colours at the same time to avoid the firestain that might occur on the exposed silver if only one colour were fired at a time.

PLACING WET ENAMELS

1 Use a small spatula – a dental spatula is ideal – to place blue flux into the etched-out area.

2 Gently tap the side of the piece with the spatula to encourage the enamel to spread and settle evenly.

3 Use the corner of an absorbent tissue to draw out excess water.

4 When the enamel is dry, hold the piece in the mouth of the kiln for a few seconds to remove all final traces of moisture. Take the piece from the kiln when the flux has fired to, or just past, the 'orange peel' stage.

5 Leave it to cool, then fill the areas with one colour. Because this piece has a base coat of flux, it is easier to fire one colour first, then apply a second colour and give the piece a second firing. Clean up the edges of the first colour with a moist paintbrush before applying the second colour.

6 Fire the first colour.

7 Fill in the rest of the area with the second colour, remembering to leave it to dry before firing it. Continue to fill in the colours until the enamel is level with, or slightly higher than, the surrounding metal.

FIRING ENAMELS

Most enamels are fired at temperatures between 750–950°C (1380–1740°F). Hard enamels are fired at the top of this range, while soft enamels are fired at 750–820°C (1380–1500°F). The time taken depends on the size of the piece and the thickness of the metal used.

Hold the enamelled piece at the mouth of the kiln for a moment or two to make sure that the enamel is dry, then place it in the kiln. Remove the piece as soon as it has a slightly 'orange peel' appearance. Leave it to cool on a rack.

When the piece is cool, apply a second coat of enamel and fire as before. The enamel should look glossy after the initial firing.

Apply several thin layers of enamel rather than one or two thick ones. This will allow you to control the colour and makes cracking less likely.

Articles to be enamelled should be placed on steel supports or on wire mesh trays, which you should place in and take out of the kiln with a long firing fork. Protect your hand with a protective glove.

COUNTER ENAMEL

As enamels are fired onto the front of a piece of metal, stresses build up in the metal that, unless balanced, will force the metal to curve toward the centre of the enamel. This can be prevented by applying a coat of enamel, known as counter enamel, to the back of the piece. The counter enamel is applied either before or after the first coat of enamel is applied to the front.

Counter enamel can spoil the appearance of the back of a piece. This can be overcome by setting the enamel piece as you would a stone so that the back is hidden. Alternatively, the metal used for the piece could be thicker than would normally be the case to prevent it from curving – for example, if the depth of the enamel for a piece of champlevé enamel was 0.3 mm, the silver could be 1.3 mm thick.

THE KILN

Kilns can be either electric or gas-fired, and they range in size from 5 × 10 × 10 cm (2 × 4 × 4 in.) to 30 × 65 × 65 cm (12 × 26 × 26 in.). A gas-fired kiln, which can run on natural or propane gas, is quick to reach the required temperature and, because the heat is reducing rather than reflective, metal is slightly less prone to oxidization. Most gas-fired kilns have a regulator or a pyrometer.

Electric kilns take longer to heat up. They can be fitted with either a regulator on a 1–10 dial or with a pyrometer, which shows the exact temperature of the kiln.

If your kiln has neither a regulator nor a pyrometer, you will be able to assess the approximate temperature by the colour, and when it gets too hot for firing, turn it off for 5 minutes until the temperature has fallen to the correct level.

APPLYING PAINTING ENAMELS

Place a small amount of powdered painting enamel on a glass tile about 10 × 10 cm (4 × 4 in.) next to a few drops of lavender oil and use a flat spatula to mix the oil into the powder. Press down the mixture to make a smooth paste.

Apply the enamel with a fine sable paintbrush. When you are painting onto opaque enamel, rub the surface of the enamel slightly with wet and dry papers to make a matt surface. Build up the colours gradually. You will find that at first they tend to fade into the background, and soft colours – red, for example – should be left until all the hard firings have been completed and the temperature of the kiln can be lowered.

Painting enamels, lustres and lining enamels must all be absolutely dry before firing. Leave them on top of the kiln until the paint looks whitish, then hold them at the mouth of the kiln so that any remaining oil evaporates.

Place the piece in the kiln and remove it when the painted enamels gloss. These enamels fire quicker than ground enamels.

As the picture is built up and more colours are added, the piece will have to be fired several times. Painted enamels are usually covered with a soft over-glaze flux, which not only gives a protective coating but also helps to create a sense of depth.

PREPARING THE METAL

Metal that is to be enamelled must be scrupulously clean. Any soldering must be completed before enamelling starts, and if hard enamels are being used, you might use enamelling solder; otherwise, use hard solder. After annealing or soldering, the piece must be cleaned. Hold it under running water and rub it all over with a glass brush until the water stays smoothly all over the surface instead of running into globules. Keep it in distilled water until you are ready to begin enamelling, when it can be dried on a paper towel and then licked – yes, licked – to make sure it is perfectly clean and neutral.

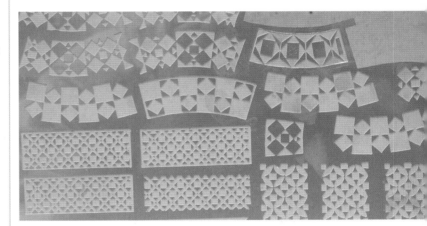

PREPARING THE METAL

1 A sheet of silver has been photoetched and is being prepared for enamelling. Pierce out the individual shape to be enamelled from the sheet.

2 Hold the metal under running water and clean it with a glass brush.

COLOUR TEMPERATURE GUIDE	
Dull red	720°C (1330°F)
Dull orange-red	750°C (1380°F)
Cherry red	790°C (1450°F)
Bright red-orange	820°C (1500°F)
Very bright orange	870–1000°C (1600–1830°F)

3 Make the background even more reflective by using a burnisher.

CLEANING PLAIN METAL
When plain metal is to be enamelled, it must be free of grease and oxides. Use a glass brush under running water until the water stays smoothly over the surface.

USING AN ENGRAVING TOOL
Use an engraving tool to give the metal a reflective texture, and remove any remaining bits of solder with a straight-edged engraver.

FINISHING A PIECE
1 When it is cool, hold the piece under running water and rub it level with a carborundum stone, which is rubbed horizontally across the piece until the enamel is level. Use wet and dry sandpapers, wrapped around the carborundum stone, still with the piece under running water.

2 Dry the piece and check to see if more depressions need to be filled. If necessary, fill and refire before rubbing down as before. Place the piece in the kiln for flash firing.

TEST PIECE
Always fire a test piece first. Use a piece of properly prepared silver, and try firing your selected colours at different temperatures. Watch to see how and when each one fires and, from the results, work out the order of firing the piece. It is a good idea to keep the results of each of your samples as a reference. Fire colours direct onto silver and on top of a clear flux, and onto silver and gold foil to assess whether you need to use flux on your piece.

TEST SAMPLE
Carrying out tests is one of the most important aspects of enamelling. You are aiming to discover how the enamel reacts to different effects. This test sample shows the effects of different firing times, temperatures, acid and polishes.

FINISHING A PIECE
When you have applied the correct amount of enamel and it is level with the cloisons or metal surrounds, the enamel must be smoothed and refired to give a neat, flat surface. When it is cool, hold the piece under running water and rub a fine carborundum stone to and fro over it until the enamel is level. Grades 280–400 of wet and dry sandpaper can be used under running water to give a finer finish. Dry the piece and check that the enamel is smooth. Any low areas can be filled with the appropriate colour and the piece refired. If the refilled areas need smoothing down, this is done now so that the enamel is completely level for the final 'flash firing', which should be done at a slightly higher temperature and more quickly than previous firings.

Enamels can also be left matt, which means that they do not need the final flash-firing after rubbing down with fine wet and dry sandpapers.

ENAMELLING TECHNIQUES
There are approximately seven different types of enamelling technique, including painting.
En bosse ronde Apply enamel directly to the surface of the metal, which can be flat, domed or repoussé.
Champlevé This French word means 'level field', which is exactly what the enamel becomes when it has been applied in layers until it is level with the surrounding metal.

Depressions in the metal are made by etching, photoetching, engraving or chiselling, or by soldering a pierced sheet about 0.4 mm (1/64 in.) thick onto a solid sheet of the same metal that is at least twice as thick. Thin layers of enamel are placed in the depressions until they are just above the surface of the metal. The enamel is then stoned to the level of the metal before flash firing.

Cloisonné The word cloison is French for 'cell', and in this technique cells are made by bending flattened cloisonné wire to make a pattern, either to fit depressions, as in champlevé, or to be placed directly on the metal as in en bosse ronde.

The wires can be soldered to the metal, but you must be careful not to let any solder show through transparent enamel. It is more usual to fire a layer of flux first, place the bent cloisonné wires on the flux, holding them in position with a little Klyrfyre glue, and then fire them in place. The wire should be as fine as possible because thick cloisonné wire can look heavy and unattractive.

The cloisons are filled with enamel, as in champlevé, but take care not to rub down the cloisonné wire enamel too soon. Little pieces of wire may get embedded in the enamel, and they will be difficult to remove.

Plique à jour In this technique, the enamel has no metal backing. A pattern is usually pierced out or it can be made by soldering cloisonné wires into the desired pattern. The wet enamel is placed in the holes and is held there by capillary action. The holes should be no larger than 1 cm (½ in.) square, and you should avoid sharp corners because the enamel will not adhere well. The pattern is either supported on steel supports or laid flat on a piece of mica.

Basse taille The French words mean 'deep cut' and refer to surface decoration of the metal before transparent enamels are applied. The decoration is usually engraved, and different tones of colour are achieved by altering the depths of the lines of the engraving. Transparent colours can be applied and merged according to the pattern beneath.

Grisaille This technique uses only black and white. The base coat is usually black, onto which white is built up in several layers. The white enamels gradually blend into the black, creating various tones of dark and light grey and white.

Gold and silver foils Foil can be applied under transparent and opalescent enamel to give a brilliantly reflective background. The gold foil brings out the true colours of the enamels, and in addition to the reflection, silver foil can be useful if you are having trouble with firestain on silver.

CLOISONNÉ

1 Use round 0.3 mm fine, silver cloisonné wire. Flatten the sides of the wire slightly by passing it through a rolling mill. The wire stands on edge, so try to make sure that the height is fractionally greater than the etched depth of the metal. Apply a base coat of flux.

2 Use round-nosed pliers and fine stainless steel tweezers to bend the cloisonné wire accurately. Keep a drawing or pattern of the design to hand so that you can measure the wires accurately and shape them carefully before dipping each piece in a little Klyfyre glue and placing it in position. The Klyrfyre will hold the wires in place until the piece is fired.

3 When the wires are in position, put the piece on a mesh tray and place it in the kiln. Fire until the flux starts to gloss and wires sink into it.

4 Any wires that do not sink into the flux can be gently pushed down with the side of a burnisher.

5 The separate colours can now be placed in the cloisons. If any colour strays into the neighbouring cloison, lift it away with the tip of a moistened paintbrush. It is easier to remove it now than later on.

6 Leave the piece on the top of the kiln to dry. Before you put it in the kiln, make sure that no foreign bodies have landed on the enamels. Carefully lift out any specks with the tip of the paintbrush.

7 After the layers have been applied and individually fired, the final layer should be fractionally higher than the edge of the piece. Rub it with a carborundum stone under running water before giving a final flash firing.

ETCHING AND PHOTOETCHING

ETCHING REMOVES ANY METAL SURFACE LEFT EXPOSED, WHEN IT IS INSERTED INTO AN APPROPRIATE ACID. A 'STOP-OUT' IS USED TO PROTECT PARTS OF THE SURFACE WHICH ARE NOT TO BE ETCHED.

'CUFFS' – CATHERINE MARCHE
These bracelets were photoetched. The etch was only required to a depth of approximately 1 mm (¹⁄₃₂ in.) to reveal the lovely patterns.

ETCHING AND PHOTOETCHING TOOLS

1 Sheet of cleaned silver;
2 tracing paper and pencils for transferring the design;
3 scribe for marking through beeswax.

ETCHING

Etching has many uses in jewellery making, and it is a quick and relatively easy process. The aim is to use an acid solution, known as a mordant, to eat or dissolve away exposed sections of metal. You can obtain different depths, depending on how long the metal stays in the mordant. If a decorative surface is required, the depth of etch need not be very great. If, however, the depression is to be used for enamelling or for laying in resins, the etch will need to be deeper – between 0.3 and 0.5 mm (¹⁄₁₀₀ and ¹⁄₅₀ in.) deep.

Always remember that the acids used in etching can be dangerous. Always handle them carefully and sensibly. Keep them in clearly labelled containers and store them under lock and key.

TYPES OF RESIST

A resist is a substance that protects the surface of the metal against the active properties in the mordant. The most common resist is called **'stop-out' varnish**, which is a thickish bitumen-based liquid painted directly onto all areas on the metal that need to be protected. Support the work on a little stand so that you can apply the varnish without having to touch the metal, and when the front is dry, turn it over and paint the other side. Remember to paint all edges with the varnish. Any cleaning up, such as

straightening wobbly lines, can be done when the varnish is dry by drawing the edge of a sharp blade down the line and gently lifting or scraping away excess varnish. Make sure that the varnish is completely dry before placing the piece in the etching fluid.

An alternative resist to varnish is **beeswax**. Melt the wax into a small tin, warm the metal and dip it in the wax, which will coat the metal in a thin, even layer. When the wax is cool, cut or draw the pattern through it.

If you want a decorative or pictorial effect on metal, you can use a **hard or a soft ground** 'stop-out'. This is a mixture of beeswax, bitumen and rosin, and it is applied to the warmed metal with either a leather dabber or a fine cloth bag containing the ground. The ground is spread evenly over the metal with a small roller. Hard ground is then treated in the smoky end of a candle flame, which is played over the 'stop-out' until it darkens. When the ground is cool, the picture or pattern can be drawn through it with the tip of a tapestry needle or a special etching needle. A coat of ordinary 'stop-out' is then painted over the sides and underside of the metal.

PREPARING THE METAL

Before you apply the resist (see below), the metal must be cleaned thoroughly with pumice powder paste or by rubbing with wet and dry

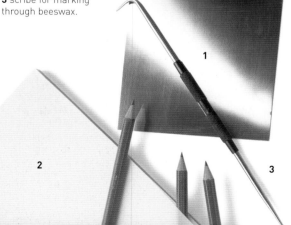

THREE ASPECTS OF A KINETIC RING – SHELBY FITZPATRICK
The flower-pattern tops of these silver rings used the photoetching process to cut away the different shapes. Photoetching is used to cut several pieces at once out of a large silver sheet. The cut-outs can be etched to a required depth or cut away entirely.

papers under running water. If the metal is not completely clean, the varnish will lift when it is left in the mordant, exposing the metal that you wanted to protect.

Depending on the intricacy of the design, the pattern is transferred to the metal either before or after it is cleaned. If the design is complex, rub the surface of the metal with putty or plasticine and trace the design onto it. Remove the tracing paper and scribe through the lines with a sharp metal point. Then clean the metal thoroughly. For a free-form design, clean the metal first, then draw on the design with a sharp lead pencil, but take care not to touch the metal with your fingers.

USING THE ETCHING FLUID

Mix up the mordant or buy it ready-mixed.

When you are working with etching fluid, always wear, in addition to protective gloves, safety glasses and an apron. Work in a well-ventilated area because the acids will give off strong fumes. Mix enough mordant to cover the piece, but do not mix more than you need. An ovenproof glass bowl is suitable for all these mordants.

Use stainless steel or plastic tweezers to place the piece of metal in the mordant, then watch the reaction of the fluid on the exposed metal. If it is too violent – that is, if a lot of bubbles rise quickly to the surface – the mordant may be too strong. Dilute it by putting 1 or 2 parts of water in another dish and carefully transferring the mordant to the new bowl. Generally, the etch will take between 15 and 30 minutes, depending on the strength of the mordant and the depth required. If you are doing a very long, gentle etch, the metal may need to be in the mordant for 3 hours.

In addition to etching downwards, the mordant bites sideways into the metal, once it has penetrated beneath the 'stop-out'. A slow etch helps to overcome this problem to some extent, but you should take this 'undercutting' into account when you prepare the design, because it can result in some fine lines becoming rather ragged.

To test the depth of the etch, remove the metal from the mordant, then rinse and dry. Run the fine point of a steel scriber over the surface and into the etched areas to get a feel for the depth achieved so far. If the piece needs further etching, check to see if the 'stop-out' needs retouching. If it does, remove any flakes of varnish, dry thoroughly and lift any raised areas with the blade of a craft knife. Repaint the area or areas with varnish. Make sure it is dry before returning it to the mordant.

CLEANING AND FINISHING

When you are satisfied with the depth of the etch, remove the piece from the mordant and rinse it thoroughly under running water. Store the etching fluid in a clearly labelled glass jar or put a lid on the bowl. Although mordant can be re-used, it will turn a clear deep blue-green when spent. When this happens, dilute it with as much water as possible and dispose of it, again in running water.

Dry the washed metal with paper towels before gently heating with your flame until all the stop-out disappears. Then quench and pickle in the usual way. Remove a beeswax 'stop-out' by holding the piece over the can of wax and heating it with a gentle flame so that the wax drips back into the can.

When all traces of 'stop-out' have been removed, clean the piece with pumice powder paste, which can be applied with a toothbrush. Clean up any ragged lines with a 'spitstick' engraving tool. If the piece is to be enamelled, rub all over the etched area with a glass-fibre brush and then use a polished burnisher to brighten the area.

SEE ALSO

- Annealing, pages 42–43
- Pickling and quenching, pages 44–47
- Polishing, pages 78–79

PREPARING THE ETCHING FLUID

You need to make up solutions of different strengths for each metal you are going to etch.

Copper	1 part nitric acid, 1 part water **or** 2 parts potassium chloride, 10 parts hydrochloric acid, 90 parts water.
Silver	3 parts water, 1 part nitric acid **or, for a longer, slower etch,** 5 or 6 parts water, 1 part nitric acid.
Gold – 18, 14 and 9 carat	8 parts hydrochloric acid, 4 parts nitric acid, 1 part iron perchloride, 40 or 50 parts water (aqua regia) **or** 2 parts nitric acid, 2 parts sulfuric (or hydrochloric) acid, 4 parts water. Gold will not dissolve in the etching fluid for silver or copper.

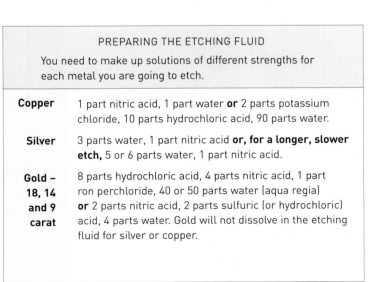

1 Stop-out varnish with paintbrushes; 2 warmed beeswax for coating the silver; 3 nitric acid solution for etching.

PHOTOETCHING

This process, which is generally carried out by commercial firms, is particularly suitable for work that is to be enamelled or that involves a lot of intricate piercing of several pieces. Photoetching involves photosensitizing metals to produce a 'resist' and to print an image that can then be attacked by a suitable etching fluid. When it is used to make jewellery, photoetching is an extremely accurate process, as long as a number of guidelines are observed.

Most photoetching firms prefer to work on a sheet of metal that is not smaller than about 30 × 46 cm (12 × 18 in.), so the design needs to be carefully considered and the number of items required needs planning to fit into the area. The etch can then be taken to an accurate depth, and if the sheet is no thicker than 1 mm (1/32 in.), the etch can pierce through the metal for either decorative purposes or to save piercing out the item later.

When you are designing for photoetching, the image should be drawn and painted to about twice the size of the finished piece. The final artwork can be reduced to half its size, either by photocopying or by the grid method. The solid, coloured area represents the metal that is going to be etched away.

When you present the finished design to the photoetching firm, remember that:
- The design should fit on a sheet about 30 × 46 cm (12 × 18 in.), with a margin of about 2.5 cm (1 in.) all around.
- The areas to be etched should be shown in solid red, and the depth of the etch required noted in writing.
- Areas to be pierced through should be shown as solid black lines.
- If you are using black lines for areas to be pierced, make sure that the metal is no more than 1 mm (1/32 in.) thick.
- If you are assembling a design from several sections, make sure that you white out all the edges, so that they do not photograph as black lines.
- Use the sheet of metal as economically as you can. It is rather wasteful if you get only two or three pieces from one sheet.

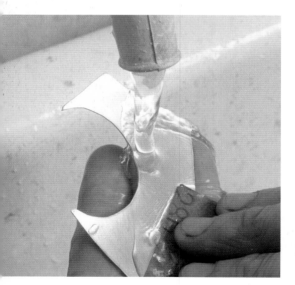

PREPARING THE METAL FOR ETCHING
1 Thoroughly clean the metal with grade 280–400 wet and dry sandpaper, holding it under running water.

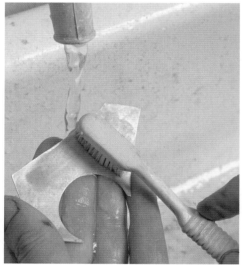

2 Mix pumice powder to a paste and use an old toothbrush to rub it all over the metal. Rinse thoroughly under running water until the water stays all over the surface. If the water forms little globules, the metal is not clean enough.

3 Use a pencil to draw the pattern on the clean silver, making sure that your fingers do not touch any of the areas to be etched.

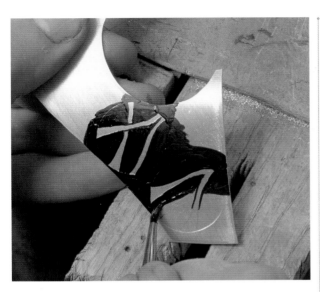

USING THE RESIST
1 Paint a coat of 'stop-out' over the areas you do not want to be etched and leave to dry.

USING THE ETCHING FLUID
1 Place the piece in the nitric acid solution and watch for bubbles to rise. To achieve an even etch, use a feather to remove the bubbles as they form.

2 When the required depth is achieved, remove the piece from the acid and rinse it under water. Remove the 'stop-out' varnish by soaking or cleaning with a rag soaked in turpentine. Alternatively, heat the piece gently with the flame until the stop-out disappears.

2 When the front is dry, turn over the piece and place it on a stand so that you can coat the back and edges with 'stop-out' varnish. Leave to dry.

CLEANING AND FINISHING
Pierce around the outside lines of the pattern.

SAFETY PRECAUTIONS

Remember that you should always add acid to water. Never add water to acid, because it may bubble and foam rapidly in the container and even spill over the top. Always wear protective gloves, and if any acid is spilled, douse the affected area with plenty of water to dilute it and mop it up with an old cloth.

CASTING

CASTING IS A TECHNIQUE BY WHICH IT IS POSSIBLE TO CREATE SHAPES THAT WOULD OTHERWISE INVOLVE AN ENORMOUS AMOUNT OF WASTE. IT IS ALSO USED TO RE-CREATE GENTLY FLOWING LINES OF THE KIND THAT ARE COMPARATIVELY EASY TO ACHIEVE IN A SOFT MEDIUM SUCH AS WAX BUT THAT ARE DIFFICULT TO REPRODUCE IN METAL. CASTING IS ALSO, OF COURSE, A MEANS BY WHICH MANY IDENTICAL PIECES CAN BE MADE, EITHER FOR THE MASS-MARKET OR TO MAKE, FOR EXAMPLE, CHAINS WITH IDENTICAL LINKS.

There are four main methods of casting. Three of these – cuttlefish casting, sand casting and the lost wax method – are available to people working at home, while the fourth involves the production of a rubber mould, which, while possible to do in the home workshop, is expensive and requires a lot of space and special equipment. It is not, therefore, a viable method unless it is being used almost every day and is most often carried out by a commercial company working from a model you have made yourself.

TOOLS AND MATERIALS

Several kinds of wax are available for creating the models used in casting. Among these are sheets of **flexible wax**, supplied in thicknesses from 3–25 mm (⅛ –1 in.); **blocks for carving**; **moulding wax**, which is worked by hand; **tubes and bars**, which can be used to make rings; and **sprue wax**, which is supplied as rods in different sizes for attaching to models. Choose the most

CASTING TOOLS
1 Selection of wax modelling tools; **2** cuttlefish bone; **3** moulding wax; **4** block of carving wax; **5** wax sheets in different thicknesses; **6** alcohol lamp for warming the modelling tools.

appropriate wax for the model you want to create.

You will also need one or two little carving tools and a craft knife. Keep a small flame burning – the pilot light of a soldering torch or a little alcohol lamp with a small wick, for example – so that you can keep warming the carving tool when you need to join pieces of wax together and to smooth over the surface of the wax. An electric 'pen' worker can be used to join different grades of wax and is useful for shaping and moulding.

CUTTLEFISH CASTING

This is a very quick and simple method and can be done in one of two ways. The first, as shown in the steps that follow, is simply to carve the required shape and depth of pattern into one side of the halved cuttlefish bone.

The alternative method consists of using a cuttlefish bone to make a model – in perspex or metal, for example – or to use a found object of a suitable shape. The bone is prepared as described in steps 1 and 2 opposite, but the object is then pushed into half the bone until it is buried to about half its depth. The model should be positioned so that its heaviest part is towards the bottom of the bone.

SET OF SILVER, GOLD AND ENAMEL RINGS – JINKS McGRATH
All these rings were modelled in wax before being cast in silver using the lost wax casting method. After each one was cast, it was then finished to the required look and sent away to have a rubber mould made and then several of each pattern cast.

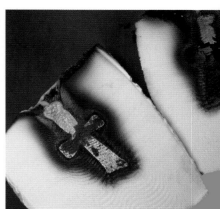

3 Use a modelling tool to carve your design directly into the bone. You will find it a very dense but soft material that carves easily. Remove the dust by blowing or with a soft paintbrush.

6 Heat the silver in the crucible. Pick up the crucible with a pair of long-handled tongs just when the silver begins to run up into a molten ball.

CUTTLEFISH CASTING

1 Use the thickest part of the bone for casting. Cut away the top and bottom ends so that it is almost square.

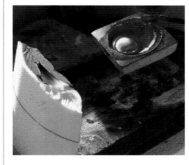

4 In the top of the bone, cut out a rounded channel. This channel, which must be slightly deeper than the design, is the duct through which the molten metal will be poured. Make it fairly large.

8 When it is cool, cut the binding wire and open the bone. The cuttlefish bone will have turned black around the area of casting and cannot be used again. Make sure the silver is quite cold before you touch it. You can hold it under cold running water to speed the cooling down process.

7 Keep the flame on the silver as you bring the crucible to the channel in the cuttlefish bone. Pour the silver into the bone.

2 Cut down through the centre of the bone. Do not exert much pressure, because the bone will cut very easily, and aim to make the cut in a single pass of the saw so that the two pieces fit together perfectly. If necessary, lay the two halves on some wet and dry sandpapers, used dry, and work in gentle circular movements until the inner surfaces are completely flat and smooth.

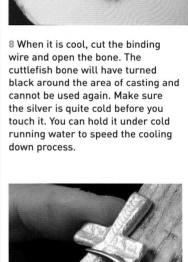

5 Place the two sections of the bone together, making sure the fit is perfect, and fasten securely with binding wire. Prop up the bone next to the soldering block. Cut up some scrap silver into little pieces and place them in a small crucible with some flux powder. It is difficult to estimate how much metal specific projects will require, but prepare more than you think will be necessary.

9 Finish the edges of the casting and burnish to highlight the high edges.

SAND CASTING

The sand-casting method uses the 'Delft' system. This consists of two aluminium rings that slot together to form a tube. The rings are packed with 'casting sand', which is a very dense, slightly oily sand. The sand cannot be carved, so this method of casting can only reproduce an object that already exists. You could make this object yourself, in wood, wax or acrylic.

SAND-CASTING TIPS

Experiment with sprueing Sand casting relies on gravity up to a point. Once the metal is poured down the channel, it then has to spread out to fill the cavity. Experiment with the sprueing; it may need to be thicker, or thinner. Make sure the air lines are clear.
Casting hollow objects Any model that is 2-mm (¹⁄₁₆-in.) thick or less will not cast well. If you want to cast something like a shell that is hollow, fill it with wax, or the sand will try to fill it and the two halves will not separate cleanly.

2 Pack the short ring with the sand, pressing it firmly down into the ring until it is slightly higher than the top. Level it off with the edge of a ruler.

3 Press the model into the sand facedown until about half its thickness is buried. It may need gentle tapping with a mallet to help it sit down into the sand. (Be sure your model is not going to crack or break if you do this.)

5 Fix the taller ring back onto the short one, lining up the two notches marked in the sides. Now fill the top ring with sand. When it is full, use a mallet to hammer the sand down so it is as dense as possible.

6 Divide the two rings again. Remove the model from the bottom ring very carefully. You should have a cavity the shape of the model in the sand on each side of the ring. Draw some air lines out from the lower cavity.

8 Where the drill has broken through, open out the area to make space for the button. If necessary, clear any sand from the sprue channel. Now you can put the two halves back together again, making sure the notches are lined up, and place the mould onto the soldering tray ready for casting.

7 Make a hole for the sprue in the top, larger half, with a drill bit 2–3 mm (¹⁄₁₆–¹⁄₈ in.) in diameter. Twist the drill up from the top of the cavity made by the model until it breaks through the top of the sand.

SAND CASTING A SIMPLE OBJECT
1 Divide the aluminium rings. Place the shorter one on a sheet of paper on the bench. The connecting lip should be uppermost.

4 Leave the model where it is and sprinkle a little baby powder over the surface of the sand. This will help the two halves to separate later. Spread the powder evenly with a paintbrush.

LOST WAX CASTING

This technique involves making a wax model that is supported on a conical stand mounted on a rubber or ceramic base. The model is surrounded by a metal sleeve or flask, which fits tightly onto the base; and a plaster/silica mix, known as investment, is poured into the flask and allowed to set. The flask is then placed in a heated kiln to melt and burn away the wax, which leaves an empty mould within the investment. The impression of the mould is left in the hardened investment. When all the wax has burned away and the investment is the correct temperature, the flask is removed from the kiln and placed into a 'centrifugal' casting machine, which is held in tension by a spring. The metal is then melted in the crucible, which is secured in place against the open end of the flask, and when it is completely molten, the heat is removed, the spring latch of the casting machine released, and the molten metal flung into the mould.

PREPARING THE WAX MODEL

When the wax model has been completed and sprued, it is weighed, and the weight of the wax is multiplied by 11 for silver, by 18 for 22-carat gold, by 14 for 14-carat gold, and by 12 for 9-carat gold to find the weight of the metal needed for casting.

PREPARING THE INVESTMENT

Mix the investment in water that is at room temperature in the proportions of 4 parts water to 10 parts investment. Once the investment has been added to the water, it must be mixed and

MIXING OF INVESTMENT	Size of flask	Quantities required	
	5 × 5 cm (2 × 2 in.)	140 g (5 oz) investment;	57 cc (3½ cubic in.) water
	5 × 6.5 cm (2 × 2½ in.)	175 g (6 oz) investment;	68 cc (4 cubic in.) water
	6.5 × 6.5 cm (2½ × 2½ in.)	280 g (10 oz) investment;	114 cc (7 cubic in.) water
	6.5 × 7.5 cm (2½ × 3 in.)	350 g (12 oz) investment;	136 cc (8¼ cubic in.) water
	7.5 × 7.5 cm (3 × 3 in.)	510 g (18 oz) investment;	205 cc (12½ cubic in.) water

poured as quickly as possible because it begins to harden after about 10 minutes. If the wax model is exceptionally detailed, apply a coat of investment before you begin pouring; this will help to prevent air bubbles from being trapped on the surface of the model, which is to be avoided at all costs because they would be cast as silver blobs.

When pouring the investment into the flask, it is important to bring as many air bubbles as possible to the surface. Hold the flask in both hands and gently bang it on your working surface a few times. Place it on a vibrating table to remove any air bubbles.

The rubber or ceramic base is then removed from the flask and the flask placed into the kiln. It should be placed with the sprue opening facing the floor of the kiln and it should be supported, either on ceramic legs or between two ceramic kiln bases, so that the wax can melt and drop out of the investment. The kiln is set to approximately 150°C (300°F) and this temperature should be held for approximately 1 hour to allow all the wax to burn out and then increased to approximately 370°C (700°F) for another hour. The temperature is then increased

further – up to approximately 700°C (1290°F) for the last two hours of the burn out.

Use long-handled tongs to remove the flask from the kiln and place it in the centrifugal machine. Place the weighed and cut-up metal in the crucible with some flux powder, and use a strong torch to melt it. Do not include any solder in the metal used for casting, and when you are

cutting up scrap, put any soldered joints back into your scrap box.

Spring the machine into position and release, and the molten metal will shoot out of the mouth of the crucible into the sprue channel of the flask. Pick up the flask with the long-handled tongs and place it in a bucket of water. The investment will break away to reveal the metal casting. Remove the sprue and file and finish the piece.

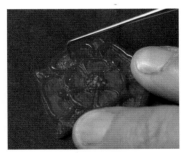

LOST WAX CASTING

1 Mark out the design on the modelling wax. The design can be accurately drawn with dividers, a scribe or something similar, and then the details of the motifs can be cut away with modelling tools. Bear in mind that the pattern can be cut and modelled very finely, and that the finished piece in silver will weight about 11 times more than the wax model.

2 When the modelling is finished, cut away the pattern from the block of wax and file away any marks made by the blade of the saw. Make any final refinements and smoothing to the wax.

3 If you wish, gently play a flame over the model to soften the edges. Attach a sprue by heating up the modelling tool in the flame and placing it smoothly between the model and the sprue. Hold them in place until the wax has set.

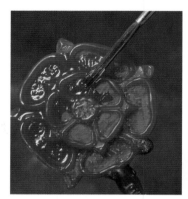

4 Melt the sprue onto the top of the base of the flask and paint the model with a wetting agent.

5 Place the flask onto the base and make sure there is space of at least 1 cm (½ in.) between the model and the sides of the flask. The model should be about 2.5 cm (1 in.) below the level of the top rim of the flask.

6 Tie a plastic bag, open at the bottom, around the flask to prevent spills, then pour the investment into the flask so that it is just over the top of the flask. Vibrate the whole thing to remove air bubbles.

7 Leave the investment to dry a little before removing the plastic bag and slicing away any excess investment at the top of the flask. Then leave to dry thoroughly, preferably overnight.

8 Give the flask and base a sharp knock to separate the two sections. If you are using a flask with a rubber base, simply peel it away. The wax sprue at the top of the channel should be visible.

9 Leave the investment to dry for 2–4 hours, then place it in a kiln so that the sprue is toward the floor of the kiln. Set the kiln to about 150°C (300°F) and leave it at that temperature for about 1 hour. Increase the temperature to about 370°C (700°F) for at least another hour. Then increase the temperature of the kiln to about 700°C (1290°F) for the last hour so that the investment is a suitable temperature when it receives the molten metal.

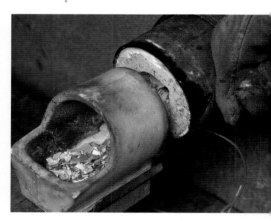

10 While the flask is in the kiln, prepare the appropriate amount of silver for the casting and place it in the crucible with some flux powder. Remove the flask from the kiln, holding it in long-handled tongs, and place it in the casting machine so that the mouth of the crucible is in a direct line with the sprue channel in the flask.

11 Melt the silver with a strong flame. You must work quickly so that the temperature of the flask does not drop too much. When the silver is molten, remove the flame and release the spring mechanism of the machine. Move away from the machine because molten silver may fly out at this point if the flask is not properly aligned or if there is some other fault with the machine or setting-up process. Allow the machine to stop completely before you remove the flask.

12 Using tongs to hold the flask, place it in a bucket of cool water. The investment will fall apart and reveal the casting. Clean away all the remaining investment with pumice paste and a toothbrush, and use a small steel tool to remove any investment that has stuck in the nooks and crannies of the design.

13 Pierce away the sprue and file the edges to make the piece ready for finishing.

COMMERCIAL CASTING

This is the process by which a rubber mould can be used many times to create large quantities of an article. In essence, a rubber mould is made around a silver or rhodium-plated model which has a sprue attached. The rubber mould is cut in half to release the model in such a way that it can be exactly relocated. Warm wax is injected into the realigned mould and removed so that more wax can be introduced to produce yet another model. All the wax models are mounted on a 'tree', which is placed in an investment and cast in the same way as the lost wax method, but on a much larger scale.

To make a good casting, you must make a really well-finished model, which is sent away to be cast commercially. If you are in any doubt about the positioning of the sprue, ask for advice from the company or leave it to the company to attach the sprue.

PREPARING A MODEL FOR COMMERCIAL CASTING

1 Make the model in nickel silver or silver and attach a sprue with easy solder. Make sure that the area around the joint has enough solder to allow a smooth flow.

2 Polish the model to give it a very smooth finish. Any scratches or file marks left at this stage will have to be removed on every piece subsequently made.

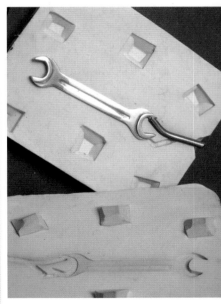

3 The commercial company makes a rubber mould around your model. This mould is then held together and injected with wax so that as many wax models as necessary can be made from just the one mould.

STONE SETTING

A STONE OR CLUSTER OF STONES IS USUALLY THE FOCAL POINT FOR A PIECE OF JEWELLERY. THE WONDERFUL VARIETY OF COLOUR, TEXTURE AND REFLECTIVE QUALITIES OF STONES IS A CONSTANT SOURCE OF PLEASURE, INSPIRATION AND BEAUTY FOR BOTH THE WEARER AND THE MAKER.

MULTICOLOURED NECKLACE – JINKS McGRATH
18-carat gold necklace with assorted semiprecious and precious stones. The large aquamarine has been claw set while the others are mainly rub-over settings.

'GRID' RING – SALIMA THAKKER
This ring is based on a mesh design, providing a decorative and airy effect. The design allows for different shapes and sizes of stone.

Many stones are quite tiny, which means that making collets, mounts and settings is a fiddly, difficult task. To begin with, it is a good idea to set some large cabochon stones into rub-over settings, then to practice on a faceted stone of a similar size. In the jewellery trade, some craftsmen specialize in making mounts for stones, while others specialize in setting them. If you are using precious stones, you should always consider sending the pieces to a specialist setter so that you can be certain that it has been properly set.

There will, however, be many occasions when it will be appropriate and when you will wish to do your own setting.

Stones can be set singly, in a group or cluster or in lines. There are two main types. Cabochon stones, which have a smooth overall surface, can be oval, round, tear-drop or curved in some other shape. Faceted stones have flat faces cut into them, in a variety of sizes and at a variety of angles, which allow the light to be reflected in different ways.

There are two types of faceted stone. The first group includes predominantly straight-sided stones. The second group includes predominantly cone-shaped stones.

Stones have different degrees of hardness and softness, which affects the ways they are set. Soft stones – opals and turquoises, for example – are vulnerable to knocks and scratches and need a more protective setting than a hard stone such as a diamond or ruby, which could be given a lighter, more open setting.

RUB-OVER SETTINGS

Cabochon stones are usually given rub-over settings. The bezel, which is the metal surrounding the stone, should extend just over the first section of the slope to hold the stone in place. If you are uncertain, measure the height of the stone and make the bezel about one-third of that measurement.

The bezel can be soldered directly to a metal backing, on which the stone sits, or a 'bearer' wire can be soldered to the lower half of the bezel to make a ledge. The stone sits on the ledge and is not in contact with the background metal.

Bezels can be decorated by having patterns pierced along their length before they are soldered into a round or oval shape. Leave at least 2 mm (¹⁄₁₆ in.) unpierced around the top of the bezel so that there is some substance to the metal when it is pushed down over the stone.

ESTIMATING THE LENGTH OF THE BEZEL FOR A ROUND STONE

To estimate the length of the bezel for a round stone, do the following calculations: **Diameter × ϖ + 2 × thickness of metal**

ESTIMATING THE LENGTH OF THE BEZEL FOR AN OVAL STONE

To estimate the length of the bezel for an oval stone, do the following calculation: **Length + width ÷ 2 × ϖ + 2 × thickness of metal**

To be absolutely certain, you can allow a little extra and pierce it away if necessary. Even if the bezel is a little large, it will still push down neatly onto the stone.

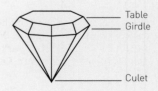

Table
Girdle
Culet

FACETED STONES

A faceted stone has a table, a girdle and a culet. The area between the girdle and the table is known as the crown, and the area from the girdle to the culet is known as the pavilion.

SETTING A CABOCHON

1 One way of finding the outside measurement of a stone is to draw around it with a pencil. Use a small piece of removable adhesive 'tack' to hold it down if necessary.

2 Cut a strip of paper and place one of the long edges against the edge of the drawn oval, using a pencil to mark both the strip and the oval. Move the strip around the oval a little at a time, marking it each time, until you have marked the complete length. Add to this figure 1.5 times of the metal you will use for the bezel.

4 Smooth the base of the oval on a flat file.

5 Place the oval on a sheet of silver, flux around the base and solder the two together.

3 Use dividers to measure the height of the bezel. It should go over the curve of the stone. Draw the dividers down a strip of metal to mark this measurement and then cut it to length. Bend into an oval and solder.

6 Pierce away the silver from around the outside of the oval.

7 Clean up the edge with a file and finish off with wet and dry sandpapers. Solder the setting to the piece, and polish and finish the piece before beginning to set the stone.

8 Use a pusher to lever the bezel over the stone. Begin at one side, then push down the opposite side. Continue in this way, making sure that the stone is securely held, before finally pushing it down all the way round.

9 Use a curved, polished burnisher to smooth the bezel.

10 Clean up the top edge of the setting with a spitstick, which can be used to level off any uneven areas.

MAKING A SETTING FOR A RAISED CABOCHON

Sometimes a cabochon stone needs to be set higher than the base of the setting. If you are soldering a setting onto a curved surface such as a ring or a dome, the base of the setting will need to be filed in a curve to fit. In order for the stone to sit straight, it needs to be raised above the curve, so in this case, a shelf was made for it to sit on.

1 Make a collet to fit the stone (see page 133). In this case the stone was 6 mm (¼ in.) in diameter, so the length of the collet was 2 cm (¾ in.). 6 x 3.142 (pi) + (twice the thickness of silver used) 1 mm (¹⁄₃₂ in.) = 19.85, rounded up to 2 cm (¾ in.).

The collet is taller than the stone so that there is room to insert the shelf and to allow for the filed curve where it is soldered to the ring.

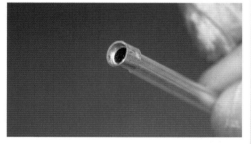

2 Here, a length of chenier fits very neatly into the inside of the collet. If chenier cannot be used, another collet is made which just fits inside the first one. It should be lower than the outer collet to allow for the stone. Solder the two together and shape the bottom to fit the ring.

3 Hold the stone with a little piece of tack above the setting and check that it fits. File any excess height from the top of the collet at this stage, and then with a flat needlefile, file at a slight angle around the top of the outside edge, to thin the metal down a little. This makes pushing the metal over onto the stone a little easier.

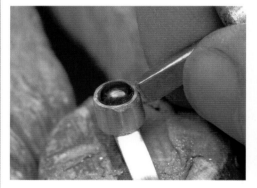

4 Use a pusher to ease the metal gently over the stone. Work from opposite sides to keep the stone steady, and when the metal is pushed evenly down over the stone, file gently around the edge to smooth it. Finish with some wet and dry papers and finally a burnisher, taking great care not to touch the stone. It is a good idea to hold the thumb right down over the stone while cleaning up around the edge.

SETTING FACETED STONES

Faceted stones can be mounted in an open claw-type setting, set in chenier, set into collets made from wire or sheet, which are then pierced and filed to allow light to reflect from the stone, or set flush with the metal in pavé settings. When you are using any of these settings, you must accurately measure the stone at the girdle and also the height from the girdle to the table and the overall length. Use a vernier or dixième tool to do this accurately. You can buy ready-made collets from a metal dealer, or you can make them yourself by bending up a sheet into a cone, which is suitable for cone-shaped stones, or by bending up wire or sheet to form rectangles, squares, triangles and so on for straight-sided stones.

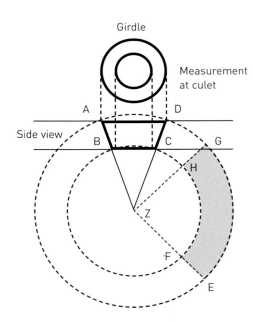

1 Pattern for a round cone mount

Drawing the pattern for a round cone mount

1. Measure the diameter of the stone at the girdle. Use this measurement to draw A–D.
2. Measure the vertical distance from the girdle to the culet, allowing extra if you are making claws as part of the cone = AB–DC.
3. Use these measurements to draw lines, continuing AB and DC to meet at Z.
4. Draw a circle, centre Z, with a radius DZ.
5. Draw a second circle, centre Z, with a radius CZ.
6. Use dividers to measure the distance AD, and mark this dimension on the outer circle starting at a point G three and one-seventh times (n), and mark this point E.
7. Draw in line GZ.
8. Draw in line EZ.
9. Make points H and F on the inner arc. The shape bounded by GEFH is the flat cone. Transfer this to the metal and cut out the shape. Anneal the metal and shape the cone on a tapered mandrel. Check the stone on the cone and adjust the shape if necessary. Solder the seam. The cone is now ready to be pierced or to have claws or a pattern on the bottom filed on it. Solder a wire ring to the bottom of the cone after it has been cut and filed to shape.

Establishing the measurements for straight-sided stones

1. Measure the square stone along one side = AD.
2. Measure the height from girdle to culet (allow extra if you are making claws or a rub-over) = AB and DC.
3. Extend lines AB and DC to meet at Z.
4. Draw a circle, centre Z, with a radius DZ.
5. Draw a circle, centre Z, with a radius CZ, and draw an arc CF.

6. For a square stone: Measure the side of your stone (i.e. AD) with dividers and mark this measurement three times on the outer circle finishing at E.

For a rectangular stone: Work as for the square stone but measure both the long and short sides of the rectangle. The measurement AD and GH will be the long side; the measurement DG and HE will be the short sides.

The shaded area within these letters is the flat pattern that can be transferred to the metal. The lines DC, GJ and HI are scored and bent up so that AB can be soldered to EF. The mount can then be filed or decorated as you wish, and outside claws can be soldered to each corner to hold the stone.

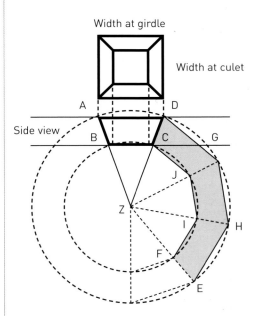

2 Measurements for straight-sided stones

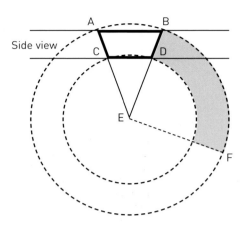

Side view

3 Pattern for a collet

DRAWING THE PATTERN FOR A COLLET

This alternative pattern (above), is perhaps a little simpler than the pattern for a round cone mount (see page 133), but is useful for a round or oval-faceted stone.

The drawing is based on two lines drawn at right angles to each other.

The shape ABCD is basically the shape of the collet that we are making. The line AB is the diameter of a round stone or the average diameter (length + width divided by two) of an oval stone. The line CD gives the height needed for the cone. This height should include the extra needed if making a claw setting.

The lines AC and BD are continued down to meet the vertical line of the right angle at E.

A pair of compasses with a sharp pencil are opened from E to B and part of a circle is drawn. Close up the compass down to ED and draw this inner part of a circle.

Work out the length of metal needed to go around the stone, i.e. the circumference plus twice the thickness of the metal. Divide this by three and open out a pair of dividers to this measurement. Place one end of the dividers on B and then walk them down the BF arc three times to give you the length required. Draw the line FE. The shaded section is the shape you need for the collet.

MAKING A TAPERED SETTING WITH CLAWS

1 The above shows the shape of the silver made from a pattern for a round cone mount (see page 133), to fit the oval-faceted stone. This needs to be cut as accurately as possible. The lines at each end of the curve need to line up for soldering, so draw the pattern carefully and then cut.

2 Anneal the silver and use a pair of round or flat-nose pliers to bring the ends of the collet together and then solder. This can then be made true with the pliers or in a collet former. If you are making the collet for an oval stone, without a collet former, make it round first and then shape it with either a gentle squeeze with the parallel pliers or by pushing it, top first, carefully down an oval mandrel.

This is now a simple tapered collet. To set the stone refer to page 138 (Setting a faceted stone in a straight-sided setting).

3 If you are making a collet with claws, divide the bottom of the collet into quarters with a pencil. Use a triangular file to make open 'V' shapes in each quarter. Finish them nicely as they will be very difficult to file and clean later.

4 Make a small jump ring to fit the bottom of the shaped collet and solder it on.

5 Mark two lines at each quarter on the top of the collet, above the filed-out areas below. These will become the claws. With a pair of dividers, one side on the top of the collet, make a mark about halfway down the side of the collet to show where the cut-out and filing for the claws will finish. Draw the shape you want the cutout to be with a pencil.

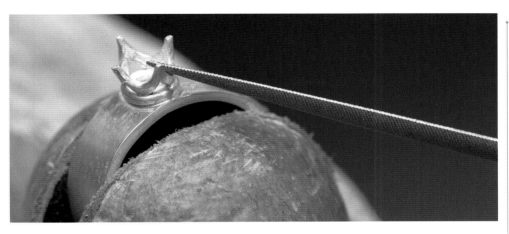

6 Follow your pencil lines to shape the collet and make the claws. The initial shape can be cut with a piercing saw but finish off with a half-round file to give you a nice shape.

SETTING A FACETED STONE IN A STRAIGHT-SIDED SETTING

1 Many round faceted stones will be able to be set into silver or gold tubing, or chenier. To assess the size of chenier needed for a particular stone, sit the stone on top of the chenier. If you can see an even area of metal around the outside of the stone, the chenier is suitable. If you cannot see any metal or only a tiny edge then the chenier is too small, so either find a larger tube, or make up the collet yourself so that the stone sits on top with the outer wall showing rather than the stone dropping down into it.

7 File a seat into the top of each claw for the girdle of the stone to sit on. Mark the position for each seat with a pair of dividers so that they are all the same distance from the top. The seat must be placed far enough down the claw to allow the prong to come over the stone, but not so far down that the culet of the stone does not sit properly in the base of the collet.

8 File the tips of the claws so that they are slightly rounded and then place the stone into the collet. Check that it is sitting level before using the pusher to push gently on each collet 'claw' to just hold it in place. Then press each one a little harder to get the claw to sit right down onto the stone. Once there are no gaps, the stone is set. Clean up carefully with a needlefile or wet and dry papers, and then finish with the burnisher.

2 Here the collet is soldered onto a pendant and is being prepared for setting the stone. The inside edge of the chenier is being removed with a bullstick. This is a small hand-cutting tool where the outside edge is sharpened, so that when it is pushed against the wall of the chenier it is able to cut away the metal at a slight angle. This angle allows for the faceted stone to sit comfortably.

If you do not have a bullstick, you can achieve a similar cut by using a tapered diamond cutter in the pendant motor. Just keep stopping to check that the angle you are cutting is correct and that you are not going too close to the outside edge.

3 Keep offering the stone up to the setting to assess how much more metal needs cutting away. Keep on cutting until the girdle of the stone is sitting below the top of the collet. You need to see at least 0.5 mm (⅕ in.) of metal above the stone before even thinking about setting it.

4 When the stone is sitting at the correct height, check that it is sitting in the collet completely straight. It should be level across the table. As you are setting the stone, keep checking that the stone remains level – there is little worse than thinking you have set the stone safely only to discover it is sitting at an angle, which means that it isn't properly set and may fall out.

5 Use a flat needlefile to gently file down around the top outer edge of the collet. Check the position of the stone and then push down around the outside edge of the collet with a burnisher to fix the stone in position. The finished look should be a smooth line of metal just over the top of the stone.

'GYPSY' SETTING A FACETED STONE

When a faceted stone is set just below the surface of the metal without any visible means of securing it in, it is called a 'gypsy' setting. It is quite a tricky setting to do well, and it can be a better idea to ask a professional setter to do it for you unless you have had lots of practice in this particular skill!

There are a few rules to remember when thinking of setting stones in this way:
• that you have enough metal for the stone to bed down into so that no part of the girdle or below is sitting above the metal;
• that the metal is deep enough to allow for the depth of the stone, in other words, the culet of the stone should not be poking through the metal underneath; and
• there must be enough metal around the stone to either file or clean up the setting.

1 Use metal thick enough and wide enough for the depth and width of the stone. To turn this metal up into a ring with just a pair of pliers may be too difficult, so use a former in the safe jaws of the vice to get the necessary curves before soldering.

2 Clean the outside of the ring with some wet and dry paper and then mark where the stone is going to be. Use a small drill to make the first hole and then gradually use larger drills to open up the hole, until it is just over half the diameter of the stone.

4 There are two ways of doing steps 4 to 6. The photograph shows method one – using a graver with a sharp but slightly rounded point, undercut a line around the inside about 1 mm (1/32 in.) down from the top. Method two is described after Step 6.

6 With a pusher, work around the top edge of the metal, all the time pushing it over and down onto the stone. You may have to push quite hard to move the metal, but if the undercut is doing its job, the metal will come over quite easily. The area around the stone will need to be cleaned up with wet and dry papers and can be polished very carefully.

3 Fasten a tapered frazier into the pendant motor and gradually open out the hole until it is the same diameter as the stone, but no bigger. This can also be opened out with a bullstick, but the outside cut needs to be kept in a true circle. The stone should just fit into the opened cone shape with the girdle sitting below the surface.

5 Take care not to remove anything from the top edge, because this would widen the area that the stone will sit in and it needs to be a close fit. Offer up the stone from time to time to get the fit as accurate as possible.

ALTERNATIVE METHOD

When you reach step 4, instead of making the undercut, use a round file on top of the metal to make a groove around the opening for the stone. The groove needs to be less than 1 mm (1/32 in.) from the edge of the opening and after filing, what looks like a little raised edge will be clearly visible. Place the stone into the setting and push the little raised edge down over the stone to hold it in place. After the stone is set, the area that was filed should be filed again until all the marks of the previous filing have disappeared. It can then be cleaned with wet and dry papers and polished carefully.

USING OTHER MATERIALS

All sorts of materials can be used in jewellery design and when selecting materials to design with there are no fixed rules. Here, wood, acrylics and fabric are explored. These sections are followed by a series of step-by-step sequences showing the potential of silver metal clay in jewellery design.

WOOD

ANY HARDWOOD CAN BE USED FOR MAKING JEWELLERY, AND VERY DENSE WOODS SUCH AS ROSEWOOD AND WALNUT ARE ESPECIALLY APPROPRIATE.

You can cut wood with a piercing saw, a coping saw, and electric bandsaw, or a laser-cutter. The required shape can be made roughly with a saw and then refined using a bench-mounted belt sander and finished by hand sanding. Automated laser-cutters, although expensive, can cut wood into very detailed shapes. A very effective way to use this in jewellery making is to create a series of thin sheets of wood in varying shapes and then laminate them together to make a three-dimensional shape.

INLAYING MATERIALS IN WOOD

Other materials such as silver, plastic or different coloured wood can be inlaid into a wooden piece. You can do this relatively easily by using silver or plastic rods inserted into holes drilled in the wood. Other shapes such as strips can also be inlaid using the same method.

'QUE?' BROOCH – CHRISTINE KALTOFT

Walnut, silver and 18-carat gold brooch, laser welded and soldered. It is part of a series of three brooches about birds. The jeweller used walnut because wood is a traditional material for depicting birds, and it also contrasts nicely with silver and gold.

BANGLE IN WOOD AND SILVER – METTE JENSEN

This sculptural bangle was shaped with steam and the ends hidden and joined with a piece of silver.

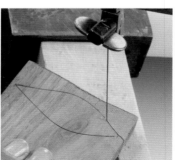

CREATING AN INLAID WOODEN PIECE

1 Draw a design on the wood using a pen or pencil. You may find it easier to cut out the design from paper and trace around it onto the wood.

2 Use a piercing saw or a coping saw to cut around the line.

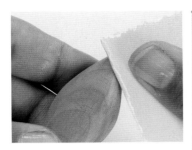

3 Shape the wood either by sanding with a bench-mounted belt sander or using coarse files. Use coarse sandpaper suitable for wood to shape it further and smooth the surface. Next, use fine-grade sandpaper and rub until the surface feels smooth and all the scratches have been removed. At this stage you can apply a finishing wax or another finishing agent to seal the surface.

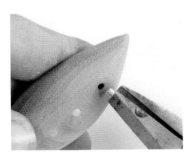

4 In this example, a piece of silver wire is being inlaid; however, other materials can be inlaid by the same method. Select a drill bit that is the same diameter as the piece to be inlaid. Drill a hole to half the depth of the wood. Cut the wire 1 mm (1/32 in.) longer than the depth of the hole. Use a pair of flat-nose pliers to hold the wire and insert it into the hole. You can apply a small amount of glue to the wire before inserting it into the hole.

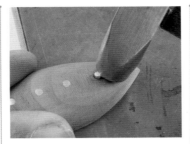

5 Place the piece on a metal block or a firm surface and use a riveting hammer to carefully tap the wire into the hole. Take care at this stage, since the wood can split if it is hammered too hard.

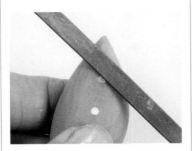

6 Hold the piece in your hand or rest it on a surface and file the top of the wire with a flat file to make it flush with the wood.

The stages of creating a solid wooden piece.

INLAYING A METAL STRIP

1 Carve a slot the same length and width as the piece to be inlaid. You can use metal burrs or a sharp knife to cut the slot.

2 Rest the wood on a metal block or firm surface and tap the metal into the slot with the riveting hammer. Apply a small amount of glue to the metal before tapping it in.

WOOD INLAID WITH A SILVER STRIP

The finished pendant has been coated with finishing wax.

WOOD INLAID WITH SILVER RIVETS

The finished piece with inlaid silver rivets running along its length.

ACRYLICS

DIFFERENT KINDS OF ACRYLIC MATERIALS CAN BE USED IN JEWELLERY TO CREATE LIGHT, CRISP AND COLOURFUL EFFECTS. YOU CAN MAKE ENTIRE PIECES FROM ACRYLIC, OR ACRYLIC CAN BE USED IN COMBINATION WITH METAL IN INGENIOUS AND SUBTLE WAYS.

You can obtain acrylics from plastics suppliers, or you may live near to a company that makes small plastic articles and that would be happy to pass on scraps to you. If you buy it from a supplier, you will be able to select from sheets, rods or tubes, circles, squares, rectangles, etc., that are clear or coloured, transparent or opaque. Acrylic is an easy material to work with, because it can be cut by hand with a piercing or coping saw and it can be filed, polished, bent in gentle heat, drilled, carved or worked on a lathe.

Acrylic can also be used as a two-part resin, which is poured or 'cast' into metal to give a finish that resembles enamel.

One problem with acrylic is that, compared with metal, it is very vulnerable, so its use needs to be carefully considered. The surface will scratch easily, and although the scratches can be easily removed, it is not always practicable to do so.

CUTTING ACRYLICS
Use an ordinary piercing saw or a coping saw to cut sheets of perspex.

CUTTING

Acrylic or perspex sheets are usually supplied with a paper covering, and you can draw the pattern directly onto the paper before you cut out the design with a piercing or coping saw. You should use a no. 0 or no. 1 blade, or an even coarser one if necessary. Make sure that you catch all the dust and swarf from the acrylic in a clean bag below the bench pin because it is irritating to have acrylic mixed with the metal scrap. As it is cut, acrylic tends to get very hot, which makes swarf melt onto the piercing blade. Cutting slowly should overcome this problem, but if you notice that the acrylic is beginning to cling to the blade, clear it by drawing the edge of a file down each side of the blade.

LINK NECKLACE – LESLEY STRICKLAND
Link necklace made from cellulose acetate, (a cotton-based plastic) in various colours and sterling silver links. Each piece of acetate is cut from sheet and shaped by filing and sanding. It is heated to form the link shapes. The silver element is interspersed throughout the chain.

TOOLS FOR ACRYLICS
1 Sheet of frosted perspex; **2** epoxy resin; **3** large flat file; **4** coloured pigment, which can be mixed into the resins to give colour.

SEE ALSO

- Filing, pages 24–26
- Drilling, pages 27–28
- Polishing, pages 78–79

FILING AND FINISHING
File the edges with a suitably shaped file and polish with wet and dry sandpapers, followed by liquid metal cleaner, applied with a cloth.

FILING AND FINISHING

Files can get clogged up quickly when they are used to smooth acrylics, and if you are going to use a lot of acrylics, it is worth keeping a separate set of files. You will need a file brush to clean them regularly. Use the files in exactly the same way as you would on metal, removing the marks made by one file with the next size down. You can get a smooth finish by working through the various grades of wet and dry sandpapers and then finishing off with a liquid metal cleaner. You can also use a polishing mop with grease-free white polish, which gives acrylic a shiny, clear surface. You must take care that it does not get too hot or the surface will start to melt and the polish will become a series of dragged black lines. Polish can be removed with detergent. Do not use acetone, turpentine, denatured alcohol or benzene on acrylic because they can damage the surface.

An effective way of finishing polished acrylics is to deliberately make them frosty. This can be done with fine steel wool and detergent and water, or with a brass brush, used with detergent and held in the pendant motor. A satin or bark finishing brush can also be used on a polishing machine to give a frosty finish. Always wear safety glasses when you use these brushes because loose pieces of steel can fly off when they are in use.

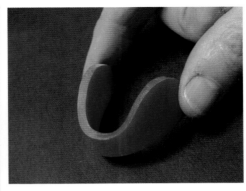

SHAPING ACRYLICS
If perspex is heated gently, it can be bent around a former or pressed into a mould.

DRILLING AND ENGRAVING

Most small holes can be drilled straight through an acrylic sheet or rod, but if you need to make a hole in a very thick sheet, you will need to lift the drill in and out several times so that the acrylic does not get too hot and the swarf does not melt on the drill. The hole will be visible as a white line or, in transparent acrylic, as an opaque line.

Engraving tools can be used on acrylics, but again, the edges of the lines will be opaque unless they can be individually polished.

CASTING

Mix the two parts of acrylic in equal proportions and add the appropriate colour. This mix can be poured into metal 'cloisons' (compartments) or into a mould. You must pour the liquid resin steadily and slowly. If you pour too quickly, heat can be generated and you may find that air bubbles appear. If you are pouring into metal cloisons, the resin is usually poured so that it is a little higher than the edge of the metal. When it is hard, it can be filed level or rubbed down with wet and dry sandpapers. Any holes that may have appeared after filing can be filled up and allowed to dry before the piece is polished.

Pouring resin into a mould has to be done in two stages. First, the mould is half-filled and allowed to set before the other half is poured in. If you try to fill the mould at once, you will generate too much heat. You can take advantage of this natural break by changing the colour or even by introducing a small object.

GLUING

When you glue acrylic pieces together or to another material, you must use a clear, compatible adhesive. Some adhesives can be coloured with dye to match the acrylic.

THERMOSETTING

Thermosetting is a process whereby acrylics and plastics can be shaped by heat. This can be done in an ordinary oven set at 175°C (350°F), over an electric hot plate, or by using a blow torch. When the plastic has reached 175°C (350°F), remove it from the heat – you must wear thick, protective gloves – and use your hands to bend it around or pour it into a mould. If you use a blow torch, use a gentle flame.

SPOTTY SCHOOL TIE CUFF LINKS – TAMSIN HOWELLS

Tamsin's designs encapsulate used and recycled fabrics into acrylic to make colourful and unique limited edition pieces. These cuff links are made from men's ties in spot designs.

MAKING A PAIR OF LATHE-TURNED ACRYLIC EARRINGS

1 Set the angle of cut on the lathe at 75 degrees and insert a round acrylic rod with a diameter of 15 mm (⅝ in.) into the chuck. Carefully turn a cone shape.

4 Use a parting-off tool, set at 90 degrees, to remove the cone from the rod. Make a second cone in exactly the same way.

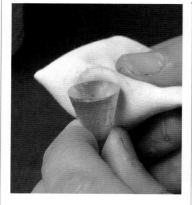

2 Use the cutter to get as smooth a finish as possible. Use water or oil as a lubricant and work slowly up the acrylic, taking off no more than 0.2 mm (¹⁄₁₀₀ in.) at a time.

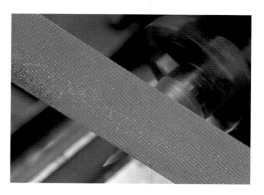

3 While the chuck is still rotating, smooth the cone still further with a single-cut 'dreadnought' file.

5 Use wet and dry sandpapers, grades 180 and 500, to smooth the acrylic even more, using the papers with water so that the work does not get too dusty. Next polish with a polishing motor with a gauze mop and grease-free polish or use a liquid metal cleaner and a rag. Polish with a clean cloth and then wash in detergent.

6 The cones are now ready to be dyed.

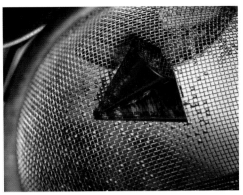

7 Mix a small amount of dye powder in cold water in a small saucepan (check the manufacturer's instructions for precise quantities). Make sure that the mix is smooth, then add a few drops each of the wetting agent and of the carrier. Add enough warm water to fill the saucepan and stir well before heating on an electric hot plate until it is nearly boiling. Place the cones in a metal sieve and lower them into the liquid. Do not allow the dye to boil or the acrylic will bend.

9 When the fluid is dry, mix a second, darker colour in the same way as the first and place the cones in the dye.

10 When the cones are cool, peel off the masking fluid and drill a 1 mm ($\frac{1}{32}$ in.) wide hole approximately 6 mm ($\frac{1}{4}$ in.) deep in the centre of the base of each cone.

8 Take the cones from the dye from time to time to check the colour. A good depth should be achieved within a few minutes. Remove the sieve and wait for a moment or two for the acrylic to cool before rinsing and drying. Use a fine paintbrush to apply strips of art masking fluid. In the example above, five parallel lines were painted on each cone.

11 Use contact cement or a two-part adhesive to glue silver wire, cut to about 4 cm (1½ in.) long, in the hole. Use your pliers to bend the wire into shape.

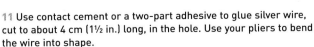

METAL CLAY

METAL CLAY IS A RELATIVELY RECENTLY INVENTED MATERIAL AND IS GROWING RAPIDLY IN POPULARITY. IT HAS A LOT TO OFFER THE JEWELLERY MAKER AND IS PARTICULARLY USEFUL FOR SCULPTED DESIGNS WHERE IT GIVES A WONDERFUL IMMEDIACY AND FREES THE ARTIST FROM THE CONSTRAINTS OF LOST WAX CASTING.

by Sue Heaser

SEASCAPE PENDANT – SUE HEASER
This seascape pendant demonstrates the rich effects of textured metal clay. The rocks are textured with a granite pebble and the sea is textured with cuttlefish bone.

METAL CLAY TOOLS
1 Silver metal clay – 10 g is sufficient for a small sculpted project; **2** small plastic or nylon rolling pin; **3** small-scale sculpting tools (stainless steel are best – do not use aluminum, which will contaminate the clay).

Metal clay is made from finely ground powdered metal such as gold or silver, combined with a binder and water to make malleable clay. After shaping or sculpting, the clay is dried thoroughly in the same way as ceramic clay to produce greenware. This can be further shaped and refined by sanding, carving, engraving, drilling and adding to. It is then fired in a kiln, with a blow torch or even on a gas hob. During the firing process, the binder burns off and the powdered precious metal sinters to produce a solid metal. Silver becomes 999 and gold 22 carat. Copper and bronze metal clays are also available. Each type of clay has its own firing requirements but the basic principles are the same.

Metal clays are normally sold in small packages of between 5 and 100 g (⅛ and 3½ oz). They have a shelf life of several years but once the packet is opened they will begin to dry out.

ADVANTAGES OF METAL CLAY
- Gives the freedom to sculpt original pieces directly in precious metal.
- The resulting fired metal is very pure and gold and silver can be hallmarked.
- Easy to engrave in the greenware state.
- Metal clay can be pushed into simple one-part moulds for rapid replication of a design.
- Many of the silver metal clays can be fired with a blow torch in only a few minutes.
- Can be used successfully as part of a design – to add embellishments or details to a precious metal piece.
- Texturing and free-form pieces are quickly made.

DISADVANTAGES OF METAL CLAY
- The fired metal is not as strong as cast metal.
- The fired metal cannot be beaten or wrought very successfully.
- The soft clay will slowly dry out in the package over time and any partly used clay must be kept wet.
- Cost: the clay is more expensive per gram than the metal it is made from.
- The techniques require soft-clay handling skills, which may be unfamiliar to jewellery makers.
- When fired, the clay shrinks between 9 per cent and 25 per cent depending on type. This has to be allowed for in ring sizing and other fitting.

TYPES OF METAL CLAY
Several different manufacturers produce a wide range of metal clays that are on the market today.

Silver metal clay
This is available in many different varieties including clay lump, clay slip in pots or in a syringe for extruding, overlay paste to apply to glass and ceramics and sheet varieties that can be treated like paper or fabric. Many of the silver clays can be fired with a blow torch.

Gold metal clay
Available in the clay lump form as well as an overlay paste. Kiln fire only.

Bronze clay and copper clay
Both available in clay lump form. These have specific needs for firing in a kiln.

1   2   3

WORKING METAL CLAY

1 Open the package and remove the clay. Knead it briefly to distribute the moisture throughout the lump. Break off sufficient clay for the first part of the project and wrap the remainder in plastic food wrap to prevent it from drying out.

4 Brush over the surface of the clay with a paintbrush dipped in water to keep the clay soft while you are working.

7 Added pieces can be cut out and textured before applying to the main piece. Here, the dorsal fin of the dolphin is cut to shape and then applied to the dolphin's back with paste. Keep brushing the piece with water while you are working.

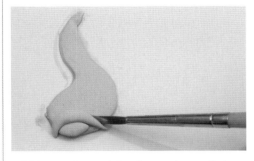

2 Shape the clay roughly into the required shape and press down on a ceramic tile. Flatten with your fingers or roll with a small rolling pin until it is the desired thickness. 2 mm (¹⁄₁₆ in.) is a good working thickness for metal clay.

5 Add extra pieces of clay that you have rolled out and shaped as required. Here the dolphin's mouth and fins are being added. Mix a slip from the clay with water and use this as a glue to attach applied pieces.

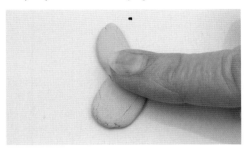

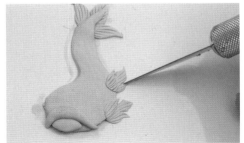

3 Trim the shape further with a knife and remove and wrap the scrap clay in clingfilm.

6 Texture the clay surface as required by impressing with a knife blade, or drawing a needle over the surface for lines.

8 Indent an eye socket with a blunt sculpting tool and form a ball of clay for an eye. Press the ball into the eye socket using paste to secure it. Add details in the soft clay around the eye with a needle tool.

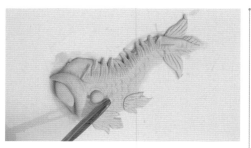

9 Texturing the surface of the soft clay adds interesting effects. Here, the eye of a needle is impressed into the clay at regular intervals to suggest scales.

10 Place the finished sculpture in a domestic oven at 150°C (300°F) for 30 minutes to dry thoroughly, or dry according to the manufacturer's recommendations. If you have worked on a tile, the piece can be dried in the oven on the tile to avoid moving the soft piece.

REFINING THE SCULPTURE IN THE GREENWARE STAGE

When the clay is bone dry, it is similar to dry plaster of Paris and relatively fragile. However, it can be sanded, drilled, filed and engraved in this state to refine the piece before firing.

1 Use a sponge-backed sanding pad of around 300–600 grit to smooth any rough areas. Take care to support the piece with your fingers to prevent it snapping.

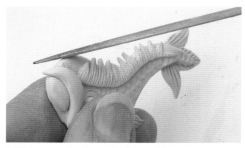

2 File any major irregularities with a fine needle file.

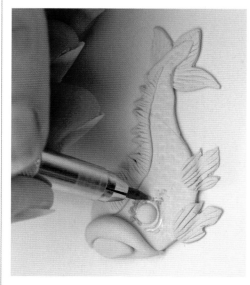

3 Use an engraving tool to accentuate any details or to engrave the piece. Light pressure and repeatedly scribing along a line will engrave deep lines into the piece. Any mistakes can be filled with slip, dried and sanded smooth. Use slip to repair any parts that break at this stage or to add findings. Dry again thoroughly in the oven after applying slip.

FIRING METAL CLAY

To kiln fire, follow the manufacturer's instructions for the particular type of clay you are using. Most types of silver metal clay can be fired using a blow torch, provided the pieces are not larger than about 50 g (1¾ oz) as follows:

1 Place the piece on a firing brick. Adjust the blow torch flame to a medium heat, and direct the flame onto the piece, rotating it all over the piece to apply an even heat.

2 After a few moments, flames will appear as the binder burns off. Continue heating the piece until it reaches a pale orange colour.

3 Hold the piece at this colour and continue firing for between 1 and 5 minutes, depending on the manufacturer's recommendations and the size of the piece. Take care not to overheat and melt the surface – if a shiny silver surface appears, pull back the torch. Leave to cool. The piece can be quenched if it consists only of silver.

POLISHING METAL CLAY
After firing, the surface of the silver will be crystalline and white. Brush over the surface with a stainless steel brush to remove this texture. Now the piece can be polished as for normal silver.

The finished dolphin pendant.

REPAIRING BREAKS IN GREENWARE
Slip or paste made from watered-down metal clay can be used to repair any breakages in the greenware state.

1 Apply slip along the break using a brush or spatula.

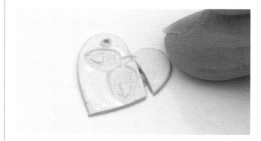

2 Push the two parts together. If the piece has a flat back, it is best to do this on a tile so that the piece can be dried in an oven without moving it.

3 Smooth the join with a fingertip or paintbrush. After drying and sanding, the join should be invisible.

REHYDRATING METAL CLAY

Metal clay dries out relatively quickly as you work, so it is worthwhile to learn how to rehydrate the clay when it begins to crack and dry out. Clay that has dried completely can be used to make slip.

3 Place the lump inside some clingfilm and knead firmly and thoroughly. Repeat as necessary until the clay is soft and workable again.

2 Apply a little water to the surface of the sheet and fold it up with the water inside.

1 Roll the drying clay into a very thin sheet on a non-stick surface with a roller. A textured plastic cutting mat or a file pocket are both ideal. Rolling will also crush any hard lumps that have formed.

4 The clay should now be smooth and workable. If the clay is too wet, roll it out inside a folded sheet of greaseproof paper to absorb some of the water.

TEXTURING METAL CLAY

Soft metal clay can be textured with texture sheets of all kinds, or a textured surface such as cuttlefish bone.

2 Smear the surface lightly with some vegetable oil.

3 Lay the clay sheet, oiled side down, on the texture surface and press firmly over the back with your fingers.

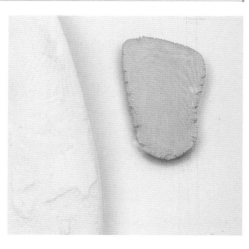

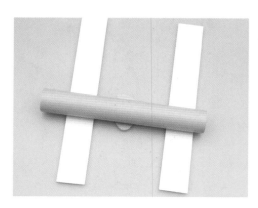

1 Roll out the metal clay into a sheet between rolling strips to ensure an even thickness.

4 Remove the clay sheet. If the impression is not deep enough, you can roll out the clay again and repeat more firmly. The textured clay sheet can now be cut out and used as required.

MOULDING METAL CLAY

Metal clay can be moulded in simple one-part silicon moulds. Here, rabbit stud earrings were sculpted in polymer clay and baked. The baked pieces were used to make a silicon mould from putty silicon moulding compound. Metal clay was pushed into the moulds to make replicas of the polymer clay originals. The pieces were dried, sanded smooth and fired. Stud earring findings were then soldered to the backs and the pieces polished.

OTHER FORMS OF METAL CLAY

Metal clay is available in an increasing number of forms that further widen the range of techniques possible. Here are two types:

SYRINGING

1 Silver metal clay is available as slip in a syringe. Fine nozzles can be attached to the syringe and the slip piped onto a lump clay backing or as freeform filigree shapes. Also available is cork clay that can be moulded into a sacrificial core that is then covered with piped filigree from the syringe. The cork burns away during firing to give hollow-form filigree pieces. This is known as hollow-form syringing.

2 The finished piece has an engraved scene with syringed flowers decorating the foreground. Oxidization accentuates the detail.

PAPER CLAY

Silver metal clay is available as a paper or sheet type that can be cut and folded like paper before firing. This can be used on its own to make jewellery or combined with other kinds of metal clay.

PAPER BRAIDING

Strips of sheet metal clay have been braided into delicate fish earrings using traditional palm braiding techniques. The piece on the right shows the braided form before the fins are trimmed to shape. After adding wire loops, the fish are fired and polished.

PAPER CUTTING

A commercial paper punch has been used to cut out tiny leaves in the silver metal clay sheet. The leaves are creased to create a realistic effect and attached with slip to an unfired silver metal clay backing. The whole piece is then fired and polished.

FURTHER TECHNIQUES

STONE SETTING

Fireable gemstones such as cubic zirconia can be pressed into soft metal clay. The clay shrinks during firing to secure the stones.

ENAMELLING

Metal clay is 999 silver after firing so it enamels particularly well with no fire stain.

ALTERATIONS

THERE WILL, INEVITABLY, BE TIMES WHEN THE SIZE OF A RING YOU HAVE MADE NEEDS TO BE ALTERED. RESIZING RINGS IS A RELATIVELY EASY PROCESS, BUT THERE ARE CERTAIN THINGS OF WHICH YOU SHOULD BE AWARE BEFORE STARTING.

If resizing your ring involves soldering, try to assess what different solders might have already been used during the construction and then make sure that anything vulnerable is protected whilst re-heating.

If you are re-sizing something you have made then knowing what solders have been used where and when is easy. Unless it looks like a very simple job, be very careful about offering to alter a ring which you have not made – it can be a little fraught when things don't quite go to plan!

MEASURING HOW MUCH

When assessing how much to add or take away it usually works out the one size is $\frac{1}{32}$ in. (1 mm). To accurately check the new size required, place the ring on the ring stick and read what the size is now.

1 Take a length of binding wire and fasten it around the ring stick at this measurement.

2 Lift the binding wire off the stick, cut it open at the top of the circle and spread it out in a straight line. Then do exactly the same with another piece of binding wire but this time on the new ring measurement you require.

3 Then do the same with another piece of binding wire but this time on the new ring measurement you require. The difference in length between the two pieces of wire is the amount you need to add or take away.

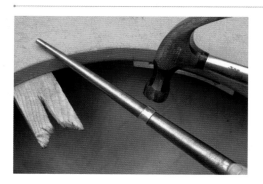

TO ENLARGE A RING

1 Place the ring on the mandrel. Use either a metal hammer or wooden mallet and hit the ring carefully while turning the mandrel, to bring it further down. Turn the ring over and hammer it down to the same point. The ring will need to be annealed before and during this process. If you stretch much more than this the metal will become quite a bit thinner and compromise the quality. If the ring has a stone set, you can still put it on the mandrel but just avoid hitting in the area of the setting. Using a metal hammer will make marks on the metal, but it will stretch it easier than a mallet.

2 You can also use a ring stretching tool. The tool stands on a bench and is usually screwed down onto it. The vertical mandrel is lettered to indicate ring sizes. It is usually made from aluminium, so this tool should not be used with a hammer or mallet. Place the ring as far down the mandrel as it will go, then push the lever back or up as far as possible. Repeat this process with the ring the other way up, then anneal the ring. Avoid hitting in the area of the setting. Using a metal hammer will make marks on the metal, but it will stretch it easier than a mallet.

SOLDERING IN AN EXTRA PIECE

1 The ring which is too small is cut open with the piercing saw along the previous join. It is then opened a little.

2 A piece of larger but similar-shaped silver is filed to make a close fit with one of the open ends of the ring. It is larger because it is easier to fit and it can be filed to the exact measurements of the ring later. Use hard solder to attach the extra piece to the ring. If the ring has a setting or any other decoration easy solder might be more appropriate.

3 With a pair of dividers, mark on the new piece where to cut so that you have the correct amount for the new size. With your piercing saw cut the piece to length. Use half round pliers to bring the end up to meet the ring for the next solder.

4 The same solder can be used for the second join, but flux the first join to allow the solder to run again if it wants. Alternatively, easy solder could be used for the second join and the hard solder join will not need refluxing.

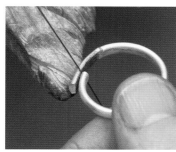

5 After pickling, rinsing and drying the additional piece is filed so that it fits neatly in with the original ring. It can then be cleaned with wet and dry papers and polished.

TO MAKE A RING SMALLER

1 The stretching tool that was used to enlarge a ring can also be used to make one smaller. At the base of the tool, there is a former with different sized tapered holes. The ring is placed in one of the holes that best fits it, and which allows the top to come a little bit higher than the top of the former.

2 The former is then turned so that the ring sits directly underneath round plate at the bottom of the mandrel. The handle is then pulled gently down towards you.

3 When the plate touches the top of the ring you will feel it through the handle. At this point, pull to put some pressure onto the ring, which will squash it slightly in the former. Take it out and turn it over and do exactly the same on the other side so that the ring comes in slightly at the top and the bottom.

4 The ring which has been reduced in this way will have a slightly curved look to it. To reduce a ring by soldering, cut through the original solder join, and measure the amount to be removed. Open out a pair of dividers to that amount and place one point of them on one edge of the opening. Use the other point to mark on the metal where to make the cut to remove the piece. Pierce that away and resolder.

TO SIZE A RING WHICH HAS A SET STONE.

This is not always a very easy thing to do. Before attempting to alter the size of a ring with a stone in make absolutely sure that no heat is allowed to come near the stone. There are some stones which don't mind the heat such as diamonds, but there is always an element of risk when a flame comes too near a stone. If you have the opportunity, it can be worth seeing just how much heat certain stones can stand, but with a very expensive stone it just isn't worth it. A very hot small flame is the best for this sort of work and if one is not available, it is better to take it to a specialist repairer who will do the job brilliantly and very quickly!

Alternatively, the stone can be removed and then altering the size is no problem.

1 Mark where the cut is to be made (take care not to cut through the hall mark) and cut the ring open with a piercing saw.

2 To resolder, isolate the stone from the heat. This shows the area of the ring where the stone has wet cotton wool wrapped around it. It has then been placed in a bed of silicone carbide soldering grain which will hold the ring steady and which does not transfer the heat. Behind the ring is a little piece of charcoal block which will reflect the heat onto the area that is being soldered. A small very hot flame is applied to the area until the solder runs. Allow to cool as it is and then remove it and clean and file as normal.

TO REMOVE THE STONE

1 The easiest way to remove a stone is to cut through the side of the collet and then peel back the metal enough to be able to push back the rest of it until the stone drops out. The collet is then pushed back together with a pair of flat or half round pliers and soldered at the same time as the resizing. If this seems too drastic a step to take, then the stone has to be released from its setting another way.

2 Bear in mind that stones may well crack or split if they are subject to pressure! With the edge of a bullstick, gently prise up one edge of the setting, taking real care not to put pressure on the stone.

3 Once you have a raised edge on the collet you can use a thin piece of silver, here solder (which has been thinned down in the rolling mill) is being used. It may take a little while to clear the stone, but the solder strip takes much less pressure than the steel tool. Once the stone is out, the sizing is done and the stone replaced. The edge of the collet will need a little tidying up, but the stone should go back and look as good as new!

SUPPLIERS AND SERVICES

TOOLS
H.S. Walsh
234 Beckenham Road
Beckenham
Kent BR3 4TS
Tel. (0208) 778 7061
or 44 Hatton Garden
London EC1N 8ER
Tel. (0207) 242 3711
Web www.hswalsh.com

ENAMELLING SUPPLIES
Vitrum Signum
Gresham Works
Mornington Road
North Chingford
London E4 7DR
Tel. (0208) 524 9546
Web www.vitrumsignum.com

PRECIOUS METALS
Cookson Precious Metals Ltd.
49 Hatton Garden
London EC1N 8YS
Tel. (0845) 100 1122
Web www.cooksongold.com

Michael Bloomstein
30 Gloucester Rd,
Brighton BN1 4AQ
Tel. (01273) 608374

Johnson Matthey Metals Ltd.
40–42 Hatton Garden
London EC1N 8EE
Tel. (0207) 269 8400
Web www.matthey.com

BASE METALS
Fays Metals
Unit 3, 37 Colville Road
London W3 8BL
Tel. (0208) 993 8883

GEMSTONES
R. Holt & Co.
98 Hatton Garden
London EC1N 8NX
Tel. (0207) 405 5284
Web www.holtsgems.com

Prabhu Enterprises
Suite D
32–34 Greville Street
London EC1N 8TB
Tel. (0207) 242 4650

A.E. Ward & Sons
8 Albemarle Way
London EC1V 4JB
Tel. (0207) 608 2703
Web www.aewgems.co.uk

CASTING
Merrell Casting
72 Warstone Lane
Birmingham B18 6NG
Tel. (0121) 236 3767

Weston Beamor
3–8 Vyse Street
Birmingham B18 6LT
Tel. (0121) 236 3688
Web ww.westonbeamor.co.uk

ELECTROFORMING
Richard Fox
8–28 Milton Avenue
Croydon
Surrey CR0 2BP
Tel. (0208) 683 3331
Web www.foxsilver.net
Electroforming, plating,
and polishing.

WATER CUTTING
SCISS Ltd.
Unit 9, Larkstore Park
Lodge Road, Staplehurst,
Kent TN12 0QY
Tel. (01580) 890582
Web www.sciss.co.uk
Precision abrasive waterjet
profile cutting.

CHEMICALS
Rose Chemicals
73 Englefield Road
London N1 4HD
Tel. (0207) 241 5100
Web www.rose-chemicals.co.uk
Wide range of chemicals for
etching and patination.

OTHER MATERIALS
4D Modelshop
The Arches
120 Leman Street
London E1 8EU
Tel. (0207) 264 1288
Web www.modelshop.co.uk
Model-making materials including
plastics, metals and silicone.
Photoetching, base metal casting
and laser-cutting services.

Pentonville Rubber
104–106 Pentonville Road
London N1 9JB
Tel. (0207) 837 7553
Web www.pentonvillerubber.co.uk
Rubber, latex, sheet and wire.

Hamar Acrylic Fabrications Ltd.
238 Bethnal Green Road
London E2 0AA
Tel. (0207) 739 2907
Web www.hamaracrylic.co.uk
Acrylic stockist; laser-cutting
service.

Alec Tiranti
27 Warren Street
London W1T 5NB
Tel. (0207) 380 0808
Web www.tiranti.co.uk
Sculptor's supplies, including
resin, silicone, ceramic clays
and patination chemicals.

Barnett Lawson (Trimmings) Ltd.
16–17 Little Portland Street
London W1W 8NE
Tel. (0207) 636 8591
Web www.bltrimmings.com
Ribbons, buttons, feathers
and millinery supplies

Stuart R. Stevenson
68 Clerkenwell Road
London EC1M 5QA
Tel. (0207) 253 1693
Web www.stuartstevenson.co.uk
Artist supplies, including gold
leaf, metallic powders and
varnishes.

Falkiner Fine Papers
76 Southampton Row
London WC1B 4AR
Tel. (0207) 831 1151
Web www.falkiners.com
Paper, bookbinding supplies,
leather and specialist adhesives.

GPS Agencies Ltd.
Unit 3–3a, Hambrook
Business Centre
Cheesmans Lane
Hambrook
West Sussex PO18 8XP
Tel. (0123) 457 4444
Web www.ivoryalternative.com
Imitation ivory, horn, ebony,
shell and marble.

ALMA
12–14 Greatorex Street
London E1 5NF
Tel. (0207) 377 0762
Fax (0207) 375 2471
Web www.almahome.co.uk
Leather.

e-Magnets UK Ltd.
Samson Works
Blagden Street
Sheffield S2 5QT
Tel. (0114) 276 2264
Web http://e-magnetsuk.com
Magnets.

CONVERSIONS

Temperatures			
°C	°F	°C	°F
0	32	593	1100
38	100	649	1200
66	150	704	1300
93	200	760	1400
121	250	816	1500
149	300	871	1600
177	350	927	1700
204	400	982	1800
232	450	1038	1900
260	500	1093	2000
288	550	1232	2250
216	600	1371	2500
343	650	1510	2750
371	700	1649	3000
427	800	1788	3250
482	900	1927	3500
538	1000	2204	4000

B&S gauge	Millimeters	Inches	
		Decimal	Fractions
–	20.0	0.787	$51/64$
–	15.0	0.591	$19/32$
1	10.0	0.394	$13/32$
4	5.2	0.204	$13/64$
6	4.1	0.162	$5/32$
8	3.2	0.129	$1/8$
10	2.6	0.102	$3/32$
12	2.1	0.080	$5/64$
14	1.6	0.064	$1/16$
16	1.3	0.050	–
18	1.0	0.040	$3/64$
20	0.8	0.032	$1/32$
22	0.6	0.025	–
24	0.5	0.020	–
26	0.4	0.016	$1/64$
28	0.3	0.013	–
30	0.25	0.010	–

TOOL SHAPES

It is always important to select the correct tool for each task as the shape of the tool will have a direct impact on the effect it makes.

Files come in many shapes, and the profile of the file determines the groove it cuts – always try to match the shape of the file to the shape of the area being filed, especially when cleaning up intricately pierced fretwork with needlefiles.

The shape of a graver determines the mark it will make when it cuts; oval or onglette gravers are used in stone setting to carve a seat for the stone and square gravers are used for engraved line work.

Seating, ball and bearing cutter burrs are all used predominantly in stone setting, and should be the same diameter as the stone. Other shaped burrs are generally used for carving or making surface textures, and all burrs come in a wide range of sizes.

FILE SHAPES

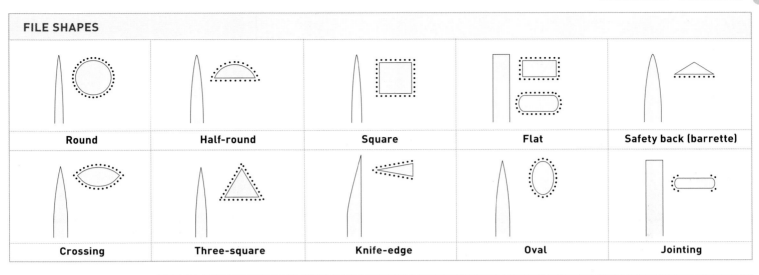

Round	Half-round	Square	Flat	Safety back (barrette)
Crossing	Three-square	Knife-edge	Oval	Jointing

GRAVER SHAPES

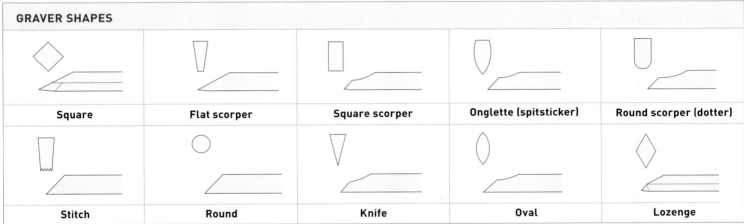

Square	Flat scorper	Square scorper	Onglette (spitsticker)	Round scorper (dotter)
Stitch	Round	Knife	Oval	Lozenge

BURR SHAPES

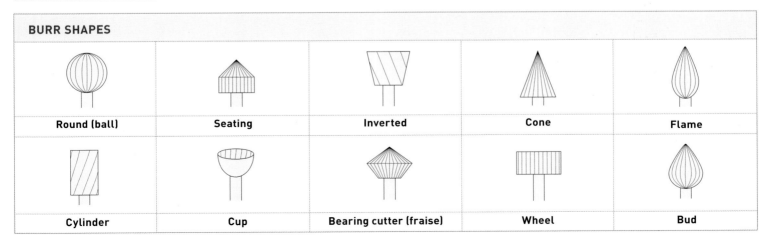

Round (ball)	Seating	Inverted	Cone	Flame
Cylinder	Cup	Bearing cutter (fraise)	Wheel	Bud

GLOSSARY

Acetone A flammable liquid solvent, used for dissolving resin, stop-out varnish, setter's wax and permanent marker-pen ink.

Alloy A mixture of metals; sterling silver is an alloy of fine silver and copper.

Annealing The process of heating and then cooling metal to make it softer and thus easier to work with. The required temperature for annealing, the duration of heating and the rate of cooling vary according to the metal used.

Arkansas stone A fine abrasive stone.

Assaying The process of determining the proportion of precious metal contained in an alloy. Most jewellery is assayed at an official Assay Office and given a hallmark that indicates the type and fineness of the precious metal.

Baguette A gemstone cut so that the shape of the top (table) is narrow and rectangular. It takes its name from the long French baguette loaf.

Base metal Non-precious metal, such as aluminium, copper, iron and nickel.

Bevelled On a slant or inclination.

Bezel The rim of metal that is used to secure a stone in a rub-over setting.

Billet A thick stack of fused metal, used in mokume gane.

Blank A flat shape cut from sheet metal.

Borax A flux commonly used when soldering jewellery. A special form of borax is produced for use by jewellers, which is easier to dissolve and melt than ordinary borax.

Burnish To polish by rubbing, usually with a polished steel tool.

Cameo A gemstone with a design cut in low relief.

Carat (1) A unit of weight, now standardized as being equal to one-fifth of a gram; this is equal to 3.086 grains Troy. The weight of gemstones is usually expressed in carats.

Carat (2) A measure of the fineness of gold or gold alloy. The number of carats is the number of parts by weight of pure gold in 24 parts of the metal. Pure gold is, therefore, described as 24 carat, and 14c gold is an alloy that contains 14 parts of pure gold in 24 parts of the alloy. In the US, the spelling 'karat' is used.

Chasing The process of punching a relief design in metal from the front.

Chenier Thin metal tube, often used for making hinges in jewellery. It can also form other parts of a piece.

Cone-shaped bezel A conical metal band that surrounds and supports a stone.

Cotter pin A double D-wire pin used to secure items. The pin is passed through a hole and the ends are spread to hold it in place.

Countersink The enlargement of the entry to a hole.

Culet The small facet on the base of some brilliant-cut stones.

Curing The process of liquid components turning solid – resin, for example.

Die A tool used for shaping by stamping or press forming, or a cutting tool used for making screw threads.

Draw plate A hardened steel plate with a series of holes of various sizes. Wire is drawn through the plate to reduce its thickness, or to change its shape. Draw plates are commonly available with round, square or triangular holes.

Electroforming The process of forming metal objects by using an electric current to deposit the metal in a mould. The mould must be coated with a substance that conducts electricity. Electroforming is sometimes used to reproduce antique pieces; the process is also used for creating new individual pieces, and for mass production.

Electroplating The process of depositing a layer of metal on an object by means of an electric current. Jewellery made from base metal is often electroplated with silver or gold to enhance its appearance. Items made from plastic or other non-metallic substances can be electroplated if they are first coated with a substance that conducts electricity.

Electrum A naturally occurring pale yellow alloy of gold and silver. The proportions of the metals vary but this alloy usually contains more gold than silver.

Engraving The process of cutting away the surface of a substance, using a sharp steel tool called a graver. Lines are often engraved in a metal surface to form a decoration or inscription. Cameos and intaglios are made by engraving gemstones.

Etching The controlled corrosion of a surface with acid. In jewellery, the process is used to form surface decoration on metal: some parts of the surface are protected by an acid-resisting substance, while others are eaten away by the acid.

Exothermic A chemical reaction that gives off heat as a by-product.

Facet A flat surface ground on a cut gemstone.

Ferrous Containing iron.

Findings Mass-produced jewellery components, such as catches, joints and clips, which are commonly used, even on handmade jewellery. When such components are made by hand, they are sometimes called fittings.

Firestain (Firescale) The black coating that forms on silver when it is heated. The coating consists of copper oxide and is formed by the copper in the impure silver combining with oxygen in the air.

Flux (1) A substance used in soldering to ensure that the solder flows. Any oxide present on the metal tends to prevent the solder from flowing. The flux is applied to the parts to be soldered and prevents air from reaching them. As a result, no oxide is formed, so the solder is able to flow and join the metal. Borax is the flux commonly used by jewellers.

Flux (2) A coulorless transparent enamel, often used as a base layer to give applied coloured enamels greater clarity, especially when enamelling on copper.

Forging The process of hammering metal to change its shape.

Former A steel shape for supporting metal while it is being hammered. Formers are also known as mandrels.

Fretwork A sheet that has been pierced with holes or shapes to make an ornamental pattern.

Fume cupboard A glass-fronted cupboard that has an extraction or air-filtration system inside, in which chemical processes such as etching are done.

Gallery (1) A wire fixed to the back of jewellery to raise the level of the metal so that there is sufficient clearance below for the stones.

Gallery (2) A mass-produced decorative metal strip, often with a series of elongated holes across the centre, usually known as a 'closed' gallery. Open galleries are made by cutting a closed gallery along the middle of the holes to produce a series of U-shapes on each piece. An open gallery can be used as a ready-made claw setting, with the arms of the 'U's forming the claws.

Gauge A standard unit of measurement of the thickness of sheet or the diameter of wire.

Gilding metal A gold-coloured alloy consisting mainly of copper and zinc. It is used to make inexpensive jewellery and is usually gilded.

Gimp A coil of very fine wire used to protect the ends of threads on which beads or pearls are strung. The ends are passed through gimps so that they cannot wear away by rubbing on the catch of the jewellery. Also called French wire.

Girdle The widest circumference of a gemstone. The girdle forms the boundary between the crown (top) and the pavilion (base).

Grain (1) A unit of weight, common to both the Troy and Avoirdupois systems. Four grains are equal to one carat, the unit of weight for precious stones and pearls.

Grain (2) A tiny ball of metal (see granulation).

Granulation The decoration or texturing of a surface by the application of tiny balls (grains) of gold or silver. Various techniques have been developed for making and attaching the grains.

Hallmark A series of impressions made in an item of gold, silver or platinum. The hallmark is an official guarantee of the fineness of the metal.

Intaglio An object with a hollowed-out design, the flat surround being the highest part. The opposite of a cameo, an intaglio is sometimes known as hollow relief. In jewellery, intaglio designs are usually made in gemstones and sometimes in metal.

Investment Fine-grade plaster used in the casting process.

Jig A tool used to form several items of identical shape.

Malleability The property, usually of a metal, of being easily hammered, rolled or pressed to shape without fracturing.

Mandrel See Former.

Marquise/Navette Any gemstone with a boat-shaped girdle. The curved sides meet at a point at each end of the stone.

Outwork Processes or special professional services that are performed by someone else, for example engraving and plating.

Pallions Small pieces of solder, taken from the French word for 'flake'.

Patina A surface finish that develops on metal or other material as a result of exposure to chemicals or handling.

Pickle A solution used during construction to clean flux and oxides from metal after heating – for example, after soldering. Pickle is also used to clean finished jewellery. Dilute sulfuric acid is often used as a pickle.

Piercing saw A saw with a blade narrow enough to be threaded through a drilled hole so that a pattern can be cut out from sheet metal or other material.

Planishing The process of hammering metal with a polished hammer to obtain an even surface.

Pleochroic A term used to describe a gemstone that appears to have two or more different colours when viewed from different directions.

Repoussé A relief design punched into thin metal from the back.

Rouge Jeweller's rouge is red iron oxide, a fine abrasive used for the final polishing stages of precious metals.

Schiller effect A sheen similar to iridescence, produced by the interference of light reflecting off internal layers within a gemstone.

Shank The part of a ring that passes around the finger.

Soldering The process of joining metal, using an alloy called solder. The solder is designed to melt at a temperature lower than the metal it is intended to join. The work and solder are heated until the solder melts. On cooling, it solidifies to form a firm joint. The terms easy, medium and hard solder describe solders with progressively higher melting points. Thus, some joints can be made at a relatively low temperature without melting earlier joints made with a higher-melting-point solder.

Sprue The unwanted piece of metal attached to a casting and formed by the access channel in the mould.

Stamping The process of forming a pattern in sheet metal, using a punch bearing the complete design. The pattern is formed by a single blow and the process is suitable for mass production.

Swaging The process of making metal U-shaped by hammering it into a U-shaped groove in a metal block.

Tap A tool used for cutting a screw thread inside a hole.

Tang The end of a file, graver or tool, which is fitted into a wooden handle.

Tempering The process of heating metal after hardening to reduce its brittleness.

Triblet A tapered steel rod on which rings are shaped.

Tripoli A coarse abrasive used in the first stages of polishing metal.

Upsetting A forging technique used to spread the end of a piece of rod.

Vulcanizing press A press used for compressing hot rubber to form moulds for casting.

Work-hardening The hardening of a metal caused by hammering or bending, which often makes the metal too hard to work with until it has been softened by annealing.

INDEX

A

acrylics 140–143
  casting 141
  cutting 140
  drilling and engraving 141
  filing and finishing 141
  gluing 141
  making lathe-turned acrylic earrings
    142–143
  thermosetting 141
alum 10
annealing 15, 42–43
  quenching temperature 43
anticlastic raising 68–69
  open forms 68

B

bending 56–59
  chenier 58
  flattening sheet metal 57
  making metal springy 57
  section wire 58
  sheet 59
  straightening wire 57
  using a former 57
binding wire 10
blanks 32–33
  making silver motifs 33
  making stainless steel blanks 32–33
borax dish and cone 10
box catches 104–105
brooches
  brooch fittings 107–108
  riveting a pin to a brooch 113
burnishing 24, 26

C

casting 124–129
  commercial casting 129
  cuttlefish 124–125
  lost wax casting 127
  preparing model for commercial
    casting 129
  preparing the investment 127–129
  preparing wax model 127
  sand casting 126
casting grain 13, 16
catches 98–105
  catches for chains 101
  hinges 102
  making a box catch 104–105
  making a figure-of-eight catch 99
  making a hinge 102–103
  making a spring catch 101–102
  making a universal joint 104
  making an interlocking catch 101
  making catches for fabric 100
  simple catch 100
  soldered catch 99
chain making 92–97
  catches for chains 101
  double-loop chain 94
  hammered chain 93
  linking chenier 96
  linking square wire 95
  loop-in-loop chain 96–97
  oval link chain 94
  planning the chain 92
  simple linked chain 93
  simple twisted chain 94
  soldering 49, 51
  soldering chains 92
  using wire and chenier 95
chamfered edges 25
charcoal 10
chasing 70–73
  holding your work 71–73
  types of punch 70
  using punches 71
chenier 23, 58, 87, 95
  linking chenier 96
  making chenier 65
chisels 29
circles 62, 64
  making a circle cutting tool 63
commercial casting 129
conversions table 154
Cooperman, Andy 'Prop' brooch 111
copper, annealing 43
cuff link fittings, attaching 109
cutting techniques
  blanks 32–33
  drilling 27–28
  engraving 38–41
  filing 24–26
  inlaying 29–31
  lathe work 34–37
  piercing 20–23
cuttlefish casting 124–125

D

Decker, Ute 48–49
  Anticlastic cuff 49
design 18–19
dies and taps 111, 113
dividers 8

Dobesova, Daniela Matching set 56
doming 62–65
  cutting circles 62, 64
  doming blocks 11
  making a circle cutting tool 63
  making a silver sphere 64–65
  making chenier 65
  shaping 62
  swaging 62, 63–64, 65
double-loop chains 94
drilling 27–28
  acrylics 141
  curved surfaces 27, 28
  drills 10
  holes 28
  making a small drill 27
  marking position 27
  small pieces 28
  using a drill 27
  using bow drill 28

E

earrings 142–143
  attaching earring fittings 107
embossing 84–85
emery boards 24
enamelling 114–119
  applying painting enamels 117
  cleaning plain metal 118
  cloisonné 119
  colour temperature guide 117
  counter enamel 116–117
  enamelling techniques 118–119
  finishing a piece 118
  firing enamels 116
  kilns 117
  lump enamels 115
  metal clay 149
  placing wet enamels 115–116
  preparing enamels 115
  preparing the metal 117–118
  test pieces 118
  types of enamels 114
  using an engraving tool 118
engraving 38–41
  acrylics 141
  cutting 38–39
  engraving design 40
  holding the tool 38
  holding the work 38
  preparing tools 39
  removing metal for inlay or enamel 41
  sharpening the graver 39

etching 120–123
  cleaning and finishing 121
  preparing the metal 120–121
  types of resist 120
  using the etching fluid 121

F

felt sticks 10
figure-of-eight catches 99
files 11, 25
  riffler files 26
filing 24–26
  acrylics 141
  burnishing 24, 26
  finishing off 26
  making a chamfered edge 25
  making an emery board 24
  using files 24, 25, 26
  using sandpapers 24
findings 106
fittings 106–110
  assembly 106
  attaching 106
  attaching cuff link fittings 109
  attaching earring fittings 107
  finishing off tie pins 109
  making a hinged pin joint 108
  making a tie clip 110
  making brooch fittings 107–108
  making chain link fittings 109
  positioning 106
  soldering 106
Fitzpatrick, Shelby
  Music and dance necklace 78
  Three aspects of a kinetic ring 120
flat metal plates 10
forging 66–69
  anticlastic raising 68–69
  simulated forging 67
fusing 52–55
  fusing gold and silver 55
  granulation 53, 55
  making a fused wire ring 54
  making a ring from scrap 53
  quenching and rinsing 52
  wire 53

G

glossary 156–157
gold 14–15, 16–17
  annealing 43
  fusing gold and silver 55
granulation 53, 55

H

hammered chains 93
hammering 60–61
hammers 11, 29, 60, 61, 75
Heaser, Sue *Seascape pendant* 144
heating techniques
    annealing 42–43
    fusing 52–55
    pickling and quenching 44–47
    soldering 48–51
Hills, Catherine *Ladybug bracelet* 98
hinges 102–103
    making a hinged pin joint 108
Howell, Tamsin *Spotty school tie cuff links* 141

I

inlaying 29–31
    choice of metal 29
    choice of wire 29
    creating an inlaid wooden piece 138–139
    inlaying a metal strip into wood 139
    inlaying metal 30, 31
    inlaying wire 30–31
inspiration 18
interlocking catches 101
investment 127–129

J

Jensen, Mette *Bangle in wood and silver* 138
joints 104
    hinged pin joints 108
jump rings 86

K

Kaltoft, Christine 19
    Doodle panel necklace 86
    'Que?' brooch 138
Kikuchi, Rui *Frills pendant* 20
kilns 117

L

Laken, Birgit *Flower brooches* 82
lathe work 34–37
    turning a silver rod 37
    turning wax for a ring 35–36
    using a lathe 35
leather sticks 10
linked chains 93
loop-in-loop chains 96–97
lost-wax casting 127

M

MacLeod, Alison *Gold keepsake earrings* 80
mallets 9, 11, 60
Marche, Catherine *'Cuffs'* 120

materials 8–11
    casting 124
May, Susan
    Forged earrings 66
    Metal earrings 76
McGrath, Jinks
    Assorted rings 66
    Double ring with moonstones 74
    Gold ring with tanzanite 60
    Multicoloured necklace 130
    Silver necklace with tourmaline 73
    Silver, gold and enamel rings 124
metal clay 144–149
    advantages 144
    disadvantages 144
    enamelling 149
    firing metal clay 146–147
    moulding 149
    paper braiding 149
    paper clay 149
    paper cutting 149
    polishing metal clay 147
    refining in greenware stage 146
    rehydrating 148
    repairing breaks in greenware 147
    stone setting 149
    syringing 149
    texturing 148
    types of metal clay 144
    working metal clay 145–146
metals 12–15
    buying metals 15
    recovering and reusing 16–17
Metaxa, Isabelle *Black collar piece* 27
moving metal
    bending 56–59
    chasing and repoussé 70–73
    doming and swaging 62–65
    forging 66–69
    hammering 60–61

N

needlefiles 11

O

Oath *Chinese circle bangles* 29
oval link chains 94

P

palladium 12–13
paper braiding 149
paper clay 149
paper cutting 149
pendant motors 76
Peters, Felicity
    Keum-boo pendant 52
    Pendant/brooch 15

Statement rings 12
Wave bangles 62
piercing saws 9
    attaching blade 20
    cutting wire and chenier 23
    holding 20
    turning corners 21
    using 21
photoetching 122
    cleaning and finishing 123
    preparing the metal for etching 122
    using the etching fluid 123
    using the resist 123
pickling 44
    alum pickle 46
    citric acid pickle 48–49
    commercial pickling solutions 46
    pickles 10
    pickling solutions 44–45
    spent pickle 46
    using pickles 45–46
    vinegar and salt pickle 49
piercing 20–23
    central areas 21, 22–23
    cutting out design 22
    large pieces 22
    piercing saws 20–21
Pittman, Sian *Copper 'collar' bracelet* 68
plagiarism 18
platinum 12
    annealing 43
pliers 8, 9
polishing 78–79
    cleaning 79
    hand polishing 78
    metal clay 147
    polishing a chain 79
    polishing a ring 79
    using a pendant motor 78, 79
    using a polishing motor 78–79
pumice powder 9
punches 11, 29
    forming with a punch 85
    stamping 82
    types of punch 70
    using punches 71

Q

quenching 43, 44, 52

R

removing stones 152
repoussé 70–73
    holding your work 71–73
    types of punch 70
    using punches 71
resist 120, 123

resizing stones 150–152
    enlarging a ring 150
    measuring 150
    sizing a ring with a set stone 151
    soldering in extra piece 151
reticulation 80–81
Richards, Loukia 18
rings
    enlarging a ring 150
    making a fused wire ring 54
    making a ring from scrap 53
    polishing a ring 79
    reducing a ring 151
    ring clamps 8
    ring mandrels 9
    ring sizers 8
    sizing a ring with a set stone 151
    turning wax for a ring 35–36
riveting 111–113
    riveting a pin to a brooch 113
    riveting links of a chain 113
    riveting sections together 112
    using taps and dies 111, 113
rolling mills 77
rulers 8

S

safety 44, 123
Sajet, Philip *Splashes* 44
sand casting 126
sandpaper 10, 24
saws 9
scrap metal 16
services 153
Sharpe, Erica *Indian Summer* 19
silver 15, 16
    annealing 15, 43
    fusing gold and silver 55
    making a silver sphere 64–65
    making ingot 17
    making silver motifs 33
    silver sheet 15
    soldering 15
    turning a silver rod 37
simple catches 100
sinusoidal stakes 69
snips 9
soldering 15, 48–51
    catch 99
    chains 49, 51
    colour changes 49
    equipment 49
    fittings 106
    fluxes 48
    joining pieces 51
    metals 49, 50
    soldering torches 10

soldering wire 10
stick soldering 51
types of solder 48–49
specialist techniques
casting 124–129
enamelling 114–119
etching and photoetching 120–123
stone setting 130–137
spring catches 101–102
stainless steel 32–33
stamping 82–85
forming with a punch 85
making a punch 83
punches 82
supports 82
steel mops 76
stone setting 130–137
cabochon 131–132
drawing pattern for collet 134
drawing pattern for round cone
mount 133
faceted stones 133–137
gypsy setting 136–137
making tapered setting with
claws 134–135
metal clay 149
raised cabochon 132
straight-sided setting 135–136
see removing stones
see resizing stones

Strickland, Lesley *Link necklace* 140
suppliers 153
surface decoration
polishing 78–79
reticulation 80–81
stamping and embossing 82–85
texturing 74–77
swaging 62, 63–64, 65

T
taps and dies 111, 113
Tavender, Faith
Disk necklaces 15
Geometric cuff links 48
Gold dipped daisy earrings 106
texturing 74–77
finishing a mixed-metal surface 74–75
metal clay 148
retexturing after assembly 75
rolling mill textures 77
texturing after polishing 74
using a hammer 75
using a pendant motor 74, 76
using a rolling mill 77
using a steel mop 76
Thakker, Salima *'Grid' ring* 130
tie clips 110
tie pins 109
tools 8–11
annealing 42

bending 56
blanking 32
casting 124
catches and joints 98
chasing and repoussé 70
doming and swaging 62
drilling 27, 28
engraving 30, 38, 39, 118
etching and photoetching 120
fusing 52
inlaying 29–30
metal clay 144
piercing 20
polishing 78
soldering 48, 49
texturing 75
tool shapes 154–155
tools for reusing metal 16
working with wire 86–87
top cutters 9
tweezers 9
twisted chains 94

U
Urino, Kyoko *Cloisonné brooch* 114

V
vices 8
Von Dohnanyi, *Babette egg pentagon
necklace* 92

W
wire 23, 86–91
bending 58
binding wire 10
catches and joints 98–105
chain making 92–97
drawing down chenier 87
drawing down wire 87
fine or cloisonné wire 89
fittings and findings 106–110
knitting with wire 89
linking square wire 95
making a helix 87
making a spiral 87
making jump rings 86
riveting 111–113
straightening 57
twisting sections in length of wire 88
twisting wire 87
wood 138–139

Y
Young, Anastasia *Spider pendant* 38

Z
Zahran, Kat *Castle ring* 24

ACKNOWLEDGMENTS

Quarto would like to thank the following artists for kindly supplying images for inclusion in this book. Artists' names appear next to their work, unless otherwise stated below:

Regina Arades (page 4) www.aradesijewellery.com

Felicity Peters (page 2) www.felicitypeters.com

Faith Tavender (page 3) www.faithtavender.com

Louika Raichards www.myprecious.gr

Christine Kalkoft (page 6) www.christinekaltoft.co.uk

Rui Kikuchi www.rubikus.net

Kat Zahran www.katzahranjewellery.co.uk

Isabella Metaxa http://2003. brilliantlybirmingham.com/

Jinks McGrath www.jinksmcgrath.com

Anastasia Young www.anastasiayoung.co.uk

Philip Sajet http://www.auquai.com

Ute Decker www.utedecker.com

Daniela Dobesova (page 2) www.danieladobesova.com

Susan May www.susanmay.org

Sue Heaser www.sueheaser.com

Sian Pittman http://sianpittman.com

Annette Petch www.annettepetchjewellery.co.uk

Shelby Fitzpatrick www.shelbyfitzpatrick.com

Alison Macleod www.alisonmacleod.com

Birgit Laken www.birgitlaken.nl

Babette Von Dohnanyi www.bd-jewellery.eu

Catherine Marche www.catherinemarche-designs.com

Catherine Hills www.designerjewellersgroup.co.uk

Andrew Cooperman (page 3, 5) www.andycooperman.com

Salima Thakker www.salimathakker.com

Mette Jensen www.mettetjensen.com

Lesley Strickland www.lesley-strickland.co.uk

Tamsin Howells www.tamsinhowells.com

Naomi James (page 2) www.naomijames.co.uk